A Text Book Of

MODERN OPERATING ENVIRONMENT AND MS OFFICE

For
BCA Semester - I (Course Code: 101)
As Per Savitribai Phule Pune University Revised Syllabus
Effective from June 2013

Gautam Bapat
M.C.A.
Asst. Professor, Computer Science & Applications
MITSOM College,
Pune

Mrs. Bhavana Chaudhary
M.Sc. (Phy.), C-DAC
Former Lecturer in Computer Science Department,
T. J. College,
Pune

N2924

Modern Operating Environment & MS Office

ISBN 978-93-83073-40-5

Second Edition : July, 2015

© : Authors

The text of this publication, or any part thereof, should not be reproduced or transmitted in any form or stored in any computer storage system or device for distribution including photocopy, recording, taping or information retrieval system or reproduced on any disc, tape, perforated media or other information storage device etc., without the written permission of Authors with whom the rights are reserved. Breach of this condition is liable for legal action.

Every effort has been made to avoid errors or omissions in this publication. In spite of this, errors may have crept in. Any mistake, error or discrepancy so noted and shall be brought to our notice shall be taken care of in the next edition. It is notified that neither the publisher nor the authors or seller shall be responsible for any damage or loss of action to any one, of any kind, in any manner, therefrom.

Published By :
NIRALI PRAKASHAN
Abhyudaya Pragati, 1312, Shivaji Nagar
Off J.M. Road, Pune – 411005
Tel - (020) 25512336/37/39, Fax - (020) 25511379
Email : niralipune@pragationline.com

Printed By :
Repro Knowledgecast Limited,
Thane

☞ **DISTRIBUTION CENTRES**

PUNE
Nirali Prakashan : 119, Budhwar Peth, Jogeshwari Mandir Lane, Pune 411002, Maharashtra
Tel : (020) 2445 2044, 66022708, Fax : (020) 2445 1538
Email : bookorder@pragationline.com, niralilocal@pragationline.com

Nirali Prakashan : S. No. 28/27, Dhyari, Near Pari Company, Pune 411041
Tel : (020) 24690204 Fax : (020) 24690316
Email : dhyari@pragationline.com, bookorder@pragationline.com

MUMBAI
Nirali Prakashan : 385, S.V.P. Road, Rasdhara Co-op. Hsg. Society Ltd.,
Girgaum, Mumbai 400004, Maharashtra
Tel : (022) 2385 6339 / 2386 9976, Fax : (022) 2386 9976
Email : niralimumbai@pragationline.com

☞ **DISTRIBUTION BRANCHES**

JALGAON
Nirali Prakashan : 34, V. V. Golani Market, Navi Peth, Jalgaon 425001,
Maharashtra, Tel : (0257) 222 0395, Mob : 94234 91860

KOLHAPUR
Nirali Prakashan : New Mahadvar Road, Kedar Plaza, 1st Floor Opp. IDBI Bank
Kolhapur 416 012, Maharashtra. Mob : 9850046155

NAGPUR
Pratibha Book Distributors : Above Maratha Mandir, Shop No. 3, First Floor,
Rani Jhanshi Square, Sitabuldi, Nagpur 440012, Maharashtra
Tel : (0712) 254 7129

DELHI
Nirali Prakashan : 4593/21, Basement, Aggarwal Lane 15, Ansari Road, Daryaganj
Near Times of India Building, New Delhi 110002
Mob : 08505972553

BENGALURU
Pragati Book House : House No. 1, Sanjeevappa Lane, Avenue Road Cross,
Opp. Rice Church, Bengaluru – 560002.
Tel : (080) 64513344, 64513355,Mob : 9880582331, 9845021552
Email:bharatsavla@yahoo.com

CHENNAI
Pragati Books : 9/1, Montieth Road, Behind Taas Mahal, Egmore,
Chennai 600008 Tamil Nadu, Tel : (044) 6518 3535,
Mob : 94440 01782 / 98450 21552 / 98805 82331,
Email : bharatsavla@yahoo.com

niralipune@pragationline.com | www.pragationline.com
Also find us on www.facebook.com/niralibooks

Preface ...

We take an opportunity to present this book entitled as **"Modern Operating Environment and MS Office"** to the students of First Semester (BCA.). The object of this book is to present the subject matter in a most concise and simple manner. The book is written strictly according to the Revised Syllabus of Savitribai Phule Pune University.

The book has its own unique features. It brings out the subject in a very simple and lucid manner for easy and comprehensive understanding of the basic concepts, its intricacies, procedures and practices. This book will help the readers to have a broader view on Modern Operating Environment and MS Office. The language used in this book is easy and will help students to improve their vocabulary of Technical terms and understand the matter in a better and happier way.

We sincerely thank Shri. Dineshbhai Furia and Shri. Jignesh Furia, the publishers, for the confidence reposed in us and giving us this opportunity to reach out to the students of management studies.

We thank Mr. Amar Salunkhe for his important inputs time to time. Mr. Akbar Shaikh painstakingly attended to all the details to make this book appear good.

We also thank Ms. Chaitali Takale, Mr. Ravindra Walodare, Mr. Mahesh Swami, Mr. Sachin Shinde, Nikunj Joshi, Nilesh Deshmukh, Ashok Bodke, Moshin Sayyed and Nitin Thorat.

We have given our best inputs for this book. Any suggestions towards the improvement of this book and sincere comments are most welcome on niralipune@pragationline.com.

AUTHORS

Syllabus ...

1. **Introduction to Computer** [6 L]

   Computer Characteristics, Concept of Hardware, Software, Evolution of Computer and Generations, Types of computer – Analog and Digital computers, Hybrid computers, General Purpose and Special Purpose Computer, Limitations of Computer Applications of Computer in Various fields.

2. **Structure and Working of Computer** [4 L]

   Functional Block diagram of Computer. CPU, ALU, Memory Unit, Bus structure of Digital Computer - Address, data and Control bus.

3. **Input /Output Devices** [5 L]

   Input device – Keyboard, Mouse, Scanner, MICR, OMR. Output devices – VDU, Printers – Dot Matrix, Daisy- wheel, Inkjet, Laser, Line printers and Plotters.

4. **Computer Memory** [6 L]

   Memory Concept, Memory cell, Memory organization, Semiconductor memory - RAM, ROM, PROM, EPROM, Secondary Storage devices - Magnetic tape, Magnetic Disk (Floppy disk and Hard disk.), Compact Disk.

5. **Computer Language and Software** [5 L]

   Algorithm, Flowcharts, Machine language, Assembly language, High Level Language, Assembler, Compiler, Interpreter. Characteristics of Good Language. Software - System and Application Software.

6. **Operating System** [6 L]

   Operating System, Evolution of Operating System, Function of Operating System, Types of Operating Systems, Detailed study of Windows Operating System, Introduction and Features of LINUX OS.

7. **Networking** [3 L]

   Concept, Basic Elements of a Communication System, Data Transmission Media, Topologies, LAN, MAN, WAN, Internet.

8. **MS-OFFICE:** Introduction to MS-office, Components and Features. [12 L]

   MS-Word: Creating Letter, Table, Fonts, Page Layout document formatting spell check, Print preview, Template, Colour, Mail merge, Auto Text, Inserting picture, Word art.

   MS-EXCEL: Introduction to Excel, Sorting, Queries, Graphs, Scientific functions.

   PowerPoint: Introduction to Power Point Creation of Slides, Inserting pictures, Preparing slide show with animation.

   MS-ACCESS: Creation and Manipulation of Files.

   ■■■

Contents ...

1. Introduction to Computer — 1.1 – 1.30

2. Structure and Working of Computer — 2.1 – 2.8

3. Input /Output Devices — 3.1 – 3.22

4. Computer Memory — 4.1 – 4.22

5. Computer Language and Software — 5.1 – 5.20

6. Operating System — 6.1 – 6.30

7. Networking — 7.1 – 7.28

8. MS-Office — 8.1 – 8.56

   Annexure A — A.1 – A.22

   University Question Papers — P.1 – P.2

■■■

Chapter 1...

Introduction to Computer

Contents ...

1.1 Introduction
    1.1.1 What is a Computer? / Meaning of Computer
    1.1.2 Definition
    1.1.3 Advantages
1.2 Computer Characteristics
1.3 Concept of Hardware and Software
    1.3.1 Computer Hardware
    1.3.2 Computer Software
1.4 Evolution of Computer and Generations
    1.4.1 Evolution of Computer
    1.4.2 Generations
1.5 Types of Computers
    1.5.1 Analog Computers
    1.5.2 Digital Computers
    1.5.3 Hybrid Computers
1.6 General Purpose and Special Purpose Computers
    1.6.1 General Purpose Computers
    1.6.2 Special Purpose Computers
1.7 Limitations of Computer
1.8 Applications of Computer in various Fields
- Questions

1.1 Introduction

- Now-a-days, computers are an integral part of our lives. They are used for the reservation of tickets for airplanes and railways, payment of telephone and electricity bills, deposit and withdrawal of money from banks, processing of business data, forecasting of weather conditions, diagnosis of diseases, searching for information on the internet, etc.
- Computers are also used extensively in schools, universities, organisations, music industry, movie industry, scientific research, law firms, fashion industry, etc.
- The term computer is derived from the Latin word compute. The word compute means to calculate.

- A computer is an electronic machine that accepts data from the user, processes the data by performing calculations and operations on it, and generates the desired output results.
- Computer performs both simple and complex operations, with speed and accuracy.
- A computer is a general purpose device that can be programmed to carry out a finite set of arithmetic or logical operations.
- A computer is an electronic device that manipulates information or data. It has the ability to store, retrieve, and process data.
- A computer is a programmable machine. The two **principal characteristics of a computer** are:
  1. Computer responds to a specific set of instructions in a well-defined manner, and
  2. Computer can execute a pre-recorded list of instructions (a program).

1.1.1 What is a Computer? / Meaning of Computer

- A computer is an advanced electronic device that takes raw data as input from the user and processes these data under the control of set of instructions (called program) and gives the result (output) and saves output for the future use.
- A computer can process both numerical and non-numerical (arithmetic and logical) calculations.
- A computer has following functions:
  1. **Input (Data):** Input is the raw information entered into a computer from the input devices. It is the collection of letters, numbers, images etc.
  2. **Process:** Process is the operation of data as per given instruction. It is totally internal process of the computer system.
  3. **Output and Storage:** Output is the processed data given by computer after data processing. Output is also called as Result. We can save these results in the storage devices for the future use.

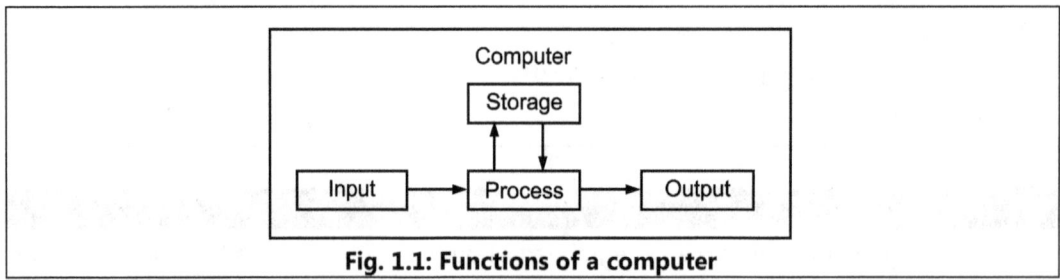

Fig. 1.1: Functions of a computer

1.1.2 Definition

- A computer is a programmable machine that can store, retrieve, and process data.

OR

- A computer is an extremely fast and accurate electronic data processing machine that receives data as input, performs arithmetic and logical operations on them according to a program stored in the memory and produces the desired output.

OR

- Computer is an electronic machine made up of various electronic devices (parts) to process the data to produce useful information.

OR

- A computer is an electronic device which is capable of receiving information (data) in a particular form and of performing a sequence of operations in accordance with a predetermined but variable set of procedural instructions (program) to produce a result in the form of information or signals.

1.1.3 Advantages

- Following list demonstrates the advantages of computers in today's arena:
    1. **High Speed:** Computer is a very fast device. It can perform millions of calculations in few seconds as compared to man who can spend many months for doing the same task.
    2. **Accuracy:** Computers are very accurate. The computer can perform calculations 100% error free.
    3. **Storage Capability:** Computers can store large amount of data using memory. Computers can store any type of data such as images, videos, text, audio and any other type.
    4. **Versatility:** A computer is a very versatile machine. Computer machine can be used to solve the problems relating to various different fields.
    5. **Automation:** Automation means ability to perform the task automatically. Computer is a automatic machine. Once, a program (instruction) is given to computer i.e. stored in computer memory, the program and instruction can control the program execution without human interaction.
    6. **Diligence:** Unlike human beings, a computer is free from monotony, tiredness and lack of concentration. Computers can work continuously without creating any error and boredom and it can do repeated work with same speed and accuracy.
    7. **Reliability:** A computer is a reliable machine and modern electronic components have failure free long lives. Computers are designed to make maintenance easy and simple.
    8. **Reduction in Cost:** Though the initial investment for installing a computer is high but it substantially reduces the cost of each of its transaction.
    9. **Reduction in Paper Work:** The use of computers for data processing in an organisation leads to reduction in paper work and speeds up the process.

1.2 Computer Characteristics

- The main characteristics (capabilities) of computer, which makes them powerful and useful are:
    1. **Automation:** Computers has automation power that means computer can perform the task automatically by using programs.
    2. **Speed:** Computers are of high speed in its operation. The speed is measured in terms of Instructions Per Second (IPS). All modern computers can process information at a speed of a couple of Million Instructions Per Second (MIPS).

3. **Accuracy:** Computers are highly accurate in its operations. They either give correct answer or do not answer at all. Errors can occur in computers but these are mainly due to human rather than technological weakness.
4. **Reliability:** It is the ability of a computer to perform the same job exactly in the same way in any numbers of times.
5. **Versatility:** A computer is capable of performing almost any task provided that the task can be reduced to a series of logical steps.
6. **Integrity:** It is the ability of a computer to carry out a sequence of instructions.
7. **No Feelings:** Computers are devoid of emotions. They have no feeling because they are machines.
8. **Diligence continuity:** A computer is free from monotony, tiredness, lack of concentration, etc. It can work for hours without creating any error.
9. **Power of Remembering:** Computers can store and recall any amount of information because of its storage capability.

1.3 Concept of Hardware and Software

- A computer system consists of hardware and software.
- The computer hardware cannot perform any task on its own. It needs to be instructed about the tasks to be performed.
- Software is a set of programs that instructs the computer about the tasks to be performed. Software tells the computer how the tasks are to be performed; hardware carries out these tasks.

1. **Relationship between Computer Hardware and Software:**
   - Hardware and Software have a symbiotic relationship, this means that without software hardware is very limited; and without hardware, software would not be able to run at all. They need each other to fulfill their potential.
   - Computer hardware and software must work together. Nothing useful can be done with the computer hardware on its own, and computer software cannot be utilized without supporting hardware.
   - The following important points show the relationships between computer hardware and software:
     (i) Both i.e. computer hardware and software are complementary to each other.
     (ii) Except for upgrades hardware is normally a one-time expense, whereas software is a continuing expense.
     (iii) Computer hardware and software are necessary for a computer to do useful job or task.
     (iv) The same hardware can be loaded with different software to make a computer system perform different types of jobs or tasks.

2. **Logical System Architecture:**
   - The logical architecture of a computer system is shown in Fig. 1.2. The architecture of computer system basically depicts the relationship among the hardware, system software, application software and users of computer system.
   - As shown in Fig. 1.2, at the center of any computer system is the hardware, which comprises of the physical devices/ components of the computer system.

- Surrounding the hardware is the system software layer, which constitutes the operating and programming environment of the computer system.
- Surrounding the system software is the application software layer, which consists of a wide range of softwares, which are designed to do a specific task, or solve a specific problem.
- The final layer is the layer of users who normally interact with the computer system via the user interface provided by the application software.

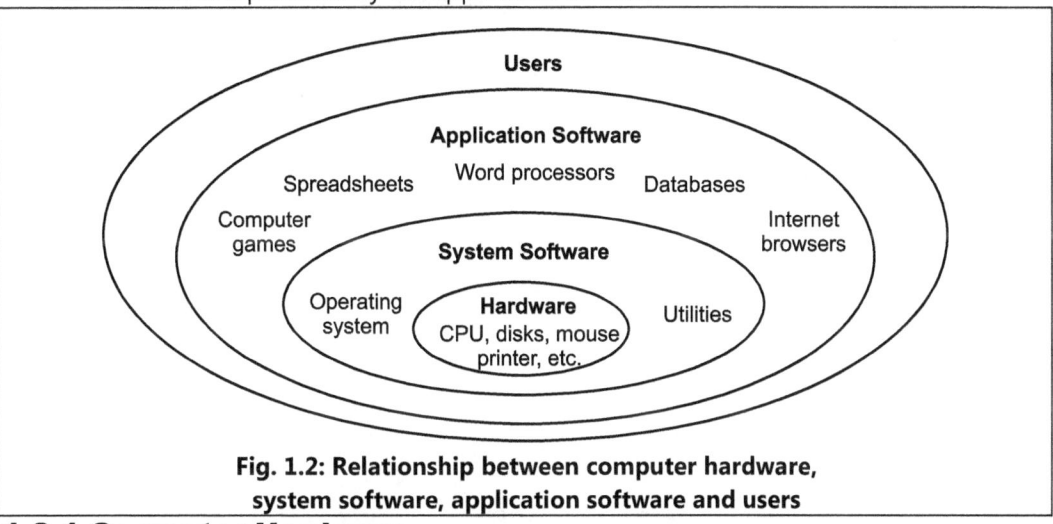

Fig. 1.2: Relationship between computer hardware, system software, application software and users

1.3.1 Computer Hardware

- The actual physical components that constitute a computer are known as Computer Hardware.
- Hardware consists of the mechanical parts that make up the computer as a machine.
- In other words, anything in the computer that you can touch and see is the hardware. For example, CPU, monitor, keyboard, ICs, resistors, etc.
- Hardware represents the physical and tangible components of the computer i.e. the components that can be seen and touched.

Components of Computer Hardware:
1. **Input/Output (I/O) Unit:** The I/O unit consists of the input unit and the output unit. CPU performs calculations and processing on the input data, to generate the output. The memory unit is used to store the data, the instructions and the output information. The user interacts with the computer via the I/O unit. The Input unit accepts data from the user and the Output unit provides the processed data i.e. the information to the user. The input unit converts the data that it accepts from the user, into a form that is understandable by the computer. Similarly, the output unit provides the output in a form that is understandable by the user.
2. **Central Processing Unit (CPU):** Central Processing Unit (CPU) controls, coordinates and supervises the operations of the computer. It is responsible for processing of the input data. CPU consists of Arithmetic Logic Unit (ALU) and Control Unit (CU).
   (i) ALU performs all the arithmetic and logical operations on the input data.
   (ii) CU controls the overall operations of the computer i.e. it checks the sequence of execution of instructions and controls and coordinates the overall functioning of the units of computer.

3. **Memory Unit:** Memory unit stores the data, instructions, intermediate results and output, temporarily, during the processing of data. This memory is also called the main memory or primary memory of the computer. The input data that is to be processed is brought into the main memory before processing. The instructions required for processing of data and any intermediate results are also stored in the main memory. The output is stored in memory before being transferred to the output device. CPU can work with the information stored in the main memory. Another kind of storage unit also referred to as the secondary memory of the computer. The data, the programs and the output are stored permanently in the storage unit of the computer. Magnetic disks, optical disks and magnetic tapes are examples of secondary memory.

- Examples of Hardware:
    - **Input devices:** Keyboard, mouse etc.
    - **Output devices:** Printer, monitor etc.
    - **Secondary storage devices:** Hard disk, CD, DVD etc.
    - **Internal components:** CPU, motherboard, RAM etc.
- Fig. 1.3 various hardware parts of a computer system.

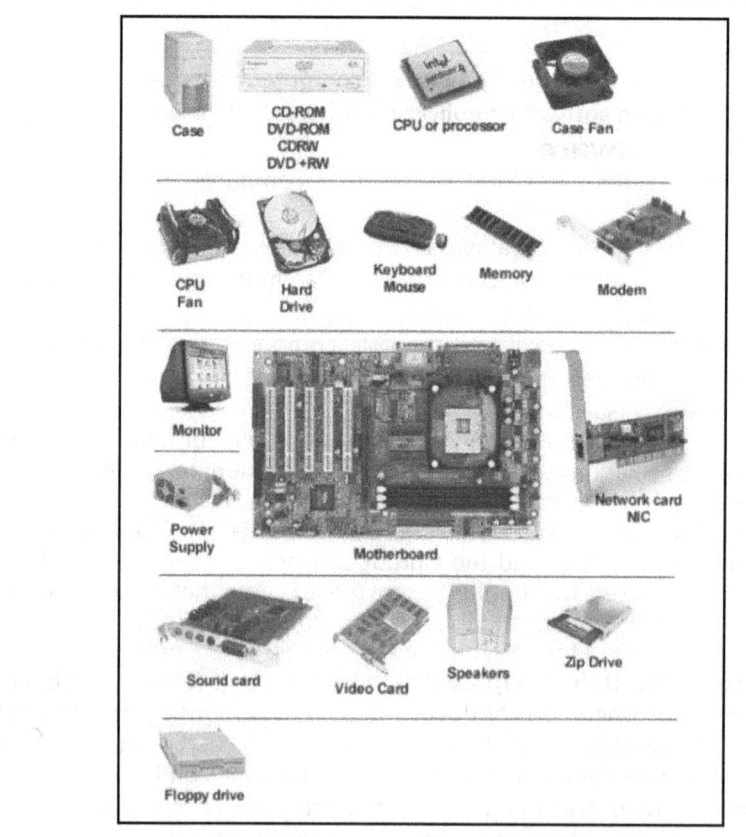

Fig. 1.3: Various hardware parts of a computer

1.3.2 Computer Software

- Software is a set of instructions that tells the computer about the tasks to be performed and how these tasks are to be performed.
- Program is a set of instructions, written in a language understood by the computer, to perform a specific task.
- A set of programs and documents are collectively called software. The hardware of the computer system cannot perform any task on its own.
- The hardware needs to be instructed about the task to be performed. Software instructs the computer about the task to be performed.

Definition:

- The instructions or programs that are required to operate the hardware are known as software.

OR

- Software is a set of instructions that are required to operate the computer hardware.
- Software is not the physical part rather they are the logical parts of a computer. For example, operating system, compiler, assemblers, etc.
- There are two types of softwares:

1. System Software:

- System software provides basic functionality to the computer. System software is required for the working of computer itself. The user of computer does not need to be aware about the functioning of system software, while using the computer.
- The system software is collection of programs designed to operate, control and extend the processing capabilities of the computer itself. System software are generally prepared by computer manufactures.
- System software controls how the various technology tools work together along with the application software. System software includes both operating system software and utility software.
- Examples of System Software are - Operating systems, Language translators like Compiler, Assembler, etc.

2. Application Software:

- The software that a user uses for accomplishing a specific task is the application software. Application software may be a single program or a set of programs.
- A set of programs that are written for a specific purpose and provide the required functionality is called as a software package.
- Application software is written for different kinds of applications—graphics, word processors, media players, database applications, telecommunication, accounting purposes etc.
- Application software are the software that are designed to satisfy a particular need of a particular environment. All softwares prepared by programmer in the computer lab can come under the category of Application software.

- Application software is used for specific information processing needs, including payroll, customer relationship management, project management, training, and many others. Application software is used to solve specific problems or perform specific tasks.
- Example of application software are: Tally for Accounting, MS-Word for word processing etc.

1.4 Evolution of Computer and Generations

1.4.1 Evolution of Computer

- In 1842, Babbage came out with his new idea of Analytical Engine, which was intended to be completely automatic. It was to be capable of performing the basic arithmetic functions for any mathematical problem, and it was to do so at an average speed of 60 additions per minute.
- Let us now briefly discuss about some of the well-known early computers.
    1. **Mark I Computer (1937–1944):** It is also known as Automatic Sequence Controlled calculator. This machine was the first fully automatic calculating machine designed by Howard A. Aiken of Harvard University, in collaboration with IBM Corporation. Its design of machine was based on the techniques already developed for punched card machinery. It was an electro-mechanical device, since both mechanical and electronic components were used in its design.
    2. **Atanasoff-Berry Computer (1939-1942):** This electronic machine was developed by Dr. John Atanasoff. It was called the Atanasoff-Berry Computer after its inventor's name and his assistant, Clifford Berry. It has used 45 vacuum tubes for internal logic and capacitors for storage.
    3. **ENIAC (1943-1946):** It was the first all electronic computer. It was constructed at the Moore School of Engineering of the University of Pennsylvania, U.S.A. ENIAC was used for many years to solve ballistic problems. It took up the wall space in a 20 × 40 square feet room and used 18,000 vacuum tubes. ENIAC performs addition of two numbers in 200 microseconds and multiplication in 2000 microseconds.
    4. **EDVAC (1946-1952):** EDVAC was designed on stored program concept. Dr. John Von Neumann also has a share of the credit for introducing the idea of storing both instructions and data in the binary form, instead of the decimal numbers or human readable words.
    5. **EDSAC (1947-1949):** The Britishers developed the Electronic Delay Storage Automatic Calculator (EDSAC). The machine executed its first program in May 1949. In EDSAC, addition operation was accomplished in 1500 microseconds and multiplication operation in 4000 microseconds. The machine was developed by Professor Maurice Wilkes at Cambridge University, Mathematical Laboratory.
    6. **UNIVAC I (1951):** UNIVAC was the first digital computer, which was not "one of a kind". The first UNIVAC machine was installed in the Census Bureau in 1951 and was used continuously for 10 years.

- In 1952, the International Business Machines (IBM) Corporation introduced the 701 commercial computer series. In rapid succession, improved models of the UNIVAC I and other 700 series machines were introduced. In 1953, IBM produced the IBM-650 and sold over 1000 of these computers.

1.4.2 Generations

- Generation in computer terminology is a change in technology a computer is/was being used.
- Initially, the generation term was used to distinguish between varying hardware technologies. But now-a-days, generation includes both hardware and software, which together make up an entire computer system.
- There are totally five computer generations known till date. Each generation has been discussed in detail along with their time period, characteristics. We have used approximate dates against each generations which are normally accepted.
- A generation in computer talk is a step in technology. Computers developed after ENIAC have been classified into five generations depending upon the technology used, processing techniques, computer languages, memory systems.
- Following are the main five generations of computers are given in Table 1.1.

Table 1.1: Generations of Computer

Sr. No.	Generations and Year
1.	**First Generation (1942-1955):** Vaccum tube based.
2.	**Second Generation (1955-1964):** Transistor based.
3.	**Third Generation (1964-1975):** Integrated Circuit based.
4.	**Fourth Generation (1975-1989):** VLSI microprocessor based.
5.	**Fifth Generation (1989-onwards):** ULSI microprocessor based.

1. **First Generation Computers (1942-1955):**

- The first generation computers were using Vacuum Tubes and machine languages were used for giving instructions. The computers of this generation were very large in size and their programming was a difficult task.
- The first commercial electronic digital computer capable of using stored programs was called "Universal Automatic Calculator" (UNIVAC) built by Macuchy and Eckert in 1951. Punched cards were used for feeding and retrieving of information.
- The major first generation computers were UNIVAC-1, IBM-701, IBM-650, ENIAC, EDVAC, EDSAC, etc.

(a) 1st generation computer   (b) Vacuum tube
Fig. 1.4

- First generation computers were the fastest calculating devices of their time. They could perform computations in milliseconds. Vacuum tube technology made possible the advent of electronic digital computers.
- The **characteristics/features of first-generation computers** are given below:
    1. The power consumption of these computers was very high.
    2. Thousands of vacuum tubes, which were used, emitted large amount of heat and burnt out frequently. Hence, the rooms/areas in which these computers were located had to be properly air-conditioned.
    3. They were too bulky in size, requiring large rooms for installation.
    4. They were the fastest calculating devices of their time.
    5. These computers required large maintenance cost.
    6. Thousands of vacuum tubes were used in making one computer, these computers were prone to frequent hardware failures as vacuum tubes and filaments have limited time period.
    7. These computers were difficult to program and use.
    8. Commercial production of these computers was difficult and costly.

Advantages:
1. First generation computers were fastest calculating devices of their time.
2. Support parallel processing.

Disadvantages:
1. Air conditioning is required.
2. Bulky in size (required large rooms) for assembly on installation.
3. Vacuum tube required very high power consumption.
4. Commercial production of these computers was difficult and costly.
5. Time consuming for assembling and installation.
6. These computers required very high constant maintenance.
7. Difficult to use and programming.

Application:

- They were used for scientific applications as they were the fastest computing device of their time.

2. Second Generation Computers (1955-1964):

- Computers are entered into second generation by the introduction of Transistors.
- Vacuum tubes were replaced by tiny solid-state components called transistors.
- Transistors were highly reliable, requires less power and faster than vacuum tubes. High Level Languages such as FORTRAN, COBOL, BASIC etc. were introduced.
- The practice of writing programs in Machine languages were replaced by High Level Languages.
- Punched cards were used for input-output operations.
- Major second generation computers were IBM-1400 series, 7000 series, Honeywell 200, CDC 3600, UNIVAC 1108 etc.

 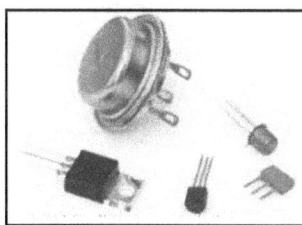

(a) 2nd generation computer   (b) Transistors

Fig. 1.5

- The **characteristics/features of second-generation computers** are as given below:
    1. They consumed much less power than the first-generation computers.
    2. They were smaller in size than first-generation computers.
    3. They were more faster than the first-generation computers.
    4. They had larger primary and secondary storage as compared to first-generation computers.
    5. They were more reliable than the first-generation computers.
    6. Commercial production of these computers was difficult and costly.

Advantages:
1. They used transistor technology as transistors are faster than vacuum tube.
2. More reliable.
3. Cheaper.
4. Smaller in size.
5. Less power consumption.
6. Support parallel processing.

Disadvantages:
1. Time consuming for assembly and installation.
2. Air-conditioning required.
3. Difficult for commercial production.
4. Costly for commercial production.
5. Maintenance is high.

3. Third Generation Computers (1964-1975):

- The third generation computers used the new technology, Transistor Integrated Circuits (IC) intended by Jack and Noyce in 1958.
- All electronic components like transistors, resistors and capacitors were fabricated on silicon chips. Computers were designed by making use of ICs.
- IC has higher speed, larger storage capacity and smaller size. Operating systems were introduced for use in computers.
- Significant advances in hardware technology made the introduction of keyboards and monitors for data input and output. More high level languages like Pascal, RPG were also introduced.
- Major third generation computers were IBM -360 series, ICL -1900 series, CDC's CYBER -175, TDC-316, IBM 370/168 etc.

(a) 3rd generation computer

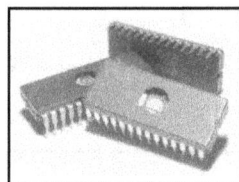
(b) ICs

Fig. 1.6

- The **characteristic/features of third-generation computers** are given below:
    1. They had faster and larger primary and secondary storage as compared to second-generation computers.
    2. They consumed much less power than the second-generation computers.
    3. They were much smaller than second-generation computers.
    4. They were much more powerful than the second-generation computers.
    5. They were totally general-purpose machines suitable for both scientific and commercial applications.
    6. The maintenance cost was much lower.
    7. Standardization of high-level programming language.

Advantages:
1. Required small space (portable).
2. More reliable.
3. Faster.
4. Support high level languages.
5. Commercial production is raised.
6. Installation is required in less time.
7. Low maintenance.

Disadvantages:
1. Air-conditioning required.
2. Cost is more than fourth generation computers.
3. Highly sophisticated technology required for the manufacturing chips.

Application:
- Computers became accessible to mass audience. Computers were produced commercially and were smaller and cheaper than their predecessors.

4. **Fourth Generation Computers (1975-1989):**
- The ICs used in third generation computers had about 10 to 100 transistors per unit.
- This technology was called Small-Scale Integration (SSI). Later, with the advancement of technology for manufacturing ICs, it is possible to integrate 10,000 transistors in an IC.
- This technology is called Large-Scale Integration (LSI). Very Large Scale Integration (VLSI) can pack a million or more transistors on a single chip. LSI and VLSI technologies led to the introduction of Microprocessors.
- Computers which are designed using Microprocessors become the fourth generation computers. Magnetic disks become the primary means for external storage.
- Intel introduced the first microprocessor 4004 using LSI. The languages C, LISP, Prolog become popular. Present day computers are fourth generation computers.
- Major fourth generation computers are IBM System 370, CRAY–MPC, WIPRO 860, IBM AS/400/B60, IBM ps/2 MODEL 80, HCL Magnum, etc.

(a) 4th generation computers

(b) Microprocessor

Fig. 1.7

- The **characteristics of fourth-generation computers** are as given below:
    1. Graphical User Interface (GUI) enabled new users to quickly learn how to use computers.
    2. Use of standard high-level programming languages.
    3. Commercial production of these systems was easier and cheaper.
    4. They were totally general-purpose machines.
    5. So they had faster and larger primary and secondary storage as compared to third generation computers.
    6. They were more reliable and less hardware failures than the third generation computers. So the maintenance cost was negligible.
    7. The PCs were smaller and cheaper than third generation computers.
    8. They were much more powerful than third generation systems.
    9. They consumed much less power than the third generation computers.
    10. No air-conditioning required for the computers.

Advantages:
1. Portable in size.
2. Cheaper.
3. More reliable.
4. Easy for installation.
5. Support high level language.
6. Support networking.
7. Support GUI (Graphical User Interface).
8. Less time required for manual assembly.

Disadvantages:
1. Air-conditioning is required.
2. Expensive.
3. Single user oriented.

Application:
- They became widely available for commercial purposes. Personal computers became available to the home user.

5. **Fifth Generation Computers (1989 onwards):**
- Fifth generation computers are capable of parallel processing, high speed computing and artificial intelligence.
- They have an architecture which allows more neural problem solving ability. These machines uses the principle of Artificial Intelligence.
- They have the ability to understand natural languages like English, Malayalam, etc. it can converse with human beings.
- Computer languages such as LISP, PROLOG, C, C++, etc., are available to program such computers.

- The goal of fifth generation computing is to develop computers that are capable of learning and self-organisation. The fifth generation computers use Super Large Scale Integrated (SLSI) chips that are able to store millions of components on a single chip. These computers have large memory requirements.

Fig. 1.8: 5th generation computer

- The **characteristics features of fifth generation computers** are as given below:
    1. They are totally general-purpose machines.
    2. Commercial production of these systems is easier and cheaper.
    3. Support of standard high-level programming languages allows programs written for one computer to be easily ported to and executed to another computer.
    4. Portable computers are much more smaller and handy than the computers of the fourth generation, allowing users to use computing facility even while travelling.
    5. They are more reliable and less prone to hardware failures than their predecessors. So the maintenance cost is negligible.
    6. They consume much less power than their predecessors.
    7. They have faster and larger primary and secondary storage as compared to their predecessors.

Advantages:
1. More smaller and handy than computers of fourth generation, allowing users to use the computing facility even while travelling.
2. Very less power required.
3. No air-conditioning required.
4. Use for large scale organisations.
5. Support standard HLL (High Level Language).
6. User friendly interface.
7. Faster in speed.
8. More reliable.
9. Easy for installation.
10. Very short time required for manual assembly.
11. Support very high powerful applications (multimedia).

1.5 Types of Computers

- Computers can be classified based on their principles of operation or on their configuration.
- By configuration, we mean the size, speed of doing computation and storage capacity of a computer.
- Types of computers according to the principles of operation and configuration are shown in Fig. 1.9.

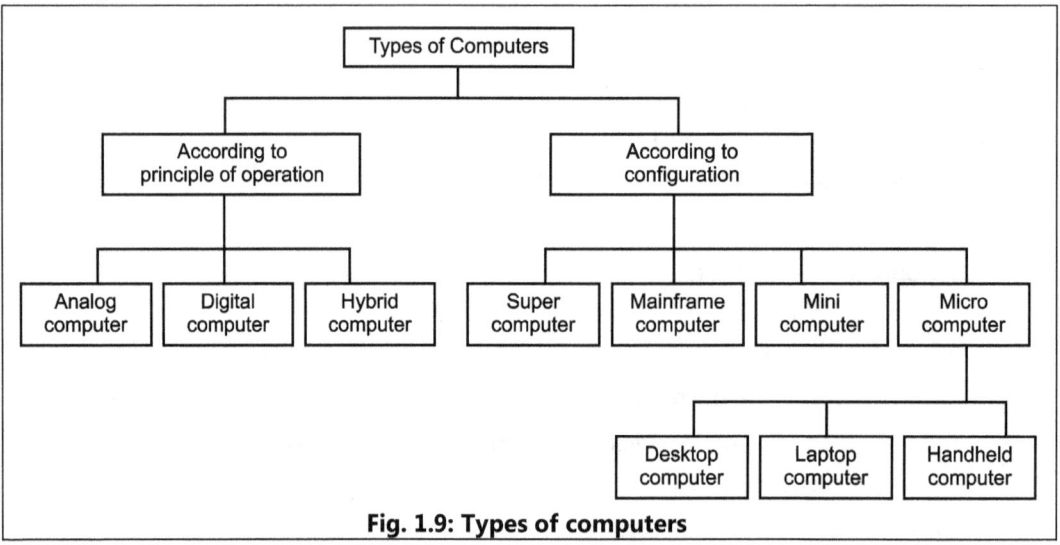

Fig. 1.9: Types of computers

1.5.1 Analog Computers

- The earliest computers were analog computers. Analog computer is a computing device that works on continuous range of values. The results given by the analog computers will only be approximate since they deal with quantities that vary continuously.
- Analog computers generally deals with physical variables such as voltage, pressure, temperature, speed, etc.
- Analog computers are used for measuring parameters that vary continuously in real time, such as temperature, pressure and voltage.
- Analog computers may be more flexible but generally less precise than digital computers.
- Slide rule, Antikythera mechanism, astrolabe, differential analyzer, Deltar, Kerrison Predictor are the example of an analog computers.

Definition:
- An analog computer (spelled analogue) is a form of computer that uses electrical, mechanical or hydraulic phenomena to model the problem being solved.

OR

- Analog computer is a mechanical, electrical, or electronic computer that performs arithmetical operations by using some variable physical quantity, such as mechanical movement or voltage, to represent numbers.

Advantages:
1. Continuous representation of all data within the range of the machine.
2. Fast and inexpensive when implemented with same technology as digital computer.
3. Parallel and real-time operation many signal values can be computed simultaneously.
4. Computation can be done for some applications without the requirement for transducers to convert the inputs/outputs to/from digital electronic form.

Disadvantages:
1. Computation elements have a limited useful dynamic range, usually not much more than 120 dB, about 6 significant digits of accuracy.
2. Useful solution of problems of any size can take an inordinate amount of setup time.
3. For a given size (mass) and power consumption, digital computers can solve larger problems.
4. Solutions appear in real (or scaled) time, and may be difficult to record for later use or analysis.
5. The range of useful time constants is limited. Problems that have components operating on vastly different time scales are difficult to deal with accuracy.

1.5.2 Digital Computers

- A digital computer uses distinct values to represent the data internally. All information are represented using the digits 0s and 1s.
- The computers that we use at our homes and offices are digital computers.
- The digital computer is designed using digital circuits in which there are two levels for an input or output signal. These two levels are known as logic 0 and logic 1. Digital computers can give more accurate and faster results.
- Digital computer is well suited for solving complex problems in engineering and technology. Hence digital computers have an increasing use in the field of design, research and data processing.
- UNIVAC, IBM-360 and other mainframe computers are examples of digital computers.

Definition:
- A computer that performs calculations and logical operations with quantities represented as digits, usually in the binary number system.

OR

- Digital computer is an electronic computer in which the input is discrete rather than continuous, consisting of combinations of numbers, letters, and other characters written in an appropriate programming language and represented internally in binary notation.

Advantages:
1. Greater flexibility and precision.
2. It can store large amount of facts, instructions, and information.

Disadvantage:
1. Its higher cost and complexity.

Difference between Digital and Analog Computers:

	Terms	Digital computers	Analog computers
1.	Definition	A computer that performs calculations and logical operations with quantities represented as digits, usually in the binary number system (0's and 1's).	Analog computer is a mechanical, electrical, or electronic computer that performs arithmetical operations by using some variable physical quantity, such as mechanical movement or voltage, to represent numbers.
2.	Computing power	Digital computers, however, are not limited specific types of applications, but have a more general purpose in terms of usage.	Analog computers are limited to performing restrictive and specialized mathematical calculations such as the measurement and analysis of electrical voltages.
3.	Output	Digital computers produce numbers as output. The computer uses display screens, printers, disc drives and other peripherals to capture this output.	Analog computers output voltage signals, and has sets of analog meters and oscilloscopes to display the voltages.
4.	Electronic circuits	Digital computers use a variety of on-off switching circuits, such as microprocessors, clock pulse generators and logic gates.	Analog computer circuits use op-amps, signal generators and networks of resistors and capacitors. These circuits process continuous voltage signals.
5.	Discrete versus Continuous signals	Digital signals have two discrete states, on or off. The off state is usually zero volts, and the on state is typically five volts.	Analog signals are continuous. They may have any value between two extremes, such as -15 and +15 volts. An analog signal's voltage may be constant or vary with time.
6.	Size	Digital computers range from tiny microchips a few millimeters square to room-sized server installations.	Analog computers vary in size from small desktop systems the size of a large book to tall racks laden with equipment.
7.	Data storage	The numeric, discrete nature of digital computers makes data storage simple. A memory circuit copies and retains the discrete states of another circuit.	For analog computers, storing data is more difficult, as they use continuous signals. A circuit that stores an analog signal is prone to drift over time.
8.	Speed and Accuracy	Digital computers can give more accurate and faster results.	Analogue computers can give less accurate and slow results.
9.	Cost	Cost is high.	Cost is low.

1.5.3 Hybrid Computers

- A hybrid computer combines the desirable features of analog and digital computers.
- Hybrid computers is mostly used for automatic operations of complicated physical processes and machines.
- Now-a-days analog-to-digital and digital-to-analog converters are used for transforming the data into suitable form for either type of computation.

Definition:

- Hybrid computer is a computer that combines the characteristics of a digital computer and an analog computer by its capacity to accept input and provide output in either digital or analog form and to process information digitally.

OR

- Hybrid computers as the name suggests are a hybrid of analog and digital computers. The analog part of the hybrid computer computes higher mathematical calculations such as differential equations while the digital part takes care of the logical computation and also controls the overall process.

Advantages:

1. Hybrid computers have tremendous computing speed enabled by the all-parallel configuration provided by the analog subsystem.
2. The results provided by hybrid computers are precise, accurate, more detailed and much more useful when compared to their earlier counterparts.

Uses:

1. One of the most widespread uses of hybrid computers is in automated assembly lines. In radar and sonar applications, signals are received in the analog form and often need to be analyzed instantaneously so that the next signal can be interpreted.
2. Other entities that use hybrid computers include the military and defense organisations of all the countries and some research labs. These military devices are a form of hybrid computers since they process analog signals with digital logical circuits.

Types of Computers based on Configuration:

(I) Super Computers:

- Super computers are one of the fastest computers currently available.
- Super computers are very expensive and are employed for specialized applications that require immense amounts of mathematical calculations (number crunching), like weather forecasting, scientific simulations, (animated) graphics, analysis of geological data etc.
- They are the best in terms of processing capacity and also the most expensive ones. These computers can process billions of instructions per second.
- Perhaps the best known super computer manufacturer is Cray Research. Some of the traditional companies which produce super computers are Cray, IBM and Hewlett-Packard.

- As of July 2009, the IBM Roadrunner, located at Los Alamos National Laboratory, is the fastest super computer in the world.

Fig. 1.10: Super computer

Advantages:
1. Super computer can solve bigger problems.
2. Run more problems in shorter time i.e. they are very fast.
3. They have very high storage capacity.

Disadvantages:
1. They require very high power.
2. Takes up a lot of space i.e. they are larger in size.
3. May only be good for specific applications.
4. They are more costly.
5. Maintenance cost is very high.
6. Difficult to assembly.
7. Air-conditioning is required.

Applications of Super computers:
1. The machine can be used in both scientific and business applications, but used mainly in scientific applications. Few large multinational banks and corporations are using small super computers.
2. Applications of super computer includes, special effects in film, collecting and processing of weather data, processing of geological data, processing of data regarding genetic decoding, aerospace (aerodynamics and structural designing), simulation, and mass destruction weapons.
3. The users include Film makers, National weather forecasting agencies, Geological data processing agencies, Genetics research organisations, Space agencies, Government agencies, Scientific laboratories, Research groups, Military and defence systems, Large time-sharing network, and Large corporations.

(II) Mainframe Computers:
- Mainframe computers, created in the early 1940s, initially were bulky machines that required cooling-sensitive rooms.
- Mainframe computers can also process data at very high speeds i.e., hundreds of million instructions per second and they are also quite expensive.

- Normally, they are used in banking, airlines and railways etc. for their applications.
- Mainframe is a very large in size and is an expensive computer capable of supporting hundreds, or even thousands, of users simultaneously.
- Mainframe executes many programs concurrently. Mainframes support many simultaneous programs execution.
- Examples of mainframe computer are DEC-1090, IBM 308-580 series, IBM 4300, ICIM 2904, etc.

Characteristics of mainframe computers:
1. Ability to run multiple operating systems.
2. Mainframes can add system capacity non disruptively and granularly.
3. Mainframes are designed to handle very high volume input and output (I/O) and emphasize throughput computing.
4. Mainframe Return On Investment (ROI), like any other computing platform, is dependent on its ability to scale, support mixed workloads, reduce labor costs, deliver uninterrupted service for critical business applications, and several other risk-adjusted cost factors.
5. Mainframes also have execution integrity characteristics for fault tolerant computing.

Fig. 1.11: Mainframe computer

Advantages:
1. Huge memory.
2. High speed compared to volume of data.
3. No virus attack so far reported in last 50-60 years.
4. Superb virtualization.
5. Huge data processing.

Disadvantages:
1. Cost of hardware is high.
2. Special operating systems/software require so higher cost.
3. Intense human attention required.
4. Intense space occupied.
5. More resource consumption.

Applications:
1. Both e-business and e-commerce use mainframe computers to perform business functions and exchange money over the internet.

2. The military one of the first users of mainframe computers continues employing this technology in combat and for keeping the country's borders secure. All branches of the armed forces use mainframes for communication among ships, planes and land; for prediction of weather patterns; and for tracking strategic locations and positions using a Global Positioning System (GPS).
3. Satellites that were once a science fiction fantasy continue to operate mainframe computers in their intelligence and spying efforts.
4. Public and private libraries, as well as colleges and universities, use mainframe computers for storage of critical data.

(III) Mini Computers:
- Mini computers are computers that are somewhere, in between a micro computer and a mainframe computer.
- Mini computers are lower to mainframe computers in terms of speed and storage capacity.
- They are also less expensive than mainframe computers. Some of the features of mainframes will not be available in mini computers. Hence, their performance also will be less than that of mainframes.
- Mini computer is a class of multi-user computers that lies in the middle range of computing spectrum, in between mainframe computers and micro computer.
- Mini computers are designed for single user.
- Examples of mini computers are Control Data's CDC 160A and CDC 1700, DEC PDP and VAX series, Data General Nova, Hewlett-Packard HP3000 series, Honeywell-Bull Level 6/DPS 6/DPS 6000 series, IBM midrange computers

Characteristics of mini computers:
1. Small in size and require small space.
2. More reliable and less power required.
3. Faster in speed.
4. Larger primary and secondary storage capacity.
5. Use for scientific and commercial use.
6. Standardization of high level language.

Fig. 1.12: Mini computer

Advantages:
1. They are faster and powerful than other computers.
2. Smaller in size.
3. Less power required.
4. Larger storage capacity.
5. Support high level language.
6. More reliable.
7. Support both scientific and commercial applications.
8. Support standardized high level languages.
9. Supports time sharing concept.

Disadvantages:
1. Air-conditioning required.
2. Cost is more than micro computer.

Applications:
1. Mini computers were often used in manufacturing sectors for process control. A mini computer used for process control has two primary functions. The first function of a process control minicomputer is data acquisition. The second function of a process control minicomputer is feedback, or, controlling a process.
2. Mini computers used for data management can be employed to acquire data, as in process control, generate data, or simply as a storage system for information.
3. Mini computers can be used as a communications tool in a larger system.

(IV) Micro Computers:
- The invention of microprocessor (single chip CPU) gave birth to the much cheaper micro computers.
- Micro computers are also known as Personal Computers (PC).
- A PC can be defined as a small, relatively inexpensive computer designed for an individual user. PCs are based on the microprocessor technology that enables manufacturers to put an entire CPU on one chip.
- Businesses use personal computers for word processing, accounting, desktop publishing, and for running spreadsheet and database management applications. At home, the most popular use for personal computers is for playing games and surfing the internet.
- Some examples of micro computers are HP 9100 A, Altair 8800 etc.
- Microcomputer is the term coined in the 1970s for a personal computer. Until that point, computers had been bulky room-sized electronics; even the smallest models were the size of large cars.
- The microcomputer has many uses, especially in the home, in business and in the medical field.

Characteristics of micro computers:
1. Support Graphical User Interface (GUI).
2. Speed is faster and larger storage capacity.
3. More powerful.
4. Smaller in size and cheaper.
5. Uses standard high level programming.
6. Use for office and homes .
7. Less power required.

Types of Micro Computers:

(i) Desktop Computers:
- Today the Desktop computers are the most popular computer systems.
- The desktop computers are also known as personal computers or simply PCs.
- They are usually easier to use and more affordable. They are normally intended for individual users for their word processing and other small application requirements.

Fig. 1.13: Desktop computer

(ii) Laptop Computers:
- Laptop computers are portable computers.
- They are lightweight computers with a thin screen. They are also called as notebook computers because of their small size.
- They can operate on batteries and hence are very popular with travellers. The screen folds down onto the keyboard when not in use.

Fig. 1.14: Laptop computer

(iii) Handheld Computers:
- Handheld computers or Personal Digital Assistants (PDAs) are pen-based and also battery-powered.
- They are small and can be carried anywhere. They use a pen like stylus and accept handwritten input directly on the screen.

- They are not as powerful as desktops or laptops but they are used for scheduling appointments, storing addresses and playing games.
- They have touch screens which we use with a finger or a stylus to be operated by user.

Fig. 1.15: Handheld computer

Advantages:
1. Smaller in size.
2. Cheaper.
3. More powerful and easy for installation.
4. Air-conditioning not required.
5. Faster in speed.
6. Larger primary and secondary storage.
7. Sharing resources in networking.
8. Does not require manual assembly.
9. More reliable and less hardware failure.

Disadvantages:
1. Non-portable.
2. Single user oriented.
3. More maintenance.

Applications:
1. Families use microcomputers for education; software can hold thousands of book volumes worth of information. Also, the first portable video games were built for the microcomputers. The home microcomputers paved the way for the invention of laptops.
2. Businesses took a huge leap forward in book-keeping, inventory and communication when microcomputers were made readily available.
3. The first microcomputer was built specifically for storing medical records. Before microcomputers were available, medical records were stored in paper form.

1.6 General Purpose and Special Purpose Computers

1.6.1 General Purpose Computers

- General purpose computers are designed to solve a large variety of problems. That is they can be given different program to solve different types of problems.
- General purpose computers can process business data as readily as they process complex mathematical formulas.
- General purpose computers can store large amount of data and the programmes necessary to process them. Because general purpose computers are so versatile, most businesses today use them.
- Most digital computers are general computers and it is mainly such computers that are used in business and commercial data processing.
- General purpose computers are used for any type of applications. They can store different programs and do the jobs as per the instructions specified on those programs. Most of the computers that we see today, are general purpose computers.
- Examples of general purpose computers include the BESM-6 computer (USSR), the ES family of computers (COMECON countries), the Atlas and System 4 computers (Great Britain), and the CDC 6600 computer and the IBM 370 family.

1.6.2 Special Purpose Computer

- Special purpose computer is one that is built for a specific application.
- Special purpose computers are designed to solve specific problems; the computer program for solving the problem is built right into the computer.
- Special purpose computers have many features of general-purpose computers but are designed to handle specific problems and are not applied to other computerized activities. For example, special purpose computers may be designed to process only numeric data or to completely control automated manufacturing processes.
- Most analog computers are special purpose computers.
- Special purpose computers are often used as training simulators.
- A simulator is a computer-controlled device for training people under simulated, or artificially created, conditions.
- The computer creates test conditions the trainee must respond to it then records and evaluates the responses, providing these results to both trainee and supervisor.
- Special purpose computers are simpler and cheaper than general purpose computers but have more limited logical and computational capabilities.

1.7 Limitations of Computer

1. **No intelligence:** A computer is a machine and has no intelligence of its own to perform any task. Each and every instruction has to be given to computer. A computer can not take any decision on its own.
2. **Environment:** The operating environment of computer should be dust free and suitable to it.
3. **No Feeling:** Computer has no feeling or emotions.
4. **Dependency:** Computer can perform function as instructed by user, so it is fully dependent on human being. Computer cannot make Judgment based on feeling, taste, experience and knowledge unlike a human being.
5. **Violation of Privacy:** It is crucial that personal and confidential records stored in computers be protected properly.
6. **Health Risks:** Prolonged or improper computer use can lead to disorders. Computer users can protect themselves from health risks through proper workplace design, good posture while at the computer and appropriately spaced work breaks.
7. **Impact on the Environment:** Computer manufacturing processes and computer waste are depleting natural resources and polluting the environment.

1.8 Applications of Computer in various Fields

- Various application of computer in various fields are listed below:

1. **Banking:**
- Today Banking is almost totally dependent on computer.
- Banks provide following facilities:
    (i) Banks, on-line accounting facility, which include current balances, deposits, overdrafts, interest charges, shares and trustee records.
    (ii) ATM machines are making it even easier for customers to deal with banks.

2. **Business:**
- Computer used in business organisation for payroll calculations, budgeting, sales analysis, financial forecasting, managing employees database and maintenance of stocks etc.

3. **Education:**
- The computer has provided a lot of facilities in the education system.
- The uses of computer provide a tool in the Education system is known as CBE (Computer Based Education).

4. **Marketing:**
- In Marketing uses of computer are following:
    - **(i) Home Shopping:** Home shopping has been made possible through use of computerised catalogs that provide access to product information and permit direct entry of orders to be filled by the customers.
    - **(ii) Advertising:** With computers, advertising professionals create art and graphics, write and revise copy, and print and disseminate ads with the goal of selling more products.

5. **Insurance:**
- Insurance companies are keeping all records up to date with the help of computer.
- The insurance companies, finance houses and stock broking firms are widely using computers for their concerns.
- Insurance companies are maintaining a database of all clients with information showing how to continue with policies, starting date of the policies, next due installment of a policy, maturity date, interests due, survival benefits bonus and so on.

6. **Communication:**
- Communication means to convey a message, an idea, a picture or speech that is received and understood clearly and correctly by the person for whom it is meant.
- Some main areas in this category are: E-mail, Chatting, Usenet, FTP, Telnet, Video-conferencing and so on.

7. **Health Care:**
- The computers are being used in hospitals to keep the record of patients and medicines. It is also used in scanning and diagnosing different diseases.
- ECG, EEG, Ultrasounds and CT Scans etc. are also done by computerised machines. Some of major fields of health care in which computer are used:
    - **(i) Pharma Information System:** Computer checks Drug-Labels, expiry dates, harmful drug side effects etc.
    - **(ii) Diagnostic System:** Computers are used to collect data and identify cause of illness.
    - **(iii) Patient Monitoring System:** These are used to check patient's signs for abnormality such as in cardiac arrest, ECG etc.
    - **(iv)** Now-a-days, computers are also used in **performing surgery**.
    - **(v) Lab-diagnostic System:** All tests can be done and reports are prepared by computer.

8. Military:

- Computers are largely used in defence. Modern tanks, missiles, weapons etc. employ computerized control systems.
- Some military areas where a computer has been used are: missile control, military communication, military operation and planning, smart weapons and so on.

9. Government Applications:

- Computers play an important role in government applications.
- Some major fields in this category are: budgets, sales tax department, income tax department, male/female ratio, computerization of voters lists, computerization of driving licensing system, computerization of pan card, weather forecasting and so on.

10. Engineering Design:

- Computers are widely used in Engineering purposes. Some fields are:
    - **(i) Industrial Engineering:** Computers deals with design, implementation and improvement of integrated systems of people, materials and equipments.
    - **(ii) Architectural Engineering:** Computers help in planning towns, designing buildings, determining a range of buildings on a site using both 2D and 3D drawings.
    - **(iii) Structural Engineering:** Requires stress and strain analysis required for design of ships, buildings, budgets, airplanes etc.

Questions

1. What is computer? Explain generations of computer.
2. Define the following terms:
   (i) Computer,
   (ii) Software, and
   (iii) Hardware.
3. What is analog computer? Explain its applications.
4. With the help of diagram describe relation between computer hardware and software.
5. Compare analog and digital computer.
6. What are the types of computers? Explain two of them in detail.
7. Describe general and special purpose computer in detail.
8. Enlist advantages of computers.
9. What is digital computer? State its applications and advantages.
10. Explain limitations of computer.
11. Enlist various application of computer in various fields like banking, business, military etc.

12. Write short note on: Evolution of computers.
13. Describe generations of computers with their characteristics, advantages and disadvantages.
14. What is super computer? State its advantages and disadvantages.
15. What is mini computer? State its advantages and disadvantages.
16. What is mainframe computer? State its advantages and disadvantages.
17. What is micro computer? State its advantages and disadvantages.
18. Distinguish between:
    (i) Mini and micro computers.
    (ii) Super and mainframe computers.
19. What are the types of micro computer?
20. Explain hybrid computer in detail.

Chapter 2...

Structure and Working of Computer

Contents ...

2.1 Introduction
2.2 Functional Block Diagram of Computer
2.3 Bus Structure of Digital Computer
    2.3.1 Address Bus
    2.3.2 Data Bus
    2.3.3 Control Bus
- Questions

2.1 Introduction

- A computer performs basically five major operations irrespective of their size and make.
- These operations are listed below:
    1. Computer accepts data or instructions by way of input,
    2. Computer stores data,
    3. Computer can process data as required by the user,
    4. Computer gives results in the form of output, and
    5. Computer controls all operations inside a computer.

2.2 Functional Block Diagram of Computer

- Fig. 2.1 shows block diagram of a computer.

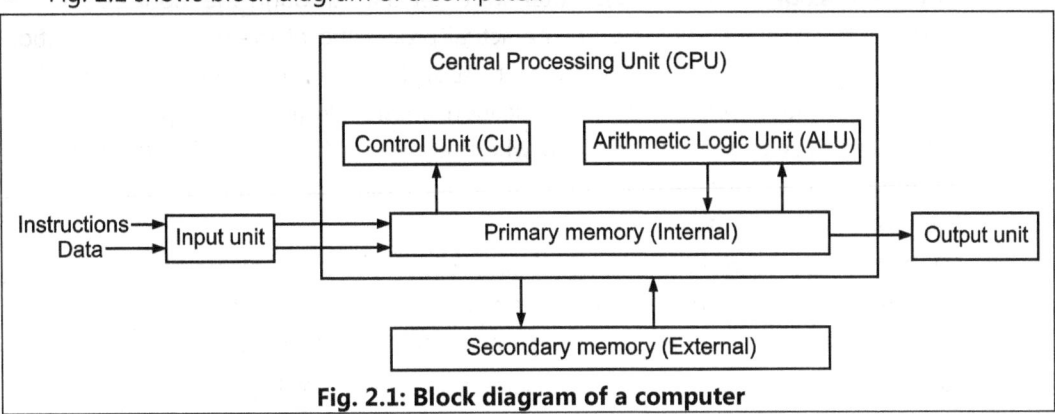

Fig. 2.1: Block diagram of a computer

- Various parts of computer are described below:

1. **Input Unit:**
- Input unit contains devices with the help of which we enter data into computer. This unit makes link between user and computer.
- The input devices translate the human readable information into the form understanddable by computer.
- Some important input devices which are used in computer systems are: keyboard, mouse, joystick, light pen, track ball, scanner, graphic tablet, microphone, magnetic ink card reader (MICR), optical character reader (OCR), bar code reader, optical mark reader (OMR).
- An input device performs the following functions:
    (i) It accepts (i.e. reads) the list of instruction and data from the user.
    (ii) It converts these instructions and data in binary form which is understood by the computer.
    (iii) It supplies the converted instructions and data to the computer for further processing.

2. **CPU:**
- The task of performing operations like arithmetic and logical operations is called processing.
- The Central Processing Unit (CPU) takes data and instructions from the storage unit and makes all sorts of calculations based on the instructions given and the type of data provided. It is then sent back to the storage unit.
- Central Processing Unit (CPU) is the heart of every computer system that performs the user instructions.
- CPU itself has following three components:
    (i) **Arithmetic Logical Unit (ALU):** After we enter data through the input device it is stored in the primary storage unit. The actual processing of the data and instruction are performed by Arithmetic Logical Unit (ALU). The major operations performed by the ALU is addition, subtraction, multiplication, division, logic and comparison. Data is transferred to ALU from storage unit when required. After processing the output is returned back to storage unit for further processing or getting stored. This unit consists of two subsection namely:
        (a) **Arithmetic section:** Function of arithmetic section is to perform arithmetic operations like addition, subtraction, multiplication and division. All complex operations are done by making repetitive use of above operations.
        (b) **Logic Section:** Function of logic section is to perform logic operations such as comparing, selecting, matching and merging of data.

- Fig. 2.2 (a) (i) shows block diagram of ALU.

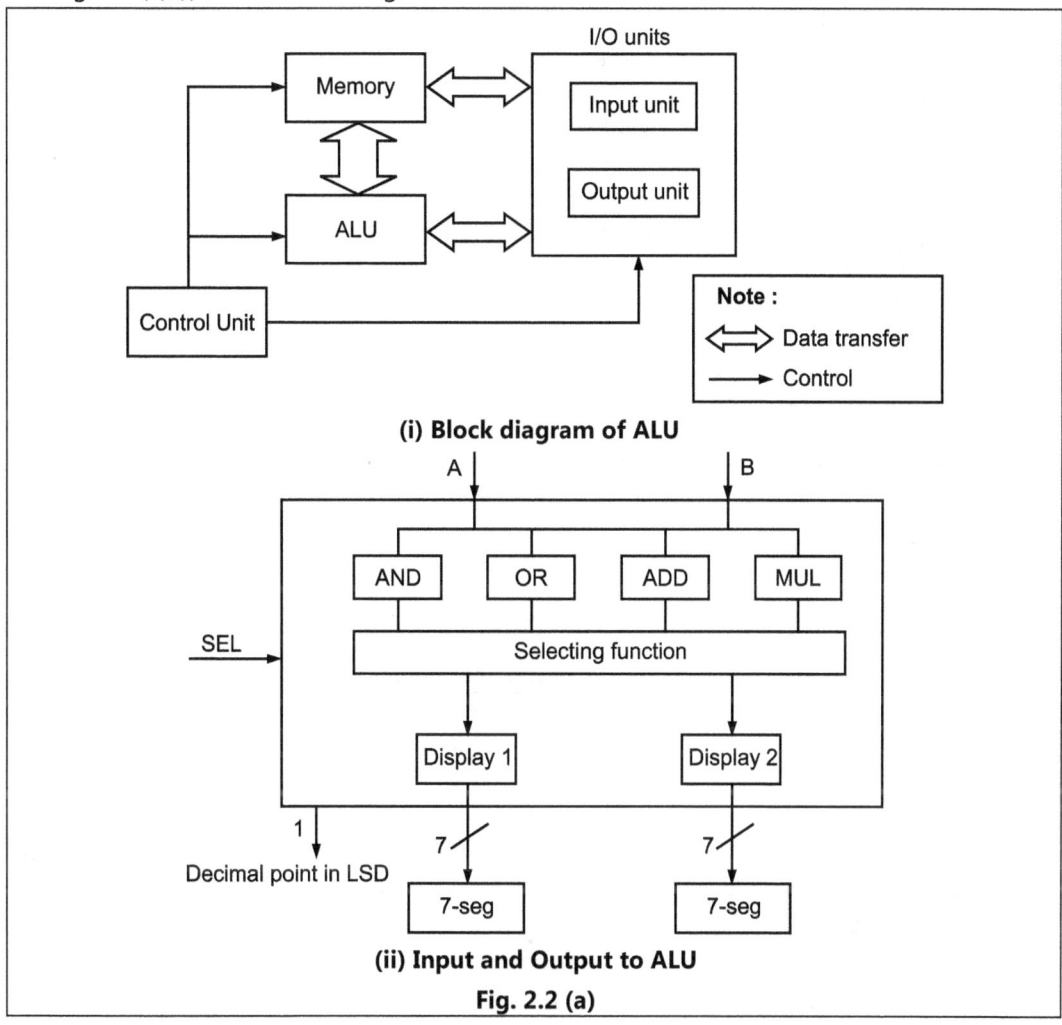

Fig. 2.2 (a)

- Input A and B as shown in Fig. 2.2 (a) (ii) are sent to the ALU.
- By selection algorithm an operation is selected to be performed on A and B.
- The selected function/operation is performed and output is sent for storage.

(ii) Control Unit (CU): The main function of control unit is to control all operations like input, processing, output etc. Control Unit (CU) acts as the supervisor seeing that things are done in proper fashion. Control Unit is responsible for coordinating various operations using time signal. The control unit determines the sequence in which computer programs and instructions are executed. Things like processing of programs stored in the main memory, interpretation of the instructions and issuing of signals for other units of the computer to execute them. It also acts as a switch board operator when several users access the computer simultaneously. Thereby it coordinates the activities of computer's peripheral equipments as they perform the input and output.

- Control unit controls the operations of all parts of computer. It does not carry out any actual data processing operations.
- **Functions of control unit** are:
    (i) It is responsible for controlling the transfer of data and instructions among other units of a computer.
    (ii) It manages and coordinates all the units of the computer.
    (iii) It does not process or store data.
    (iv) It obtains the instructions from the memory, interprets them and directs the operation of the computer.
    (v) It communicates with Input/Output (I/O) devices for transfer of data or results from storage.

- Fig. 2.2 (b) shows block diagram of CU.

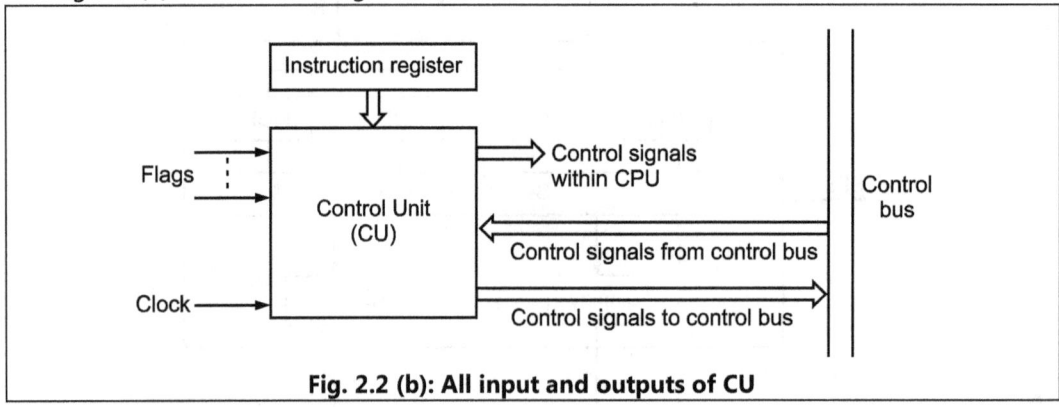

Fig. 2.2 (b): All input and outputs of CU

- Fig. 2.2 (b) shows the following inputs and outputs for CU.
- The inputs of CU are:
    1. **Clock:** It is how the control unit "keeps time".
    2. **Instruction register:** The opcode and addressing mode of the current instruction are used to determine which micro operations to perform during the execute cycle.
    3. **Flags:** Flags are needed by CU to determine the status of the processor and the outcome of previous ALU operation.
    4. **Control signals from control bus:** The control bus portion of the system bus provides signals to the CU.
- The outputs are:
    1. **Control signals within the processor:** These are two types:
        (i) those that cause data to be moved from one register to another, and
        (ii) those that activate specific ALU functions.
    2. **Control signals to control bus:** These are controls signals to memory and control signals to the I/O modules.

3. **Memory or Storage Unit:**
   - Memory unit can store instruction, data and intermediate results. This unit supplies information to the other units of the computer when needed.
   - It is also known as internal storage unit or main memory or primary storage or Random Access Memory (RAM).
   - Its size affects speed, power and capability. There are two types of memories in the computer namely primary memory and secondary memory.
   - **Function of memory unit** are:
     (i) It stores all the data to be processed and the instructions required for processing.
     (ii) It stores intermediate results of processing.
     (iii) It stores final results of processing before these results are released to an output device.
     (iv) All inputs and outputs are transmitted through main memory.

4. **Secondary Memory (Storage):**
   - To supplement the limited storage capacity of the primary storage section, most computer have secondary storage capabilities.
   - These devices are connected directly to the processor which accept data/program instructions for the processor, retain them, and then write them back to the processor as needed to complete the processing tasks.
   - Magnetic tape, disks are the examples of secondary storage.

5. **Output Unit:**
   - Output is the process of producing results from the data for getting useful information. Similarly the output produced by the computer after processing must also be kept somewhere inside the computer before being given to you in human readable form. Again the output is also stored inside the computer for further processing. The result of computer processing is called as output. This result is communicated to user through a device called output devices.
   - Output unit consists of devices with the help of which we get the information from computer. This unit is a link between computer and users.
   - Output devices translate the computer's output into the human readable form.
   - Few of the important output devices which are used in computer systems are: Monitors, Graphic plotter, Printer etc.
   - The following **functions are performed by an output** unit:
     (i) It accepts results produced by the computer which are in binary coded form and hence cannot be understood by user.
     (ii) It converts these coded results to human readable form.
     (iii) It supplies the converted form to the user.

- Fig. 2.3 shows the functional view of the computer.
- A computer must be able to process data and it is essential that a computer store data.
- A computer must be able to move data between itself and the outside the world and computer must have control over three units as shown below.

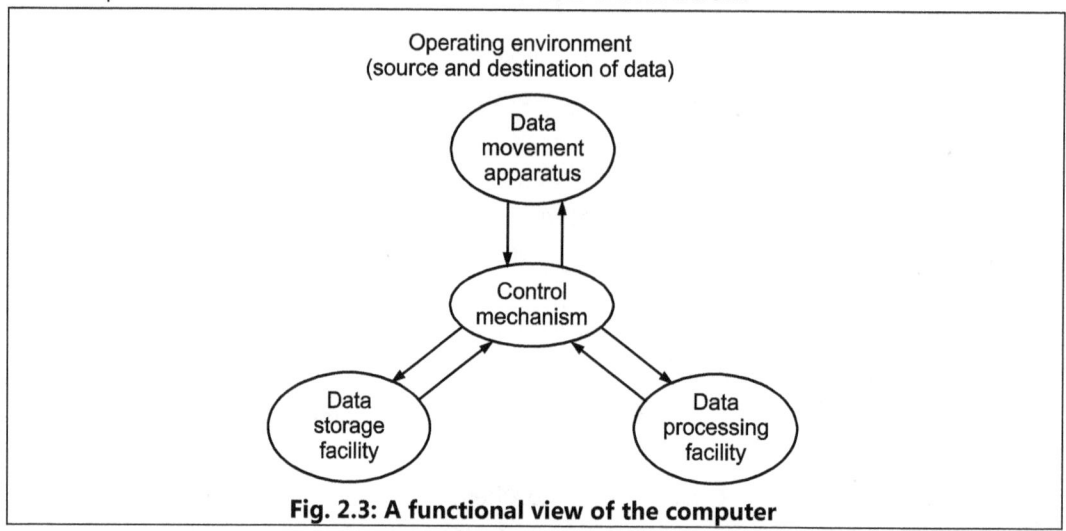

Fig. 2.3: A functional view of the computer

2.3 Bus Structure of Digital Computer

- CPU sends data, instructions and information to the components inside the computer as well as to the peripherals and devices attached to it.
- Bus is a set of electronic signal pathways that allows information and signals to travel between components inside or outside of a computer.
- The different components of computer, i.e., CPU, I/O unit, and memory unit are connected with each other by a bus. The data, instructions and the signals are carried between the different components via a bus, (See Fig. 2.4).
- A system bus is a single computer bus that connects the major components of a computer system.
- A bus is a communication pathway connecting more than two devices.
- The key characteristic of a computer bus is that, it is a shared transmission medium.
- Multiple devices connect to the bus and a signal transmitted by any one device is available for reception by all other devices attached to the bus.
- Typically a bus consist of multiple communication pathways or lines and each line is capable for transmitting signals representing binary 1 and 0.
- The **features and functionality of a bus** are as follows:
    1. A bus is a set of wires used for interconnection, where each wire can carry one bit of data.
    2. A bus width is defined by the number of wires in the bus.

3. A computer bus can be divided into two types i.e. internal bus and external bus.
4. The internal bus connects components inside the motherboard like, CPU and system memory. It is also called the System Bus.
5. Fig. 2.4 shows interaction between processor, memory and I/O with bus.

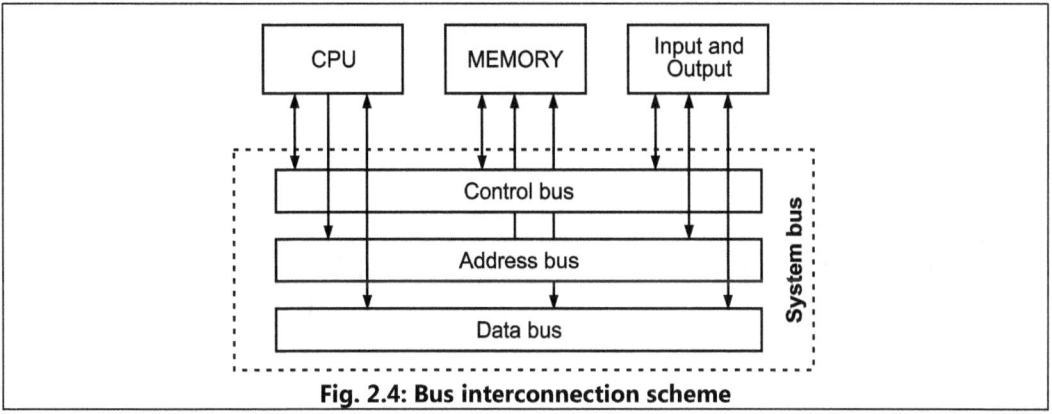

Fig. 2.4: Bus interconnection scheme

- A bus that connects major computer components like processor, I/O, memory is called a system bus (See Fig. 2.4).
- A system bus or expansion bus comprise of three kinds of buses - data bus, address bus and control bus.

2.3.1 Address Bus

- The address of I/O device or memory is carried by the address bus.
- An address bus is a computer bus (a series of lines connecting two or more devices) that is used to specify a physical address.
- The address bus is used to designate the source or destination of the data on the data bus.

2.3.2 Data Bus

- The data to be transferred is carried by the data bus.
- A data bus is a group of electrical wires used to send information (data) back and forth between two or more components.
- A data bus is a computer subsystem that allows for transferring of data from one component to another on a motherboard or system board, or between two computers.
- Data bus can include transferring data to and from the memory, or from the central processing unit (CPU) to other components. Each one is designed to handle so many bits of data at a time. The amount of data a data bus can handle is called bandwidth.
- Data bus provide a path for moving data among system modules.
- The data bus may consist of 32, 64, 128 or even more separate lines, the number of lines being referred to as the width of the data bus.

2.3.3 Control Bus

- The command to access the memory or the I/O device is carried by the control bus.
- A control bus is (part of) a computer bus, used by CPUs for communicating with other devices within the computer.
- Control bus is used to control the access to and the use of data and address lines.
- While the address bus carries the information on which device the CPU is communicating with and the data bus carries the actual data being processed, the control bus carries commands from the CPU and returns status signals from the devices, for example if the data are being read or written to the device the appropriate line (read or write) will be active (logic zero).

Questions

1. What is meant by bus?
2. Describe functional block diagram of computer.
3. Define bus. Explain its types.
4. Explain the following terms:
   (i) Input unit,
   (ii) Storage unit, and
   (iii) Output unit.
5. What is ALU and CU? What are its function.
6. With the help of diagram describe bus structure of digital computer.
7. What are the types of buses? Explain two of them in detail.
8. What is data bus and control bus?
9. Write short note on: address bus.

■■■

Chapter **3**...

Input/Output Devices

Contents ...
3.1 Introduction
3.2 Input Devices
    3.2.1 Keyboard
    3.2.2 Mouse
    3.2.3 Scanner
    3.2.4 MICR
    3.2.5 OMR
3.3 Output Devices
    3.3.1 Monitor/VDU
    3.3.2 Printers
        3.3.2.1 Dot Matrix Printer
        3.3.2.2 Daisy Wheel Printer
        3.3.2.3 Line Printers
        3.3.2.4 Inkjet Printers
        3.3.2.5 Laser Printers
    3.3.3 Plotter
- Questions

3.1 Introduction

- The terms input and output are used both as verbs to describe the process of entering or displaying the data, and as nouns referring to the data itself entered into or displayed by the computer.
- Input devices allow us to enter raw data into a computer. The computer processes the data and then produces outputs that we can understand using an output device.

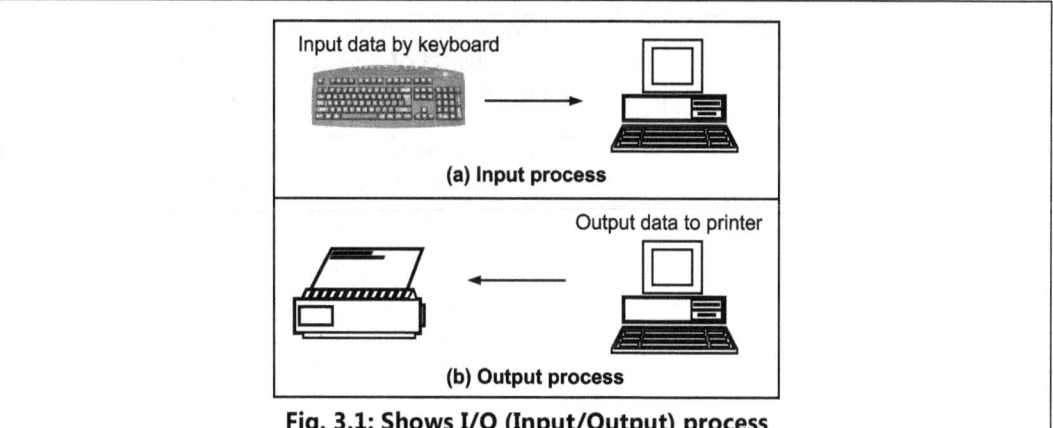

Fig. 3.1: Shows I/O (Input/Output) process

- Any information or data that is entered or sent to the computer to be processed is considered input and anything that is displayed from the computer is output.
- Therefore, an input device such as a computer keyboard is capable of having information sent to the computer, but does not display (output) any information.
- An output device such as a computer printer can print information from the computer but does not send any information (input) to the computer.

3.2 Input Devices

- The devices which are used to input the data and the programs in the computer are known as Input Devices.
- Input device can read data and convert them to a form that a computer can understand and use.
- An input device is equipment used to capture information and commands.

3.2.1 Keyboard

- Keyboard is most common input device is used today. Keyboard are used for inputting data to computer.
- The data and instructions are input by typing on the keyboard. The message typed on the keyboard reaches the memory unit of a computer. It is connected to a computer via a cable. Apart from alphabet and numeral keys, it has other function keys for performing different functions.
- The layout of the keyboard is like that of traditional typewriter, although there are some additional keys provided for performing some additional functions.
- Keyboard are of two sizes 84 keys or 101/102 keys, but now 104 keys or 108 keys keyboard is also available for Windows and Internet.
- The keys are following:

Sr. No.	Keys	Description
1.	Typing Keys	These keys include the letter keys (A-Z) and digits keys (0-9) which are generally arranged in same layout as that of typewriters.
2.	Numeric Keypad	It is used to enter numeric data or cursor movement. Generally, it consists of a set of 17 keys that are laid out in the same configuration used by most adding machine and calculators.
3.	Function Keys	The twelve functions keys are present on the keyboard. These are arranged in a row along the top of the keyboard. Each function key has unique meaning and is used for some specific purpose.
4.	Control keys	These keys provides cursor and screen control. It includes four directional arrow key. Control keys also include Home, End,Insert, Delete, Page Up, Page Down, Control (Ctrl), Alternate (Alt), Escape(Esc).
5.	Special Purpose Keys	Keyboard also contains some special purpose keys such as Enter, Shift, Caps Lock, Num Lock, Space bar, Tab, and Print Screen.

- Fig. 3.2 shows a keyboard with its keys.

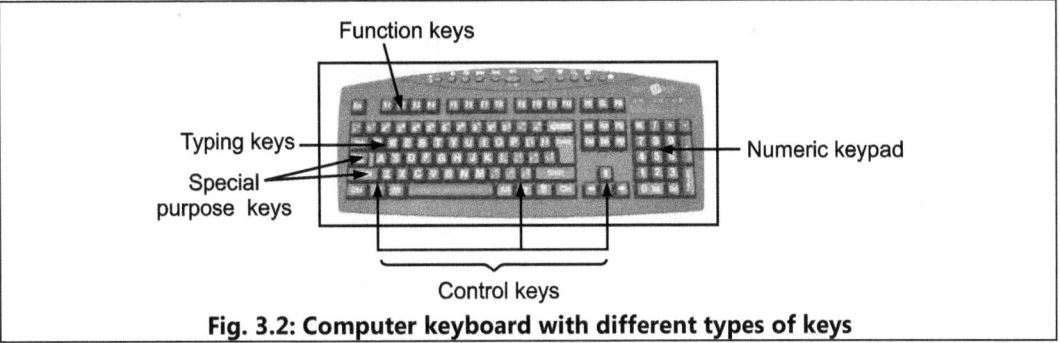

Fig. 3.2: Computer keyboard with different types of keys

3.2.2 Mouse

- Mouse is most popular pointing device.
- Mouse is a very famous cursor-control device.
- Mouse is a small palm size box with a round ball at its base which senses the movement of mouse and sends corresponding signals to CPU on pressing the buttons.
- Generally it has two buttons called left and right button and scroll bar is present at the mid wheel, (See Fig. 3.3).
- Mouse can be used to control the position of cursor on screen, but it cannot be used to enter text into the computer.

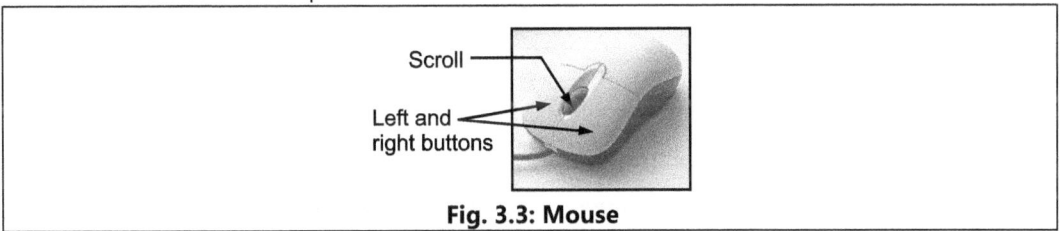

Fig. 3.3: Mouse

Advantages:
1. Easy to use.
2. Not very expensive.
3. Moves the cursor faster than the arrow keys of keyboard.

3.2.3 Scanner

- Scanner is an input device which works more like a photocopy (Xerox) machine.
- Scanners are used to enter information directly into the computer's memory.
- The scanner converts any type of printed or written information including photographs into digital pulses, which can be manipulated by the computer.
- Scanner is used when some information is available on a paper and it is to be transferred to the hard disc of the computer for further manipulation.
- Scanner captures images from the source which are then converted into the digital form that can be stored on the disc. These images can be edited before they are printed.

Fig. 3.4: Scanner

3.2.4 MICR

- MICR is an input device.
- MICR is a very fast and reliable as a means of entering data into a computer.
- Magnetic Ink Card Reader (MICR) input device is generally used in banks because of a large number of cheques to be processed every day.
- The bank's code number and cheque number are printed on the cheques with a special type of ink that contains particles of magnetic material that are machine readable.
- This reading process is called Magnetic Ink Character Recognition (MICR). The main advantage of MICR is that it is fast and less error prone.
- MICR is a character recognition system that uses special ink and characters.

Fig. 3.5: MICR

3.2.5 OMR

- Optical Mark Reader (OMR) is the process of gathering data with an optical scanner by measuring the reflectivity of light at predetermined positions on a surface.
- OMR is a special type of optical scanner used to recognize the type of mark made by pen or pencil.
- OMR is used where one out of a few alternatives is to be selected and marked.
- OMR is specially used for checking the answer sheets of examinations having multiple choice questions.

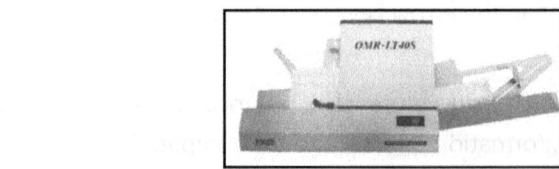

Fig. 3.6

Other important Input Devices:

1. **Digital Camera:**
- Digital camera is an input device.
- Digital cameras are becoming increasingly popular as they become cheaper and photo sharing websites become common.

- Digital camera is a device that captures digital photographs. Most digital cameras do not directly input data into a computer - they store photographs on memory cards.
- The photographs can later be transferred to a computer. A modern digital camera can capture 10 Megapixels or more per photograph - that's 10,000,000 colored dots (pixels) in every photo.

Fig. 3.7: Digital camera

2. **Digitizer:**
- Digitizer is an input device which converts analog information into a digital form.
- Digitizer can convert a signal from the television camera into a series of numbers that could be stored in a computer.
- Digitizer can be used by the computer to create a picture of whatever the camera had been pointed at.
- Digitizer is also known as Tablet or Graphics Tablet because it converts graphics and pictorial data into binary inputs.
- A graphic tablet as digitizer is used for doing fine works of drawing and image manipulation applications.

Fig. 3.8: Digitizer

3. **Joystick:**
- Joystick is also a pointing device which is used to move cursor position on a monitor screen.
- Joystick is a stick having a spherical ball at its both lower and upper ends. The lower spherical ball moves in a socket. The Joystick can be moved in all four directions.
- The function of joystick is similar to that of a mouse.
- Joystick is mainly used in Computer Aided Designing (CAD) and playing computer games.

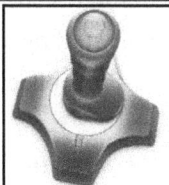

Fig. 3.9: Joystick

4. **Light Pen:**
- Light pen is an input device which is used to draw lines or figures on a computer screen.
- Light pen is a pointing device which is similar to a pen. It is used to select a displayed menu item or draw pictures on the monitor screen.
- Light pen consists of a photocell and an optical system placed in a small tube.
- When light pen's tip is moved over the monitor screen and pen button is pressed, its photocell sensing element detects the screen location and sends the corresponding signal to the CPU.

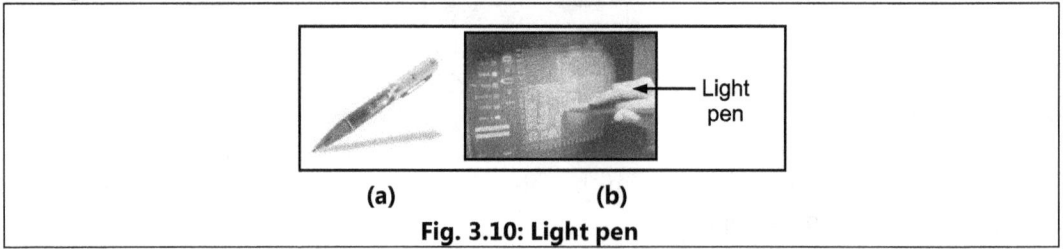

Fig. 3.10: Light pen

5. **Track Ball:**
- Track ball is an input device that is mostly used in notebook or laptop computer, instead of a mouse.
- This is a ball which is half inserted and by moving fingers on ball, pointer can be moved.
- Since, the whole device is not moved, a track ball requires less space than a mouse. A track ball comes in various shapes like a ball, a button and a square.
- Track ball is similar to the upside-down design of the mouse.
- The user moves the ball directly, while the device itself remains stationary. The user spins the ball in various directions to effect the screen movements.

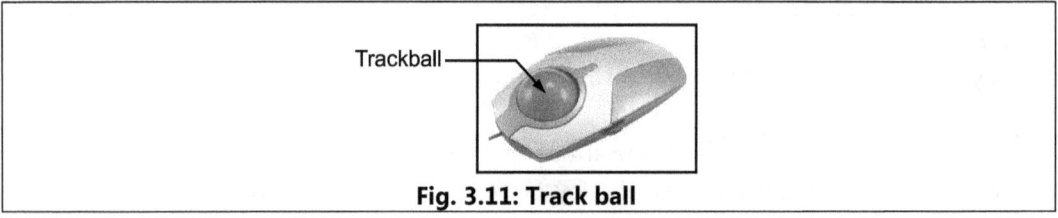

Fig. 3.11: Track ball

6. **Optical Character Reader (OCR):**
- OCR is a device which detects alpha numeric characters printed or written on a paper.
- The text which is to be scanned is illuminated by a low frequency light source.
- The light is absorbed by the dark areas but reflected from the bright areas. The reflected light is received by the photocells.
- OCR is an input device used to read a printed text.
- OCR scans text optically character by character, converts them into a machine readable code and stores the text on the system memory.

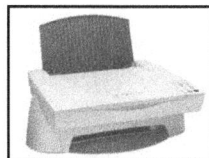
Fig. 3.12: OCR

7. Bar Code Readers:
- A bar code reader reads bar codes and coverts them into electric pulses to be processed by a computer. A bar code is nothing but data coded in form of light and dark bars.
- Bar coded data is generally used in labelling goods, numbering the books etc. It may be a hand held scanner or may be embedded in a stationary scanner.
- Bar code reader scans a bar code image, converts it into an alphanumeric value which is then fed to the computer to which bar code reader is connected.

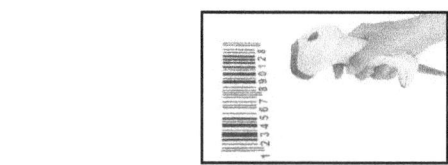
Fig. 3.13: Barcode reader

3.3 Output Devices

- Output device can produce the final product of machine processing into a form usable by users. It provides machine to man communication.
- The output devices accept the results after processed by the CPU, converts it into human acceptable form and supplies it to the user.
- An output device is equipment used to see, hear, or otherwise accept the results of information processing requests.

3.3.1 Monitor/VDU

- Monitor commonly called as Visual Display Unit (VDU) is the main output device of a computer.
- Monitor forms images from tiny dots, called pixels, that are arranged in a rectangular form. The sharpness of the image depends upon the no. of the pixels.
- The monitor displays the video and graphics information generated by the computer through the video card.
- Monitors are very similar to televisions but usually display information at a much higher resolution.
- The monitor is also known as screen, display, video display or video screen.
- Monitors come in two major types i.e. LCD and CRT.

1. CRT (Cathode Ray Tube):

- CRT monitors look much like old-fashioned televisions and are very deep in size. A monitor contains a Cathode Ray Tube (CRT), hardware to control an electronics beam and a power supply.
- A CRT is used to display numbers, letters and graphics.
- In the CRT display is made up of small picture elements called pixels for short. The smaller the pixels, the better the image clarity, or resolution. It takes more than one illuminated pixel to form whole character, such as the letter e in the word help.
- A finite number of characters can be displayed on a screen at once. The screen can be divided into a series of character boxes - fixed location on the screen where a standard character can be placed.
- The most screens are capable of displaying 80 characters of data horizontally and 25 lines vertically.

Fig. 3.14: CRT monitor

How CRT Monitor works?

- CRT monitor looks like TV screen. This kind of screen uses the Cathode Ray Tube (CRT) technology.
- CRT is a partially evacuated glass tube which is filled with an inert gas at very low pressure.
- Images are formed in this CRT by an electron gun shooting a stream of electrons at the surface of phosphorescent. Deflection coils are used to divert electron beam and strike on the exact position of phosphorescent surface.
- The CRT screen can be classified into two types in terms of colors capability:

    (i) Monochrome Monitor: Monochrome monitor actually displays only two colors, one for the background and other for the foreground.

    (ii) Color Monitor: Color Monitor display color but the number of colors they can display depends on the video adaptor capabilities as well as the monitors. Color monitor can display from 1 to 16 million different colors. Color monitor are sometime called RGB monitors because they accept three separate signal RED, GREEN and BLUE.

- Fig. 3.15 shows structure of CRT.

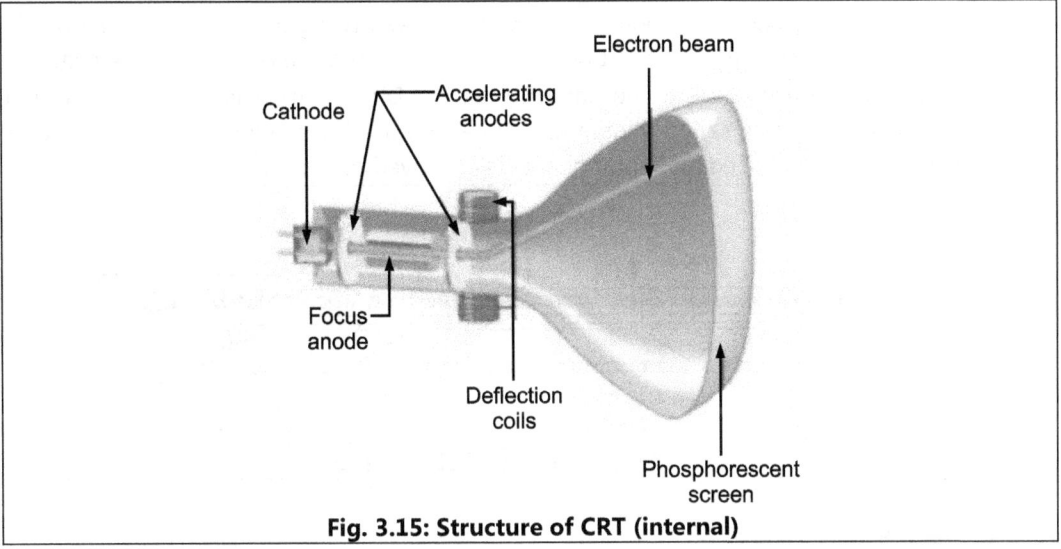

Fig. 3.15: Structure of CRT (internal)

- There are some disadvantage of CRT
  (i) Large in Size, and
  (ii) High Power consumption.

2. **LCD:**
- LCD stands for Liquid Crystal Display. LCD monitors are much thinner, use less energy, and provide a greater graphics quality.
- LCD monitors have completely obsoleted CRT monitors due to their higher quality, smaller footprint on the desk, and decreasing price.
- The flat-panel display refers to a class of video devices that have reduced volume, weight and power requirement compared to the CRT.
- You can hang them on walls or wear them on your wrists. Current uses for flat-panel displays include calculators, videogames, monitors, laptop computer, graphics display.

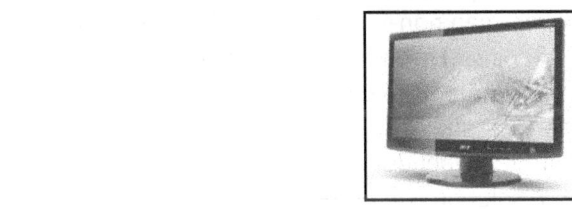

Fig. 3.16 (a): LCD monitor

- The flat-panel display are divided into two categories:
  (i) Emissive Displays: The emissive displays are devices that convert electrical energy into light. Example are plasma panel and LED (Light-Emitting Diodes).
  (ii) Non-Emissive Displays: The Non-emissive displays use optical effects to convert sunlight or light from some other source into graphics patterns. Example is LCD (Liquid-Crystal Device).

How LCD Monitor Works?

- In LCD or liquid crystalline material is sandwich between two glass or plates as shown in Fig. 3.16 (b) (LCD monitor). The front plate is transparent and the back plate is reflective.
- The less expensive LCD's are called passive matrix LCD's. The expensive LCD's are called active matrix LCD's (also called thinfil transistor - TFT) used transistor to control the color of each screen pixel. Speed and color quality is improved on passive matrix LCD's.

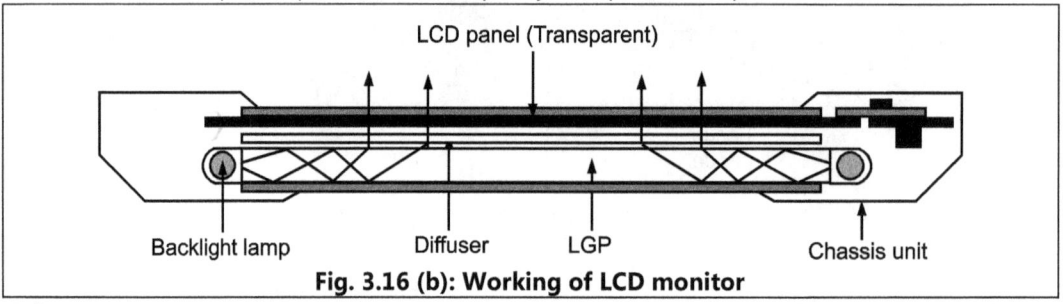

Fig. 3.16 (b): Working of LCD monitor

Advantages:
  (i) Power consumption is low.
  (ii) Cost is less.

Disadvantages:
  (i) Turn-on and Turn-off is large hence they are slow devices.
  (ii) Their life span is less when used on DC.
  (iii) They occupy large area.

- Most monitors are in a widescreen format and range in size from 17" to 24" or more. This size is a diagonal measurement from one corner of the screen to the other.

3.3.2 Printers

- Printer is a peripheral which produces a hard copy (permanent readable text and/or graphics) of documents stored in electronic form, usually on physical print media such as paper or transparencies.
- Printer is the most important output device, which is used to print information on paper.
- The quality of printer depends on following factors:
  1. **Speed:** The impact printer is slower than non-impact printer. The speed of dot matrix printer depends on number of pins. The expensive printer is faster than non-expensive printers. Generally, color printer is also slow.
  2. **Resolution:** The sharpness of text and image per inch is called resolution of computer. The quality of output depends on resolution. The high-resolution computer is expensive than low-resolution computers.
  3. **Memory:** The costly input/output device has own local memory to hold data at the time of processing. The printer is slower than the processor so, if it has its own memory to hold processed data, the speed can be increased. So, high memory printer is preferred for quality and fast printings.
  4. **Color:** The color is a part of information. The colorful text and graphics are more attractive than plain text and graphics. So, color printer is also a part of quality printings.

- Fig. 3.17 shows types of printer.

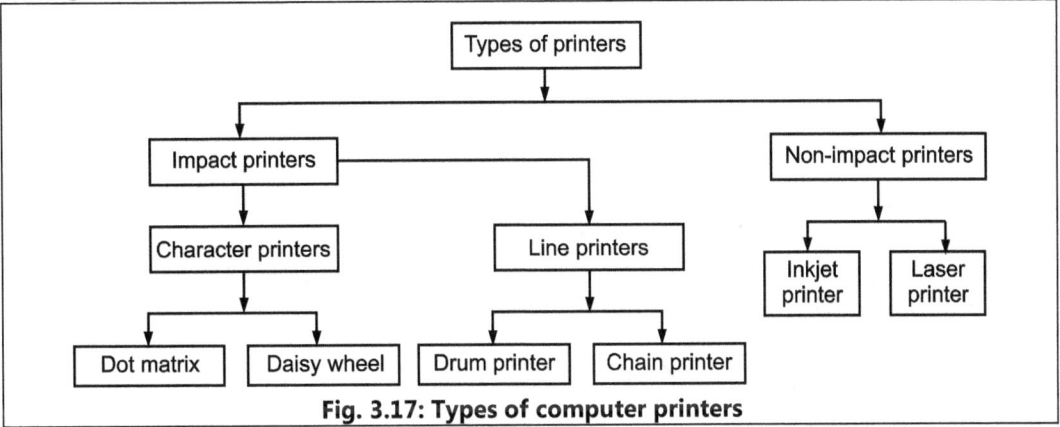

Fig. 3.17: Types of computer printers

1. Impact Printers:
- The printers that print the characters by striking against the ribbon and onto the paper, are called impact printers.
- An impact printer is like a typewriter and the characters are formed by physically striking the type devices against an inked ribbon.
- Impact printers can produce a page, a line, or a character at a time. Print quality is low, but these printers are mainly used for printing backup copies of large amounts of data.
- Some of the examples of impact printers are: Dot matrix printer, Daisy wheel printers, Drum printers and Chain printers.

Characteristics of Impact Printers:
    (i) Very low consumable costs.
    (ii) Impact printers are very noisy.
    (iii) Useful for bulk printing due to low cost.
    (iv) There is physical contact with the paper to produce an image.
- Impact printers are of two types:
    - **(i) Character printers:** Character printers are printers which print one character at a time. These are of further two types Dot Matrix Printer (DMP) and Daisy wheel printer.
    - **(ii) Line printers:** A line printer is a high-speed printing device that is able to store and print a complete line of information at a time. Line printers are printers which print one line at a time. Large computer system typically use line printer. Line printers are of further two types Drum printer and Chain printer.

Advantages of Impact Printers:
    (i) Design and functioning of this kind of printer is easier than that of non-impact printer.
    (ii) Since, the image is produced as a result of impact, multiple copies can be produced by the use of carbon paper.

Disadvantages of Impact Printer:
    (i) They are noisy in operation.
    (ii) The wear and tear of printer head causes the periodical replacement of the printer head.

2. Non-impact Printers:

- Non-impact printers generally, use specially coated or sensitized papers that respond to thermal or electrostatic stimuli to form an image.
- The printers that print the characters without striking against the ribbon and onto the paper, are called non-impact printers.
- Non-impact printers print a complete page at a time, also called as page printers.
- Non-impact printers, used almost everywhere now, are faster and more quiet than impact printers because they have fewer moving parts.
- Non-impact printers are of two types Laser printers and Inkjet printers.

Characteristics of Non-impact printers:
 (i) Faster than impact printers.
 (ii) They are not noisy.
 (iii) High quality.
 (iv) Support many fonts and different character size.

Advantages of non-impact printer:
 (i) Soundless operation.
 (ii) High quality output.

Disadvantages of non-impact printer:
 (i) Multiple copies cannot be produced in a single pass.
 (ii) They are costly.

3.3.2.1 Dot Matrix Printer

- In the general sense many printers rely on a matrix of pixels, or dots, that together form the larger image. However, the term dot matrix printer is specifically used for impact printers that use a matrix of small pins to create precise dots.
- A dot matrix printer or impact matrix printer refers to a type of computer printer with a print head that runs back and forth on the page and prints by impact, striking an ink-soaked cloth ribbon against the paper, much like a typewriter.
- Dot matrix technology uses a series or matrix of pins to create printed dots arranged to form characters on a piece of paper. Because the printing involves mechanical pressure, these printers can create carbon copies and carbonless copies.
- The print head mechanism pushes each pin into the ribbon, which then strikes the paper. Many offices and government agencies use them because they can make multiple copies at lowest cost.

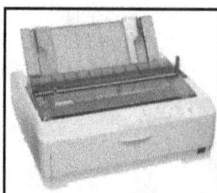

Fig. 3.18: Dot matrix printer

Working of Dot Matrix Printers:

- Fig. 3.19 shows working of dot matrix printer.
- Dot matrix refers to the way the printer creates characters or images on paper.
- This is done by several tiny pins, aligned in a column, striking an ink ribbon positioned between the pins and the paper, creating dots on the paper.
- Characters are composed of patterns of these dots by moving the printhead laterally across the page in very small increments.
- The pins, contained in the printhead, are about one inch long and are driven by several hammers which force each pin into contact with the ink ribbon (and paper) at a certain time.
- The force on these hammers comes from the magnetic pull of small wire coils (solenoids) which are energized at a particular time, depending on the character to be printed.
- Timing of the signals sent to the solenoids is programmed into the printer for each character, and translated from information sent by the computer about which characters to print.

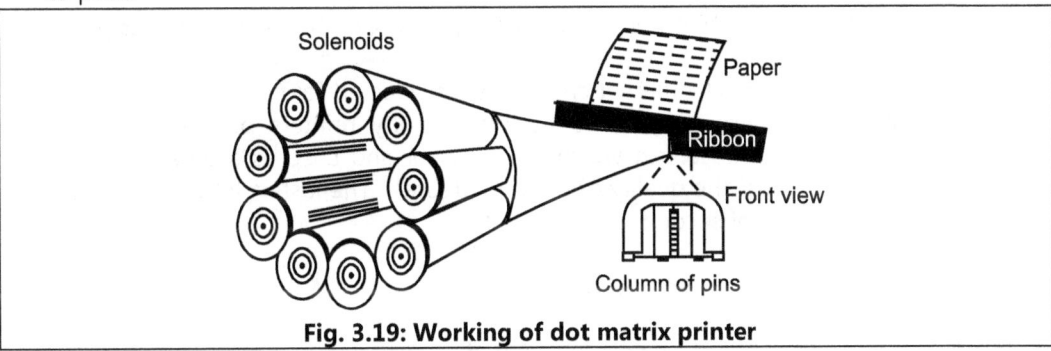

Fig. 3.19: Working of dot matrix printer

Advantages:
1. They can print on multi-part stationary or make carbon copies.
2. Low printing cost.
3. They can bear environmental conditions.
4. Long life.

Disadvantages:
1. These printers are noisy.
2. Low resolution.
3. Very limited color performance.
4. Low speed.
5. Servicing cost of this printer is more than buying a new one.

3.3.2.2 Daisy Wheel Printer

- A daisy wheel printer is an electronic device that can be connected to a word processor or computer to allow documents to be printed from that machine.
- The basic functionality of these devices is similar to other printers, such as dot matrix or inkjet printers, though the way in which a document is printed is quite different.

- A daisy wheel printer uses a printing mechanism known as a "daisy wheel," which consists of numerous raised letters and numbers arrayed in a circle.
- Head is lying on a wheel and Pins corresponding to characters are like petals of Daisy (flower name) that is why it is called Daisy Wheel Printer.
- These printers are generally used for word-processing in offices which require a few letters to be send here and there with very nice quality representation.

Fig. 3.20: Daisy wheel

Working of Daisy wheel printer:
- Daisy wheel printers operate in much the same fashion as a typewriter. A hammer strikes a wheel with petals (the *daisy wheel*), each petal containing a letter form at its tip.
- The letter form strikes a ribbon of ink, depositing the ink on the page and thus printing a character.
- By rotating the daisy wheel, different characters are selected for printing.
- These printers were also referred to as letter-quality printers because, during their heyday, they could produce text which was as clear and crisp as a typewriter (though they were nowhere near the quality of printing presses). The fastest letter-quality printers printed 30 characters per second.

Advantages:
1. More reliable than dot matrix printers.
2. Better quality.
3. The fonts of character can be easily changed.

Disadvantages:
1. Slower than dot matrix printers.
2. Noisy in operation.
3. More expensive than dot matrix printers.

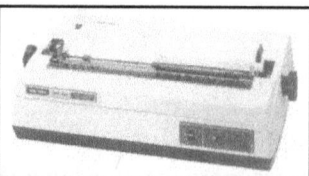

Fig. 3.21: Daisy wheel printer

3.3.2.3 Line Printers

1. Drum Printer:
- Drum printer is like a drum in shape so it called drum printer.
- Drum Printer consists of a drum which consists of a number of characters; those are printed on the drum. And the number of characters or number of tracks are divided, after examining the width of the paper.

- The surface of drum is divided into number of tracks. Total tracks are equal to size of paper i.e. for a paper width of 132 characters, drum will have 132 tracks.
- A character set is embossed on track. The different characters sets are available in market 48 character set, 64 and 96 characters set. One rotation of drum prints one line.
- Drum printers are fast in speed and speed is in between 300 to 2000 lines per minute.

Working of Drum Printer:
- In a typical drum printer design, a fixed font character set is engraved onto the periphery of a number of print wheels, the number equals the number of columns (letters in a line) the printer could print.
- The wheels, joined to form a large drum (cylinder), spin at high speed and paper and an inked ribbon are stepped (moved) past the print position.
- As the desired character for each column passes the print position, a hammer strikes the paper from the rear and presses the paper against the ribbon and the drum, causing the desired character to be recorded on the continuous paper.
- Because the drum carrying the letterforms (characters) remains in constant motion, the strike-and-retreat action of the hammers had to be very fast.

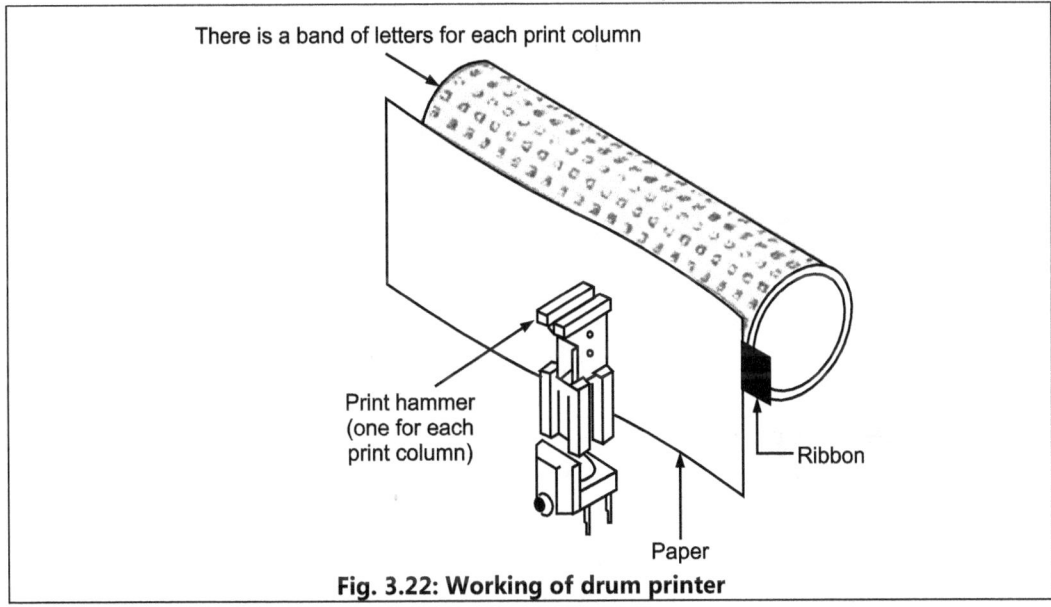

Fig. 3.22: Working of drum printer

Advantages:
   (i) Very high speed.

Disadvantages
   (i) Very expensive.
   (ii) Characters fonts can not be changed.

2. Chain Printer:
- In this printer chain of character sets are used so it is called chain printers.
- A standard character set may have 48, 64, 96 characters.
- These are also line printers, which print one line at a time. All the characters are printed on the chain and the set of characters are placed on the chain.

- There are 48 and 64 and 96 characters set printers are available. There are also some hammers, those are placed in front of the chain, and paper is placed between the hammer and the inked ribbon.
- The total number of hammers will be equal to the total number of print positions.

Working of Chain Printer:
- Chain printers (also known as train printers) placed the type on moving bars (a horizontally-moving chain).
- As with the drum printer, as the correct character passed by each column, a hammer was fired from behind the paper. Compared to drum printers, chain printers had the advantage that the type chain could usually be changed by the operator.
- By selecting chains that had a smaller character set (for example, just numbers and a few punctuation marks), the printer could print much faster than if the chain contained the entire upper - and lower - case alphabets, numbers, and all special symbols.

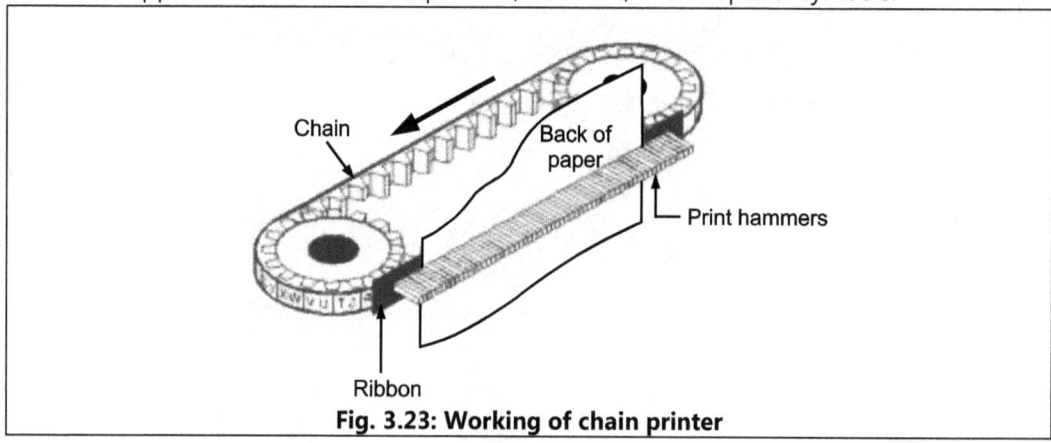

Fig. 3.23: Working of chain printer

Advantages:
(i) Character fonts can easily be changed.
(ii) Different languages can be used with the same printer.

Disadvantages:
(i) Noisy in operation.
(ii) Do not have the ability to print any shape of characters.

3.3.2.4 Inkjet Printers
- Inkjet printers are non impact character printers based on a relatively new technology.
- Inkjet printer print characters by spraying small drops of ink onto paper.
- Inkjet printers produce high quality output with presentable features.
- Inkjet printer make less noise because no hammering is done and these have many styles of printing modes available.
- Using inkjet printer, colour printing is also possible. Some models of Inkjet printers can produce multiple copies of printing also.

Fig. 3.24: Injet printer

- An inkjet printer is a type of computer printer that creates a digital image by propelling droplets of ink onto paper.
- Inkjet printers are the most commonly used type of printer and range from small inexpensive consumer models to very large professional machines that can cost up to thousands of dollars. Its consumable is called inkjet cartridge.

Working of Inkjet Printers:
- Inkjet printers operate by propelling variably-sized droplets of ink onto almost any sized page. They are the most common type of computer printer for the general consumer due to their low cost, high quality of output, capability of printing in different colors.
- A typical inkjet receives control info from your printer driver/PC, or may process the printout in its onboard electronics. Either way, rollers advance a page from your paper tray (1) under a sliding printhead/cartridge assembly (2). Then, the printhead stepper motor (3), kicks in, drawing the assembly on a sliding rod (4), to its starting position, usually via a belt (5).
- The printhead (6) proper is an incredible piece of miniaturization, in some cases fabricated via an etching process similar to semiconductor manufacture. On some printers, the head and ink cartridge (7) are one unit.
- The head's microscopic nozzles (8) anywhere from dozens to literally thousands-are outlets for incredibly tiny ink chambers (9), which are fed by the cartridge's reservoirs. Microscopic droplets (10), measured in millionths of a millionth of a liter, fire through the nozzles.

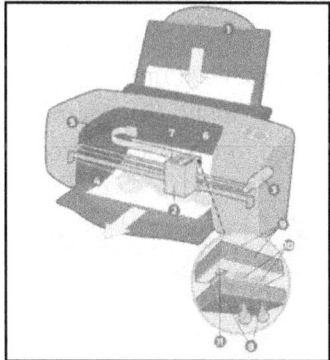

Fig. 3.25: Working of inkjet printer

Advantages:
1. High quality printing.
2. More reliable.
3. Low printer cost.
4. Compact size.
5. Low noise.

Disadvantages:
1. Expensive as cost per page is high.
2. Slow as compare to laser printer.
3. The ink is often very expensive.
4. Lifetime of inkjet prints produced by inkjet printer is limited. They will eventually fade and the color balance may change.
5. Easily get blur if get water drop.
6. Easy to get clogging on inkjet nozzles.

3.3.2.5 Laser Printers

- Laser printers are non impact printers.
- Laser printers use laser lights to produces the dots needed to form the characters to be printed on a page.

Fig. 3.26: Laser printer

- Laser printing is the most advance technology.
- In laser printing, a computer sends data to the printer. Printer translates this data into printable image data. This kind of printers use xerographic principle.
- A laser beam discharges photo sensitive drum.
- A latent image is created on drum, during development process toner is attracted to the drum surface and then transferred to the paper. Its consumable called toner cartridge or laser toner.

Working of Laser Printer:
- Static electricity is the principle behind laser printers.
- A revolving drum or cylinder builds up an electrical charge.
- A tiny laser beam pointed at the drum discharges the surface in the pattern of the letters and images to be printed creating a surface with positive and negative areas.

- The surface is then coated with toner, a fine powder that is positively-charged so it clings only to the negatively-charged areas, and is then passed onto the paper to form the positive image.
- The paper then passes through heated rollers fusing the toner to the paper. Color lasers make multiple passes, in order to mix the different color toners.

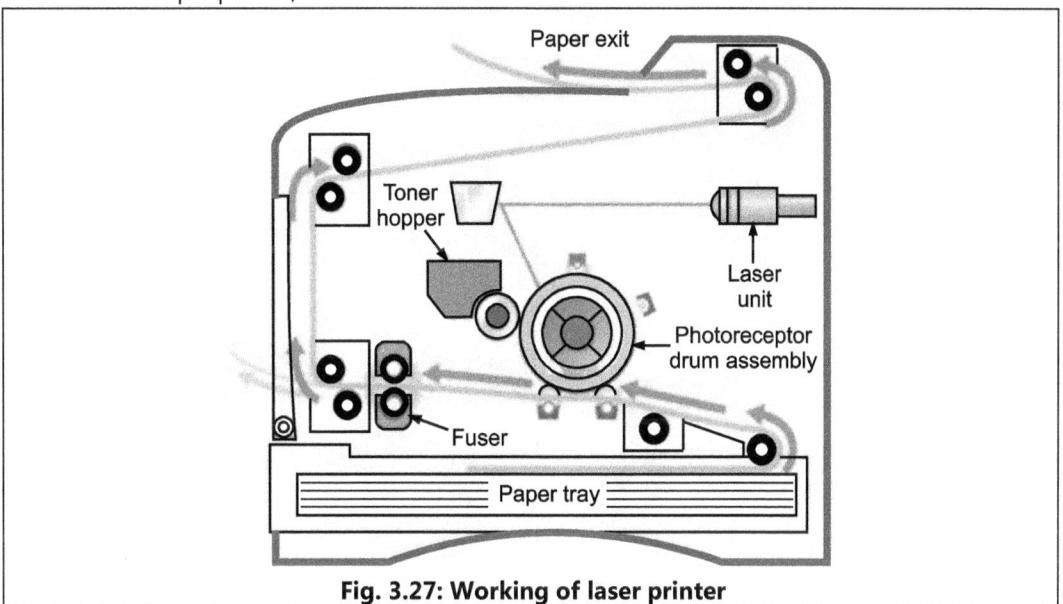

Fig. 3.27: Working of laser printer

Advantages:
1. Very high speed.
2. Very high quality output.
3. Low noise in printing operation.
4. Support many fonts and different character size.
5. Low cost per page. Compare to inkjet printer.
6. Give good and high graphics quality.

Disadvantages:
1. Laser printers are more expensive, but getting more affordable these days.
2. Cannot be used to produce multiple copies of a document in a single printing.
3. Their size is generally larger.

3.3.3 Plotter

- A plotter is a device that draws images on paper after receiving a command from a computer.
- A plotter is a special output device used to produce hardcopies of graphs and designs on the paper.

- A plotter is typically used to print large-format graphs or maps such as construction maps, engineering drawings and big posters.
- Plotters are divided into two types drum plotter and flatbed plotter.

1. Drum Plotter:
- A drum plotter is also known as roller plotter.
- Drum plotter consists of a drum or roller on which a paper is placed and the drum rotates back and forth to produce the graph on the paper.
- Drum plotter also consists of mechanical device known as Robotic Drawing Arm that holds a set of colored ink pens or pencils.
- The robotic drawing arm moves side to side as the paper are rolled back and forth through the roller. In this way, a perfect graph or map is created on the paper. This work is done under the control of computer.
- Drum plotters are used to produce continuous output, such as plotting earthquake activity.

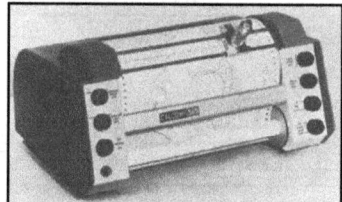

Fig. 3.28: Drum plotter

2. Flatbed Plotter:
- A flatbed plotter is also known as table plotter.
- Flatbed plotter plots on paper that is spread and fixed over a rectangular flatbed table.
- The flatbed plotter uses two robotic drawing arms, each of which holds a set of colored ink pens or pencils. The drawing arms move over the stationary paper and draw the graph on the paper. Typically, the plot size is equal to the area of a bed.
- The plot size may be 20 by 50 feet. It is used in the design of cars, ships, aircrafts, buildings, highways etc. Flatbed plotter is very slow in drawing or printing graphs. The large and complicated drawing can take several hours to print.
- The main reason of the slow printing is due to the movement mechanical devices.

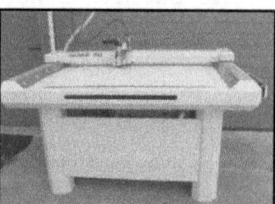

Fig. 3.29: Flatbed plotter

- Today, mechanical plotters have been replaced by thermal, electrostatic and inkjet plotters. These systems are faster and cheaper. They also produce large size drawings.

Advantages:

1. Plotters are faster than other types of printing machines, including the desktop printer.
2. The versatility of plotters is another major advantage. A plotter can be hooked up to any computer. There are a number of plotter configuration options as well, depending on the model and series we buy.
3. Plotter allows us to print and manipulate the plotter in a number of ways, and it also allows it to be connected to any type of machine. Plotters also have their own interfaces in some cases, which allow the user to operate and control them without resetting the paper or having to maintain the plotter during operation.
4. The precision of the plotter is the main advantage for engineering drawings. Plotters have advanced technology that allows them to print more precise lines. When printing a set of drawings for a bridge or skyscraper, it is imperative that each line be precise.
5. Color accuracy and picture quality are also improved with the overall precision of the plotter. This is an advantage for a business looking for an inexpensive and efficient way to print promotional materials, banners and more.

Questions

1. What is input and output? Explain meaning of input and output device.
2. What is scanner? What are its types?
3. What are the types of printers? Explain two of them in detail.
4. What is monitor? What are its types.
5. Explain the term keyboard in detail.
6. With the help of diagram describe working of following:
   (i) Laser printer, and
   (ii) Daisy wheel printer.
7. Compare impact and non impact printers.
8. What is OMR? How it works? Explain in brief.
9. Write short note on: Plotter.
10. With the help of diagram describe working of dot matrix printer.
11. Explain working of CRT and LCD diagrammatically.
12. Describe the term MICR in detail.
13. Explain working of inkjet printer.
14. What are the types of line printers?
15. Distinguish between character printer and line printer.

16. Explain the following term:
    (i) Mouse, and
    (ii) Drum printer.
17. What is MICR? State its advantages.
18. With the help of diagram describe keyboard.
19. Compare printer and plotter.
20. Distinguish between inkjet and laser printers.
21. Explain the following terms in short:
    (i) Digitizer,
    (ii) Joystick,
    (iii) Digital camera,
    (iv) OCR.
22. Write short note on: Bar code reader.

Chapter 4...

Computer Memory

Contents ...

4.1 Introduction
4.2 Memory Concept
4.3 Memory Cell
4.4 Memory Organisation
4.5 Semiconductor Memory
    4.5.1 RAM
    4.5.2 ROM
        4.5.2.1 MROM
        4.5.2.2 PROM
        4.5.2.3 EPROM
        4.5.2.4 EEPROM
4.6 Secondary Storage Devices
    4.6.1 Magnetic Tape
    4.6.2 Magnetic Disks
        4.6.2.1 Floppy Disk
        4.6.2.2 Hard Disk
    4.6.3 Optical Disks
        4.6.3.1 CD
        4.6.3.2 DVD
- Questions

4.1 Introduction

- Computer memory is any physical device capable of storing information temporarily or permanently.
- Computer data storage, often called storage or memory, is a technology consisting of computer components and recording media used to retain digital data.
- Various forms of storage, divided according to their distance from the central processing unit.
- Fig. 4.1 shows storage hierarchy.

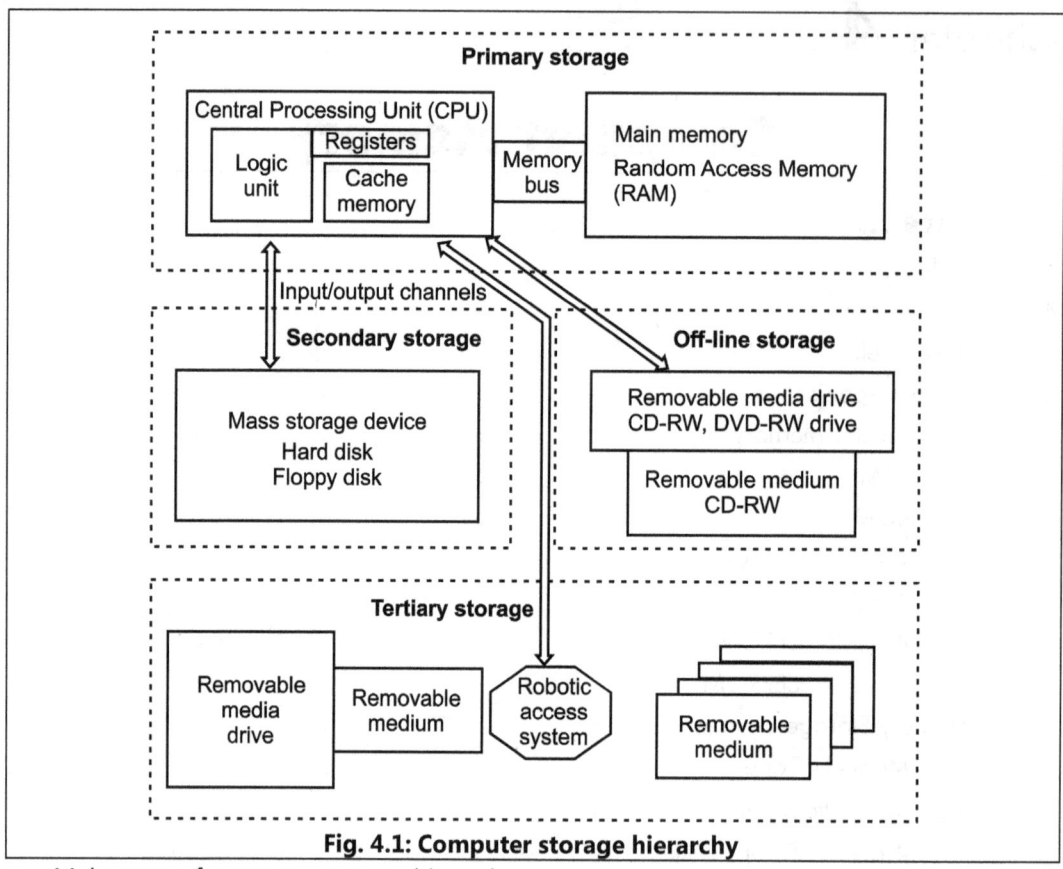

Fig. 4.1: Computer storage hierarchy

- Main parts of computer storage hierarchy are:
  1. **Primary (Temporary Storage):** Primary memories are generally a part of a system, that are used to functionate system. These memories help system to store intermediate data or some specific data as instructions that are necessary to make system run. Typical examples include RAM, ROM.
  2. **Secondary (Permanent Storage):** Secondary memories are abstract from any system like one can carry this memory any where. A data is permanently stored in this types of memories for long period. Typical examples include hard disk, floopy disk etc.
  3. **Tertiary Storage:** Tertiary memory (storage) provides a third level of storage. Typically it involves a robotic mechanism which will mount (insert) and dismount removable mass storage media into a storage device according to the system's demands; these data are often copied to secondary storage before use. Typical examples include tape libraries and optical jukeboxes.

4.2 Memory Concept

- Memory refers to the physical devices used to store programs (sequences of instructions) or data (e.g. program state information) on a temporary or permanent basis for use in a computer or other digital electronic device.

- The main function of memory is to store the information or data.
- Basically, memory is a means for storing data or information in the form of binary words. It is made up of storage locations in which numeric or alphanumeric information or programs (sets of instructions that a computer executes to achieve a desired result) may be stored.
- A memory is just like a human brain. It is used to store data and instruction. Computer memory is the storage space in computer where data is to be processed and instructions required for processing are stored.
- The memory is divided into large number of small parts. Each part is called cell. Each location or cell has a unique address which varies from zero to memory size minus one.
- The memory used to store data is called data memory, and the memory used to store programmes is called program memory. The sub-system of a digital processing system which provides the storage facility is called memory.
- There are two types of memories:
  1. **Volatile memory** is a type of memory (storage) whose contents are erased when the system's power is turned off or interrupted.
  2. **Non-volatile memory** is any memory or storage that will be saved regardless if the power to the computer is on or off.

Comparison between Volatile and Non-volatile memories:

Volatile Memories	Non-volatile Memories
1. Information stored is lost when power is switched OFF.	1. Information stored is retained even after power is switched OFF.
2. All RAMs are volatile memories.	2. ROMs, EPROMS are non-volatile memories.
3. Stored information is retained as long as power is ON.	3. No effect of power, on stored information.
4. Used for temporary storage of information.	4. Used for permanent storage of information.

- Fig. 4.2 shows classification of memories.

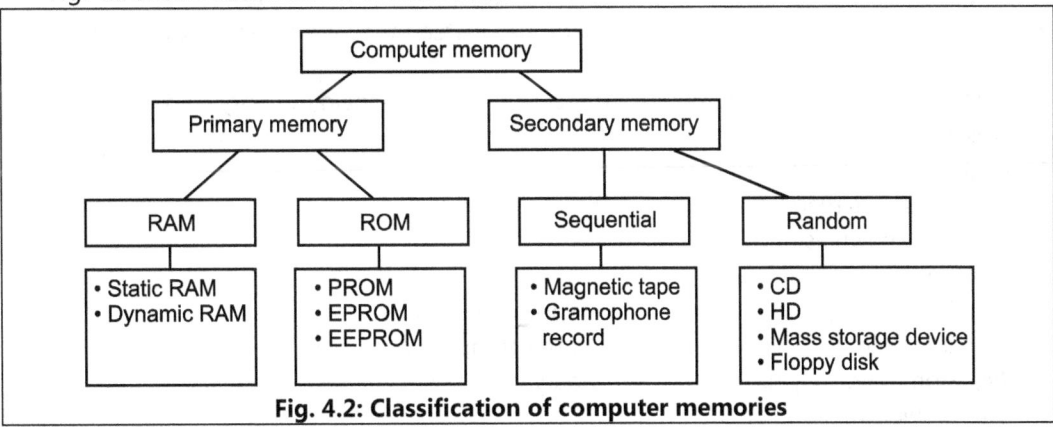

Fig. 4.2: Classification of computer memories

- Now we discuss computer storage in detail:

1. Primary storage:
- Primary storage (or main memory or internal memory), often referred to simply as memory, is the only one, directly accessible to the CPU.
- The CPU continuously reads instructions stored there and executes them as required.
- Any data actively operated on is also stored there in uniform manner.
- Primary memory holds only those data and instructions on which computer is currently working. It has limited capacity and data get lost when power is switched off.
- It is generally made up of semiconductor device. These memories are not as fast as registers. The data and instruction required to be processed earlier reside in main memory.
- Primary memory is divided into two subcategories RAM and ROM.

Characteristic of main memory:
  (i) Primary memories are semiconductor memories.
  (ii) Usually volatile memory.
  (iii) Data is lost in case power is switched off.
  (iv) It is working memory of the computer.
  (v) Faster than secondary memories.
  (vi) A computer cannot run without primary memory.

2. Secondary storage:
- Secondary storage (also known as external memory or auxiliary storage), differs from primary storage in that it is not directly accessible by the CPU.
- The computer usually uses its input/output channels to access secondary storage and transfers the desired data using intermediate area in primary storage.
- Secondary storage does not lose the data when the device is powered down—it is non-volatile. Per unit, it is typically also two orders of magnitude less expensive than primary storage.
- Consequently, modern computer systems typically have two orders of magnitude more secondary storage than primary storage and data are kept for a longer time there.
- Secondary memory is slower than main memory.
- CPU directly does not access these memories instead they are accessed via input-output routines.
- Contents of secondary memories are first transferred to main memory, and then CPU can access it. For example: disk, CD-ROM, DVD etc.

Characteristic of secondary memory:
  (i) These are magnetic and optical memories.
  (ii) It is known as backup memory.
  (iii) It is non-volatile memory.
  (iv) Data is permanently stored even if power is switched off.
  (v) It is used for storage of the data in the computer.
  (vi) Computer may run without secondary memory.
  (vii) Slower than primary memories.

Comparison between Primary and Secondary storages (Memories):

Primary Storage	Secondary Storage
1. It is a part of CPU.	1. It is not a part of CPU.
2. It is the internal or main memory.	2. It is the external memory and resides on disk.
3. The access time is less a few nanoseconds.	3. The access time is more a few milliseconds.
4. It is a medium capacity memory.	4. It is a high capacity memory.
5. It is further classified as RAM and ROM.	5. There are different types of secondary storage devices such as hard disk, floppy disk, CD-ROM etc.
6. Most Primary Storage is temporary.	6. All secondary storage is permanent.
7. Primary storage is expensive and smaller.	7. Secondary storage is usually cheaper and large.
8. Primary storage is usually faster therefore more expensive.	8. Secondary storage connects to the CPU via cables and therefore is slower.

4.3 Structure of Memory Cell

- A memory cell is the smallest unit of information storage and holds a single 0 or 1.
- Memory cells are often grouped together to form words.
- The location of each cell in the memory is specified by its address, which is called a physical address to distinguish it from the logical address of an operand generated by the computer.
- The information is stored in an array of memory cells. Regardless of the technology, all RAM (Random Access Memory) cells must provide these four functions: Select, DataIn, DataOut, and R/$\overline{W}$.

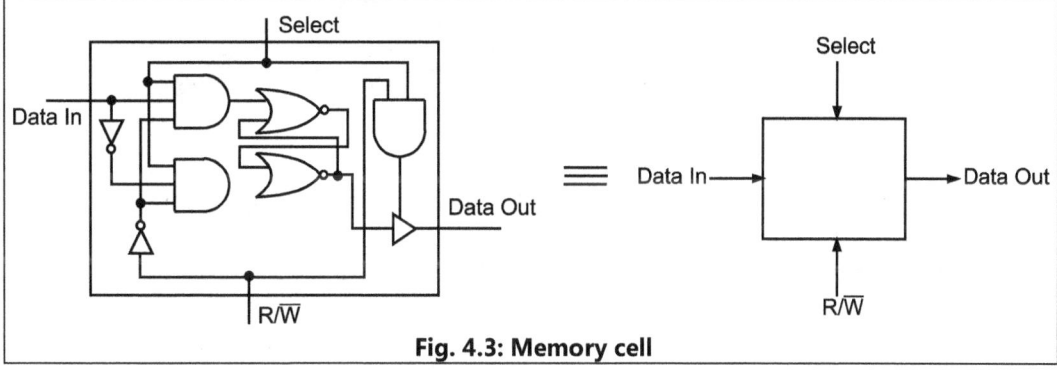

Fig. 4.3: Memory cell

- The internal structure shown in Fig. 4.3 is not realistic for actual implementations, but is functionally correct.
- The memory array is built out of such basic cells. In addition to the cell array, an address decoder and I/O buffers are needed in all memory designs.

- The following is an example of 4 x 8 bit memory to illustrate the structure.

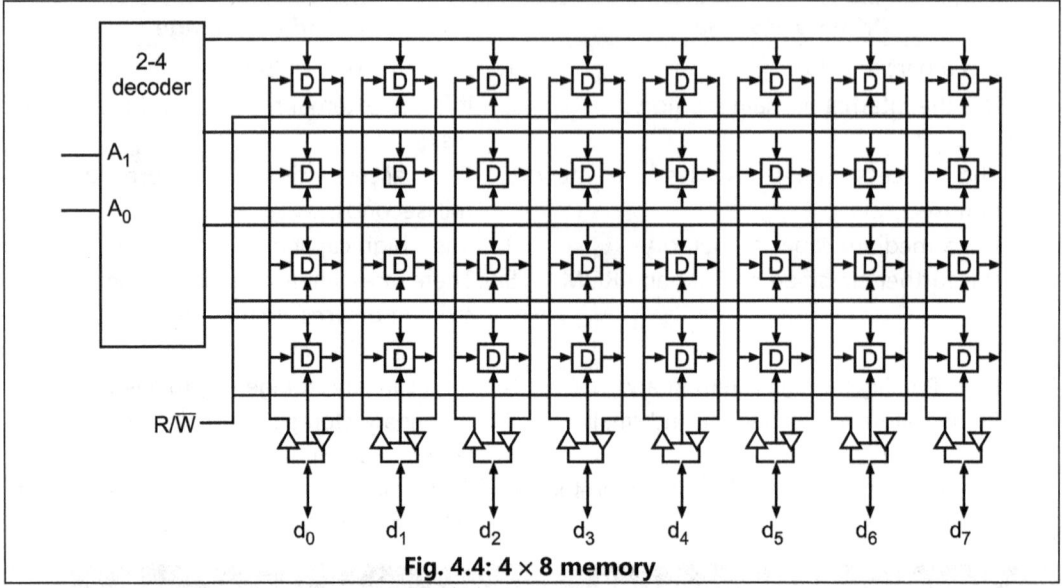

Fig. 4.4: 4 × 8 memory

- A 2-to-4 decoder selects one of the four rows to be accessed. The R/W line is common for all cells, but is applied only in the cells on the selected row. The data interface is a bi-directional 8-bit bus.

4.4 Memory Organization

- Memory types in a computer are CPU registers, main (primary) memory, secondary memory and cache memory.

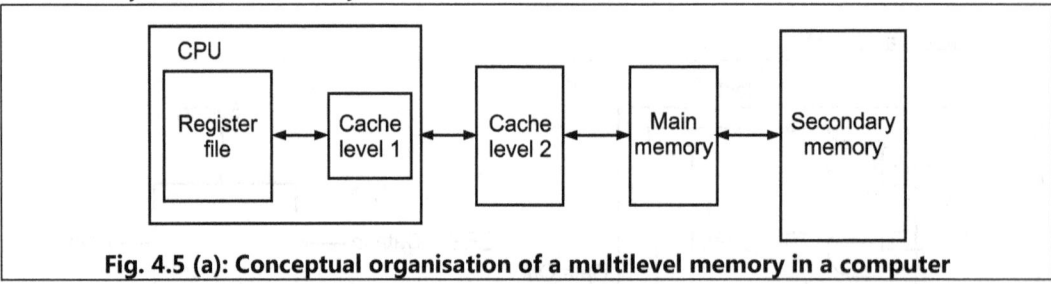

Fig. 4.5 (a): Conceptual organisation of a multilevel memory in a computer

- Storage devices are an essential component in any computer system.
- They enable the user to recall information that has already been entered.
- All computers have primary memory – otherwise known as main memory, typically referred to as Random Access Memory (RAM); on a temporary basis, as long as nothing interrupts the operation of the computer, this could be classed as a storage medium.
- However, when the power to the computer is lost the contents of this memory are lost. Memory that has this characteristic is often called volatile.
- Secondary storage devices are used as a more permanent (non-volatile) form of data storage.

- Secondary storage include magnetic disks, optical discs, magnetic tape etc.
- We know that a flip-flop is a 1-bit memory cell. Hence the flip-flop is the basic element of the semiconductor memory.
- The information is stored in the binary form. There are number of locations in a memory chip, each location being meant for one word of digital information. The number of locations and number of bits comprising the word vary from memory to memory.
- The size of the memory chip is specified by two numbers M and N as M × N bits. The number M specifies the number of locations available in the memory and N is the number of bits at each memory location.
- The commonly used values of the number of words per chip are 64, 256, 512, 1024, 2048, 4096 etc. Whereas the common values for the word size are 1, 4 and 8 etc.
- The block diagram of a memory device is shown in Fig. 4.5 (b). Each of the M locations of the memory is defined by a unique address and therefore for accessing any one of the M locations, n inputs are required, where $2^n = M$. These n number of input lines are referred to as address bus. The address is specified in the binary form. Octal and hexadecimal representations can also be employed.

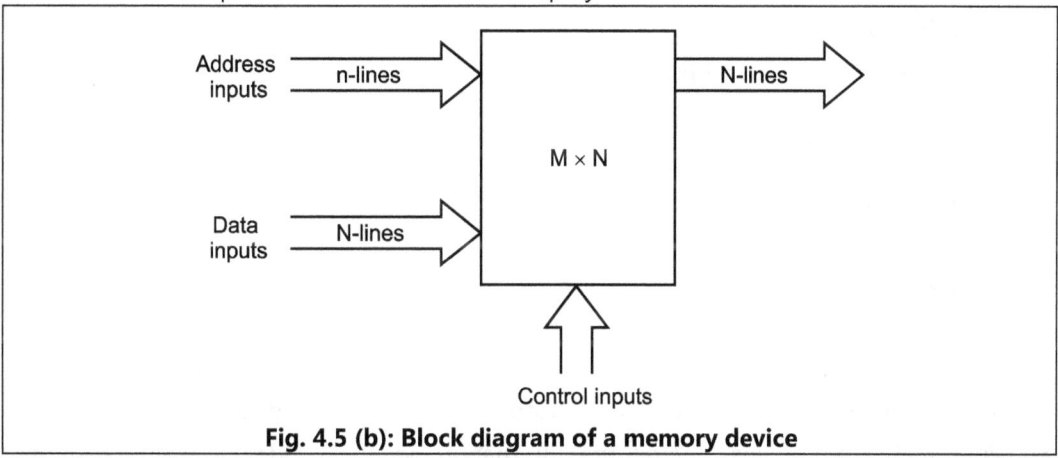

Fig. 4.5 (b): Block diagram of a memory device

4.5 Semiconductor Memory

4.5.1 RAM

- RAM stands for Random Access Memory.
- A RAM constitutes the internal memory of the CPU for storing data, program and program result. It is read/write memory.
- RAM is volatile, i.e. data stored in it is lost when we switch off the computer or if there is a power failure. Hence, a backup Uninterruptible Power System (UPS) is often used with computers. RAM is small, both in terms of its physical size and in the amount of data it can hold.
- This memory is accessible from any memory location anytime. one can switch to one place to another place in memory randomly.

Fig. 4.6: RAM chips

- RAM is of two types i.e. Static RAM (SRAM) and Dynamic RAM (DRAM).

1. SRAM:

- SRAM (Static Random Access Memory) is a type of semiconductor memory where the word static indicates that, it does not need to be periodically refreshed, as SRAM uses bistable latching circuitry to store each bit.
- SRAM is volatile in the conventional sense that data is eventually lost when the memory is not powered.
- Static RAM is used as cache memory needs to be very fast and small.

Characteristic of the Static RAM:

(i) It has long data lifetime.
(ii) There is no need to refresh.
(iii) Faster.
(iv) Used as cache memory.
(v) Large size.
(vi) Expensive.
(vii) High power consumption.

2. DRAM:

- DRAM (Dynamic Random Access Memory) is a type of random access memory that stores each bit of data in a separate capacitor within an integrated circuit.
- Since, real capacitors leak charge, the information eventually fades unless the capacitor charge is refreshed periodically. Because of this refresh requirement, it is a dynamic memory as opposed to SRAM and other static memory.

Characteristic of the Dynamic RAM:

(i) It has short data lifetime.
(ii) Need to refresh continuously.
(iii) Slower as compared to SRAM.
(iv) Used as RAM.
(v) Lesser in size.
(vi) Less expensive.
(vii) Less power consumption.

Comparison between Static RAM and Dynamic RAM:

Static RAM (SRAM)	Dynamic RAM (DRAM)
1. Each static RAM cell is a flip-flop.	1. A dynamic RAM cell consists of a MOSFET and a capacitor.
2. Less number of memory cells/unit area.	2. More number of memory cells/unit area.
3. More number of components per cell.	3. Only two components per cell.
4. Does not require refreshing.	4. Require refreshing.
5. Faster memories.	5. Slower memories.
6. Power consumption is less.	6. More power consumption.

4.5.2 ROM

- ROM stands for Read Only Memory.
- The memory from which we can only read but cannot write on it.
- This type of memory is non-volatile. The information is stored permanently in such memories during manufacture.
- Read only memory, also known as firmware, is an integrated circuit programmed with specific data when it is manufactured. ROM chips are used not only in computers, but in most other electronic items as well like washing machine and microwave oven.
- A ROM, stores such instruction as are required to start computer when electricity is first turned on, this operation is referred to as bootstrap.

Advantages of ROM:
1. Non-volatile in nature.
2. These can not be accidentally changed.
3. Cheaper than RAMs.
4. Easy to test.
5. More Reliable than RAMs.
6. These are static and do not require refreshing.
7. Its contents are always known and can be verified.

4.5.2.1 MROM

- MROM stands for Masked ROM.
- The very first ROMs were hard-wired devices that contained a pre-programmed set of data or instructions.
- These kind of ROMs are known as masked ROMs.
- MROM is inexpensive ROM.

4.5.2.2 PROM

- PROM stands for Programmable Read Only Memory.
- PROM is read-only memory that can be modified only once by a user. The user buys a blank PROM and enters the desired contents using a PROM programmer.

- Inside the PROM chip there are small fuses which are burnt open during programming. It can be programmed only once and is not erasable.
- A Programmable Read-Only Memory or Field Programmable Read-Only Memory (FPROM) is a form of digital memory where the setting of each bit is locked by a fuse or antifuse.

4.5.2.3 EPROM

- EPROM stands for Erasable and Programmable Read Only Memory.
- An EPROM is a type of memory chip that retains its data when its power supply is switched off. The EPROM can be erased by exposing it to ultra-violet light for a duration of up to 40 minutes. Usually, a EPROM eraser achieves this function.
- During programming an electrical charge is trapped in an insulated gate region. The charge is retained for more than ten years because the charge has no leakage path.
- For erasing this charge, ultra-violet light is passed through a quartz crystal window (lid). This exposure to ultra-violet light dissipates the charge. During normal use the quartz lid is sealed with a sticker.

4.5.2.4 EEPROM

- EEPROM stands for Electrically Erasable and Programmable Read Only Memory. EEPROM also written as E^2PROM.
- EEPROM is a type of non-volatile memory used in computers and other electronic devices to store small amounts of data that must be saved when power is removed,
- The EEPROM is programmed and erased electrically. It can be erased and reprogrammed about ten thousand times. Both erasing and programming take about 4 to 10 ms (milli second).
- In EEPROM, any location can be selectively erased and programmed. EEPROMs can be erased one byte at a time, rather than erasing the entire chip. Hence, the process of re-programming is flexible but slow.

Comparison between E^2PROM and EPROM:

E^2PROM	EPROM
1. E^2PROM stands for Electrically Erasable Programmable Read Only Memory.	1. EPROM stands for Erasable Programmable Read Only Memory.
2. Can be programmed and erased electrically.	2. Cannot be erased electrically and require UV rays to erase the EPROM.
3. Can be erased in a small time of 10 ms.	3. Requires 20 to 30 min. for erasing the contents.
4. Not required to remove the chip from the circuit for erasing and reprogramming.	4. Chip has to be removed from the circuit for erasing and reprogram-ming.
5. Low density	5. High density
6. Expensive than EPROM.	6. Cheaper than E^2PROM.

Difference between RAM and ROM:

RAM	ROM
1. RAM stands for Random Access Memory.	1. ROM stands for Read Only Memory.
2. It is temporary memory.	2. It is permanent memory.
3. RAM is volatile memory.	3. ROM is non-volatile memory.
4. Information stored by user.	4. Information stored by manufacturer.
5. Read/write operations can be performed.	5. Only read can be performed.
6. Every location can be accessed directly or randomly.	6. Longer access time.
7. RAM stores data, program instructions during program execution.	7. ROM stores system software are programs for basic operations.

Cache Memory:
- Cache memory is a very high speed memory placed in between RAM and CPU. Cache memory increases the speed of processing.
- Cache memory is a storage buffer that stores the data that is used more often, temporarily, and makes them available to CPU at a fast rate.
- During processing, CPU first checks cache for the required data. If data is not found in cache, then it looks in the RAM for data.
- To access the cache memory, CPU does not have to use the motherboard's system bus for data transfer.
- Cache memory is built into the processor, and may also be located next to it on a separate chip between the CPU and RAM.
- Cache built into the CPU is faster than separate cache, running at the speed of the microprocessor itself. However, separate cache is roughly twice as fast as RAM.

Flash Memory:
- It is an extension of EEPROMs.
- It uses floating gate principle.
- It is designed such that large blocks of memory can be erased all at once rather than just one word at a time.

Applications:
1. To store photograph in a digital camera.
2. To store voice in compressed form in a voice recorder.
3. To store message in mobile phone.

4.6 Secondary Storage Devices

4.6.1 Magnetic Tape
- Magnetic tape is now principally used only as a backup medium. It is also used to archive records of past transactions for long-term storage, as it is cheap, robust and easily used to store large quantities of data.

- Magnetic tape is a recording medium consisting of a thin tape with a coating of a fine magnetic material, used for recording analog or digital data.
- A device that stores computer data on magnetic tape is a tape drive.

Fig. 4.7: Magnetic tape

- The magnetic tape drive is similar to the audio tape recorders. Before the data on magnetic tape can be processed, the tape must be placed in a machine called tape drive or tape transport.
- We can read/write data from the tape. Writing data on the tape destroys the previous tape contents.
- When the tape is accelerated to its full speed no recording can be done. The distance traversed by the tape during this time is called as Inter Block Gap (IBG). The beginning of the tape is indicated by a metal foil called a marker.
- When a write command is given, the block of data is written on the tape and after the IBG the next block of data is written. A metal foil is used again to indicate the end of tape. The data which is stored on the tape has to be accessed sequentially.

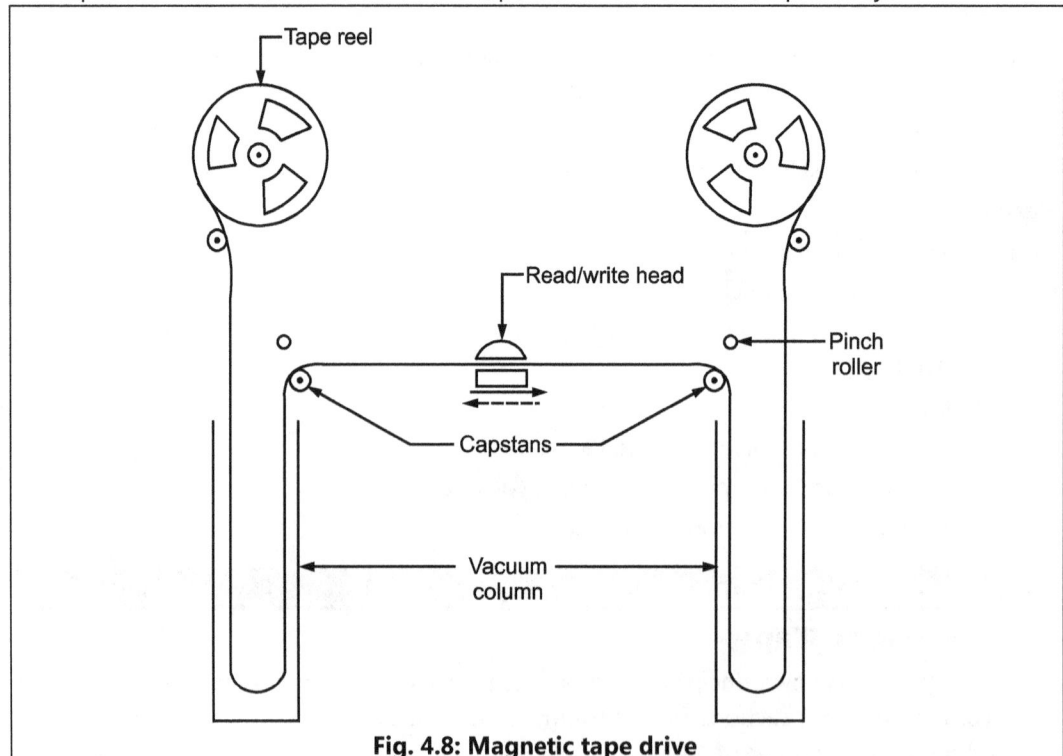

Fig. 4.8: Magnetic tape drive

4.6.2 Magnetic Disks
4.6.2.1 Floppy Disk
- The floppy disk is made up of thin flexible plastic (Mylar) material of circular shape. As the thickness of the Mylar is few thousands of an inch it is called floppy.
- The information can be stored on single side or both sides of the disk. Depending on the recording technique used, they are classified as single density and double density diskettes.
- The different sizes available are:
    1. 8" disk which is used in order computers which is presently obsolete.
    2. $5^1/_4$" disk having capacity 1.2 MB called mini floppy.
    3. $3^1/_2$" disk having capacity 1.44 MB called micro floppy.

Fig. 4.9: A floppy

- **Construction of floppy disk:** The floppy disk is coated with magnetic material and enclosed in a protective jacket. There is a large slot on jacket through which head reads and writes data on the disk.

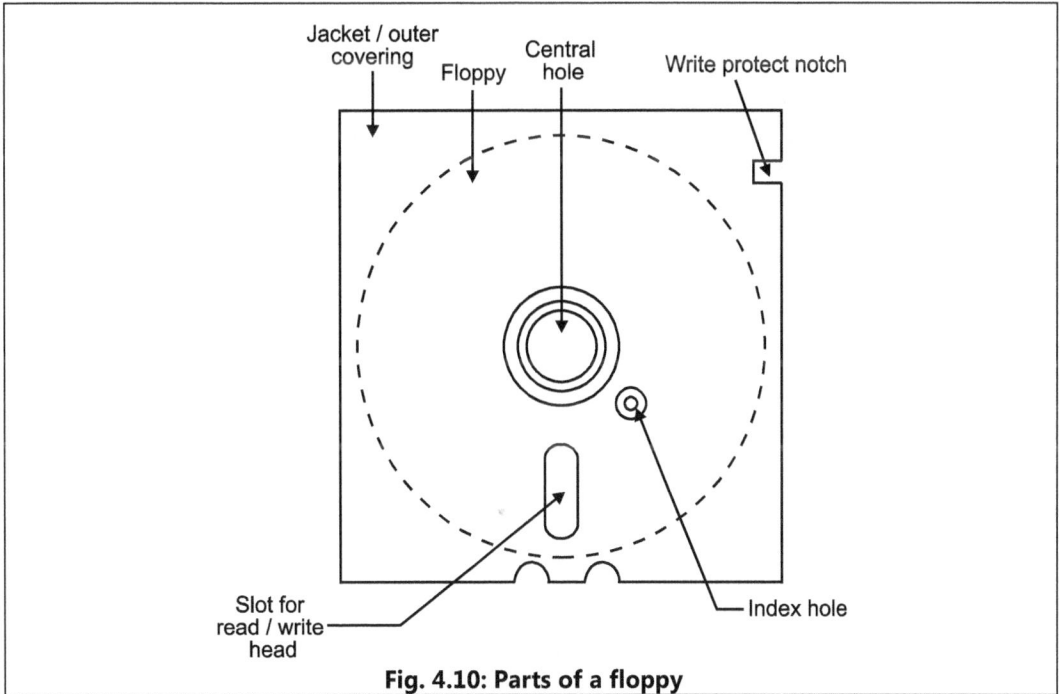

Fig. 4.10: Parts of a floppy

- A hole is provided at the centre called hub for clamping the floppy so that it can rotate easily without slipping. Near the centre a small hole is punched on the diskette called index hole.
- This hole indicates the beginning of a track. Writing is done on the floppy disk only after sensing the index hole.
- A write protect notch is provided. If this notch is open, writing on diskette is permitted. If this notch is covered by a paper or sticker then writing is not permitted.
- Principle of working: Floppy is made of number of tracks and each track is divided into a number of sectors. Data is stored on the track bit by bit using electromagnetic techniques, the data is read (or stored) from (on) the disk.
- There are two heads, one for writing on the top side of the disk and the other on the bottom side of the disk. In a write operation the write data line contains both clock pulses and data pulses.
- Current is passed through read/write head and flux transition is created for each clock or data pulse. In read operation e.m.f. is induced into the read head because of rotation of floppy disk which causes flux transitions. The induced e.m.f. is amplified and shaped by the amplifier circuit in FDD.
- In a write operation the data pulses as well as the clock pulses are stored on the disk or else it becomes difficult to differentiate between no data and zero data.

1. Micro Floppy:

- It is of the size $3^1/_2$ inch and its capacity is 1.44 MB. The 3.5" is so designed that one end is truncated which prevents improper insertion of the diskette.
- There is a round plastic sheet (mylar), coated with magnetic material and is enclosed in a hard plastic jacket. It uses a more finely grained medium with buffer magnetic properties so its capacity is more.
- A hole with slider is provided along the side of the plastic jacket. One can read/write if the hole is blocked by the slider. One can only read the data if the hole is visible.

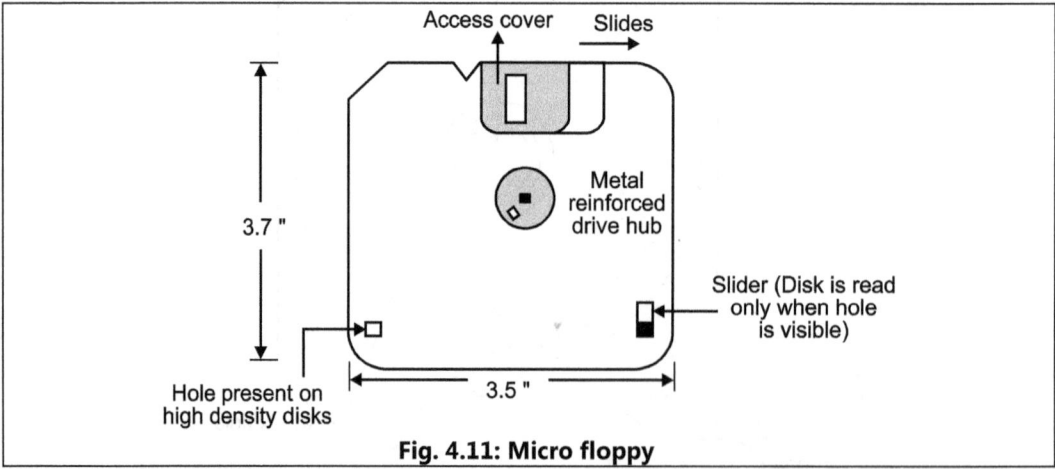

Fig. 4.11: Micro floppy

- It uses a metal hub so the disk can be centered very easily. If one more hole is provided it indicates the diskette has double density.

2. Mini Floppy:

- A mini floppy is of size of $5^{1}/_{4}$ inch floppy disk. A floppy diskette is an ultra thin plastic piece in circular shape.
- It is coated with a magnetic material and enclosed in a protective jacket. An oval access hole is made on the jacket so as to provide contact between the read/write head and the diskette.
- On floppy there is write protect notch. If this notch is kept uncovered then you can write to the floppy, but if it is covered by a sticker then floppy becomes read only and you cannot write on to it.
- When index hole of upper cover and mini floppy matches each other then there is first block/sector on read/write head slot. It is widely used in present day computers including PCs, PC-XTs, PC-ATs, etc.

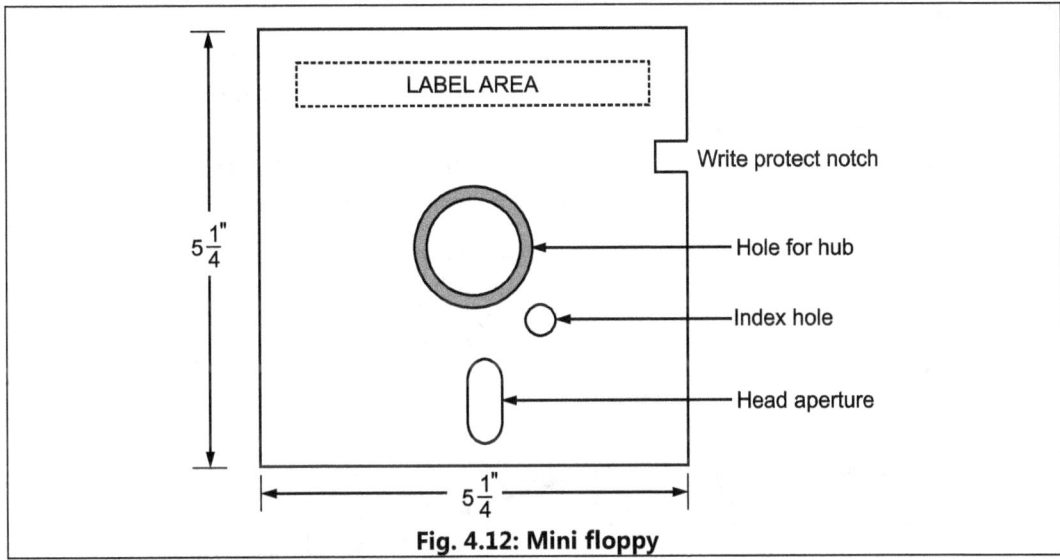

Fig. 4.12: Mini floppy

Advantages of Floppy Disk:
1. Information can be directly encoded onto the disk.
2. Bulky media is not used, so ease in handling and transportation.
3. Used for storage, input and output.
4. It is cheap.
5. Density is high.
6. It can be reused many times.

Disadvantages of Floppy Disk:
1. It should be handled carefully.
2. It is sensitive to environment conditions such as heat, dust etc.

4.6.2.2 Hard Disk

- The hard disk is the most widely used mass storage device for PCs. On the hard disk all the programs and data are stored which can be accessed instantly thus making the system faster.
- The hard disk drive or hard disk is the main, and usually largest data storage device in a computer.
- It is a non-volatile, random access digital magnetic data storage device.
- A hard drive is made up of platters which stored the data, and read/write heads to transfer data.
- A hard drive is generally the fastest of the secondary storage devices, and has the largest data storage capacity, approximately the same as magnetic tapes. Hard drives however, are not very portable and are primarily used internally in a computer system.

Construction of Hard Disk:

- Hard disks use a circular hard platters to store data on. They are in pristine condition with a mirror like finish to them. These platters are locked away inside a steel casing as unclean air can easily ruin a hard disk.
- This is why we should never remove the casing from the hard disk as it is very unlikely that we will be able to put it back together as a working component.

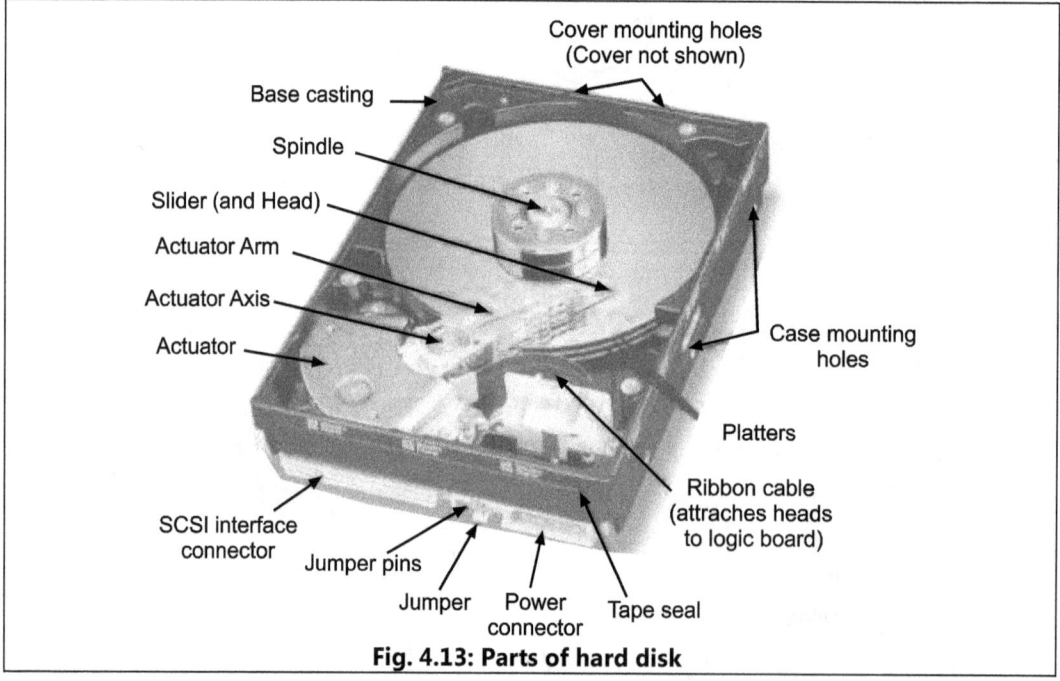

Fig. 4.13: Parts of hard disk

- Fig. 4.13 shows a labelled diagram of a hard disk.
- The model is a SCSI (Small Computer Scientific Interface) shows the hard platters on top of each other with a set of arms which hold the read/write head.

- The speed of the arm is truly amazing as well as the accuracy of the head which can read and write to perfection on a platter which is rotating around 7200 rpm.
- The hard disk looks a very simple idea and probably is, however a lot goes on before the simple writing to the disk itsself.
- Hard disk should have two parts: Physical part like platter read/write head and Logical parts like track, Sector, Pie, Shape and Cylinder.
- A hard disk is divided into tracks and sectors, data on this hard disk is positioned into these tracks and sectors so they can be easily read by the heads and also to help reduce fragmentation on the hard disk.
- Fig. 4.14 depicts how a hard disk is divided into tracks and sectors.

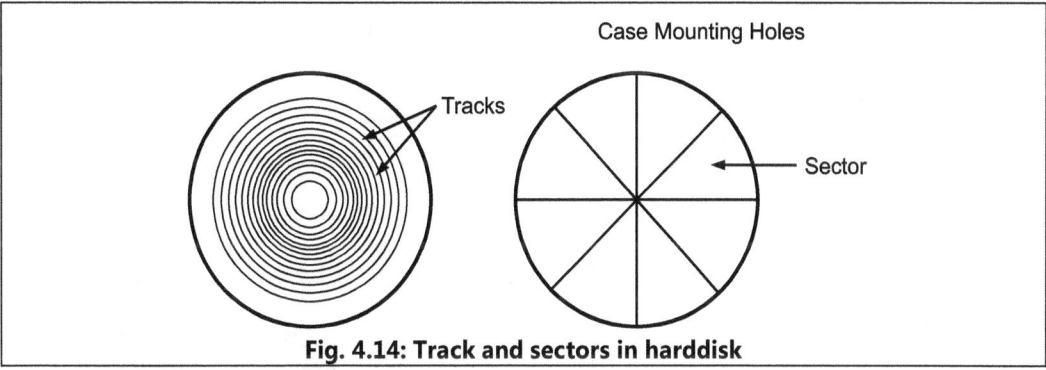

Fig. 4.14: Track and sectors in harddisk

- Data on a hard drive are accessed by two methods:
  1. **Fixed Head:** Hard disks with fixed heads have a read/write head for each track on the hard disk, since there is no moving of heads to access data, the data access time is generally faster for fixed head hard drives.
  2. **Moving Head:** A moving head hard disk is one in which one or more read-write heads are attached to a movable arm which allows each head to cover many tracks of information.
- Each access to the hard drive to read or write data causes the read/write heads to burst into a furious flurry of movement – which must be performed with microscopic precision. The tolerances in a disk drive are equivalent to a jumbo jet flying at an altitude of less than a centimetre.
- Data is stored in a very orderly pattern on each platter. Bits of data are arranged in concentric, circular paths called tracks. Each track is broken up into smaller areas called sectors. Part of the hard drive stores a map of sectors that have already been used up and others that are still free.
- When the computer wants to store new information, it takes a look at the map to find some free sectors
- Typically, data up to 100 GB's can be stored on single platter.
- With so much information stored in such a tiny amount of space, a hard drive is a remarkable piece of engineering.

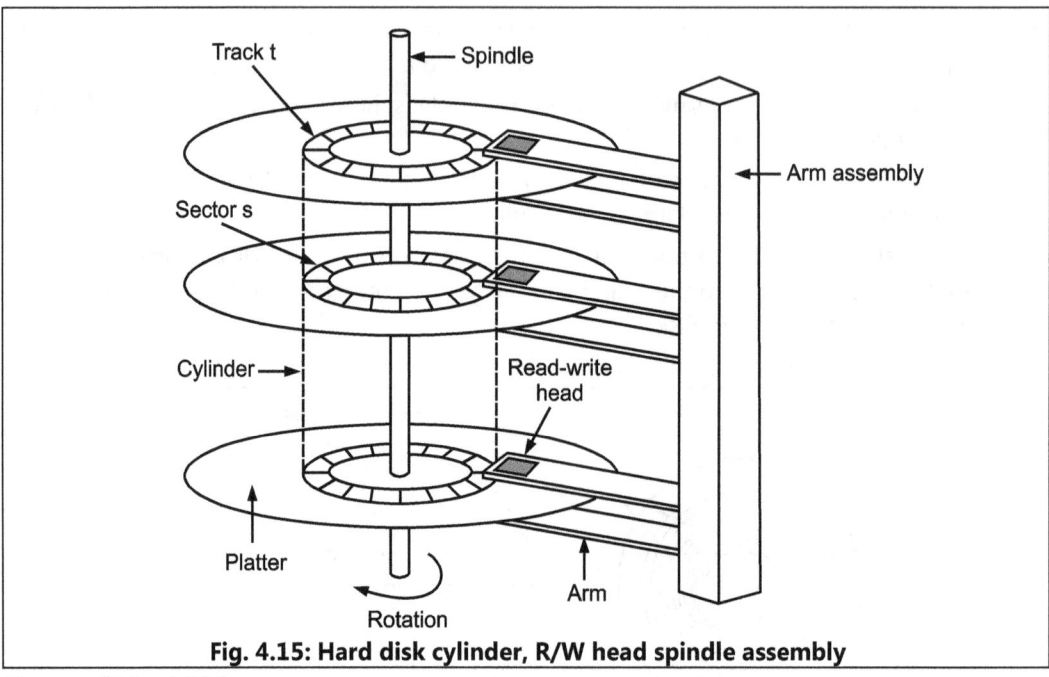
Fig. 4.15: Hard disk cylinder, R/W head spindle assembly

Types of Hard Disk:
1. **Removable and Fixed:** In a removable hard disk, the disks can be removed and placed in a cupboard or other computer similar to a floppy. In a fixed hard disk the disks cannot be removed.
2. **Moving head and Fixed head:** In moving head hard disk, the read/write head moves from one track to another track as controlled by the computer. In fixed head hard disk, as the name indicates heads are fixed.
3. **Single head and Dual head assembly:** In single head assembly there is one head for each surface. In a dual head assembly there are two heads for each surface.
4. **Winchester and Non-Winchester:** Winchester was introduced by IBM in 1973, all the disks before 1973 were of non-Winchester type. The head in a Winchester disk is attached to airfoil. The head is kept floating a few micro inches above the surface of the disk. So there is no wear of the disk surface.

Terms Related to Hard Disk:
1. **Seek Time:** It is the time taken to position the heads over the required track. It depends upon where the arm assembly is when read-write command is received.
2. **Search or Latency Time:** Time taken to locate actual data on a track. Once, the head assembly is positioned the head corresponding to specified surface is switched. Once, the head is switched it has to wait until the required record comes under the head. This average rotational delay is called latency time.
3. **Access Time:** It is the summation of seek time, latency time and the time for reading/writing on the disk.
4. **Average Latency Time:** It is half the time, the read/write head requires for one revolution of the disk.

Comparison between Tape drive and Hard disk/Floppy disk:

Tape drive	Hard disk/Floppy disk
1. Data cannot be accessed directly, it has to be accessed sequentially.	1. Data can be accessed directly or sequentially
2. The data cannot be accessed and immediately updated.	2. The data can be accessed and updated in a few milliseconds.
3. It is cheaper than magnetic disks.	3. It is nearly 20 times more expensive than tape drive.
4. Easy to maintain security of tape files than files stored on a disk.	4. Security of files is less compared to tape drive.

Difference between Floppy disk and CD ROM:

Floppy disk	CD ROM
1. It has lower storage capacity 1.44 MB.	1. It has higher storage capacity upto 700 MB.
2. It uses magnetic technology.	2. It uses laser technology.
3. Data is recorded on both sides.	3. Data is recorded on one side.
4. It is affected by dust, moisture.	4. It is not affected by dust, mositure.
5. It is read/write medium.	5. It is read only medium.
6. Used to store low volumes of data.	6. Used to store high volumes of data such as encyclopaedia, telephone, directory etc.

Difference between Floppy disk and Hard disk:

Floppy disk	Hard disk
1. It is a removable, low storage capacity secondary storage medium.	1. It is not easily removable, high capacity secondary storage medium.
2. It provides off-line storage of data.	2. It can provide on-line storage of data.
3. It has more access time, but it is cheaper.	3. The access time is less but it is costly.
4. It has a write-protect notch.	4. It does not have a notch.
5. There are two read/write heads in the drive, one for each side of the floppy.	5. There are many read/write heads in the drive because the disk contains many plotters.
6. The read/write head touches the surface of floppy.	6. The read/write head never touches the surface.

4.6.3 Optical Disks

- Optical disk is an electronic data storage medium from which data is read and written to by using a low-powered laser beam.
- It is flat, circular, plastic or glass disk on which data is stored in the form of light and dark pits.
- There are three basic types of optical disks: Read-Only Optical Disks, Write Once Read Many Optical Disks and Rewritable Optical Disks.
- Two main types of optical disks are CD and DVD.

4.6.3.1 CD

- CD stands for Compact Disk.

Fig. 4.16: A CD

- CD is an abbreviation of Compact Disk, and is a form of data storage that can transfer data up to the speed of 7800 KB/s.
- A standard 120 mm CD holds up to 700 MB of data, or about 70 minutes of audio. There are two types of CD: CD-ROM and CD-RW.
- CD-ROM are stands for CD-Read Only Memory and they function the same way Read Only Memory does.

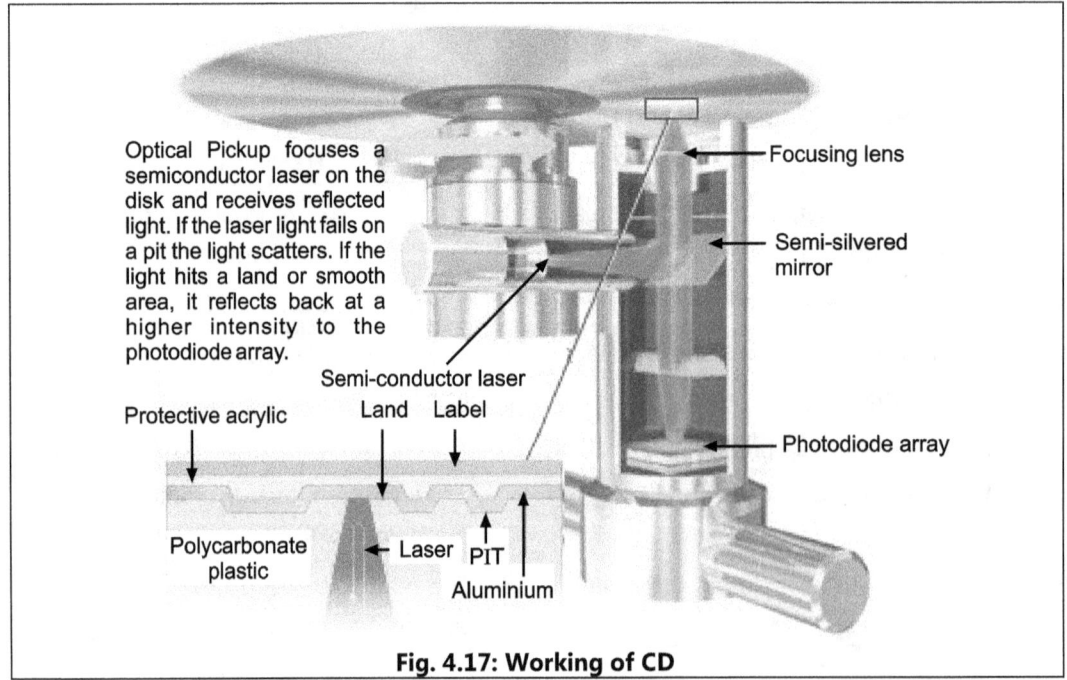

Fig. 4.17: Working of CD

- CD-RW stands for CD-Rewritable, these disks can be erased and rewritten at any time.
- The Compact Disk (CD) is storage media that hold content in digital form and that are written and read by a laser; these media include all the CD and DVD variations, as well as optical jukeboxes and autochangers.
- Optical media have a number of advantages over magnetic media such as the floppy disk. Optical disk capacity ranges up to 6 gigabytes; that's 6 billion bytes compared to 1.44 megabytes (MB) – 1,440,000 bytes – of the floppy.
- One optical disk holds about the equivalent of 500 floppies worth of data. Durability is another feature of optical media; they last up to seven times as long as traditional storage media.

4.6.3.2 DVD

- DVD is an abbreviation of Digital Versatile Disc, and is an optical disc storage media format that can be used for data storage.
- The DVD supports disks with capacities of 4.7 GB to 17 GB and access rates of 600 Kbps to 1.3 mbps.
- A standard DVD disc store up to 4.7 GB of data. There are two types of DVD's: DVD-ROM and DVD-RW.
- DVD-ROM are stands for DVD-Read Only Memory and they function the same way Read Only Memory does.
- DVD-RW stands for DVD-Rewritable, these disks can be erased and rewritten at any time.

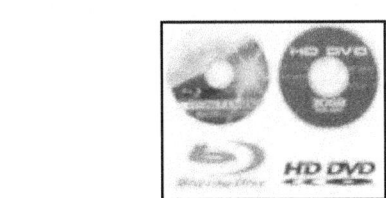

Fig. 4.18: DVDs

- A DVD is composed of several layers of plastic, polycarbonate base, totaling about 1.2 millimeters thick. Writing data to the DVD is done by a red laser beam modulated by the serial data stream. When the beam turns on and hits the dye layer, a distortion (known as a pit) on the surface is made.
- Dual layer recording allows DVD-R and DVD+R discs to store significantly more data, up to 8.54 GB's per side, per disc, compared with 4.7 GB's for single-layer discs. While you will need as much as 300 DVD's to be able to store that data.

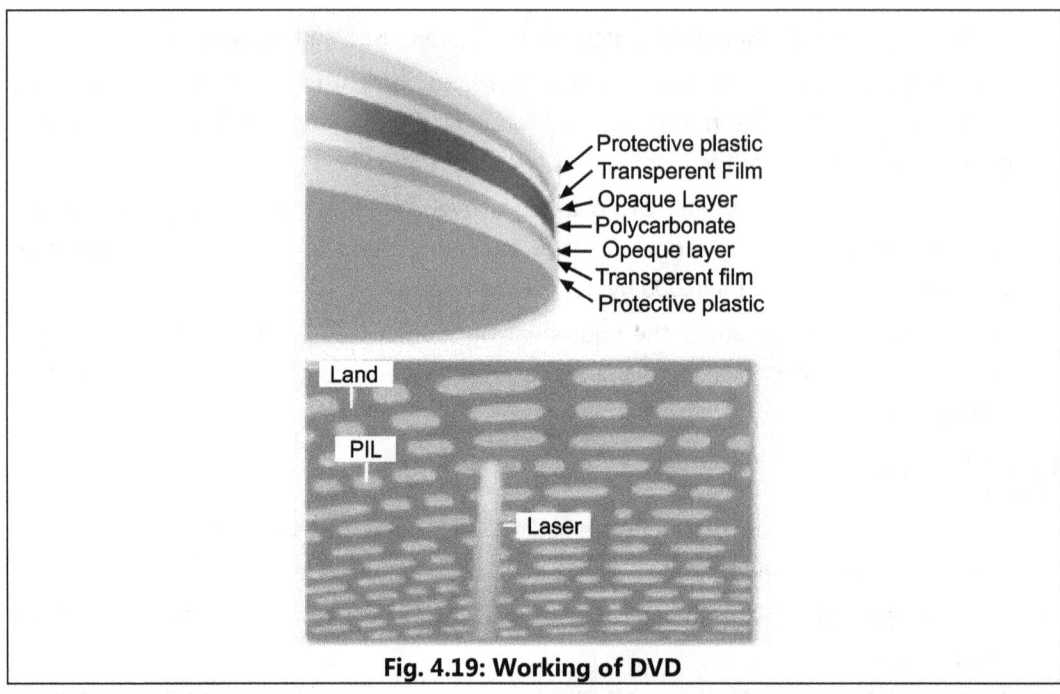

Fig. 4.19: Working of DVD

Questions

1. What is computer memory?
2. What are the types of memory?
3. With the help of diagram describe memory cell.
4. Explain memory organisation in detail.
5. What is meant by primary and secondary memory? Compare them.
6. What is hard disk? Explain its construction in detail.
7. What is RAM and ROM? State its characteristics.
8. Enlist characteristics of primary and secondary memory.
9. What is CD? How it works? Explain diagrammatically.
10. Differentiate between RAM and ROM.
11. What is floppy disk? How it works?
12. Compare hard disk and floppy disk.
13. Write short note on DVD.
14. Describe magnetic tape in detail.
15. With the help of diagram describe classification of memory.
16. Distinguish between magnetic tape and magnetic disks.
17. What is meant by volatile and non-volatile memories?
18. With the help of diagram describe computer memory hierarchy.

■■■

Chapter 5...

Computer Language and Software

Contents ...

5.1 Introduction
5.2 Algorithm
    5.2.1 Definition
    5.2.2 Characteristics
    5.2.3 Advantages
    5.2.4 Examples
5.3 Flowchart
    5.3.1 Definition
    5.3.2 Principles
    5.3.3 Examples
    5.3.4 Advantages and Disadvantages
5.4 Computer Languages
    5.4.1 Machine Language
    5.4.2 Assembly Language
    5.4.3 High Level Language
5.5 Assembler
5.6 Compiler
5.7 Interpreter
5.8 Characteristics of a Good Language
5.9 Software
    5.9.1 System Software
    5.9.2 Application Software
    • Questions

5.1 Introduction

- As we human beings communicate with each other in different languages such as Marathi, Gujarati, Punjabi and Arabic etc., similarly, to communicate with the computers we have to use specific languages.
- A computer language means, a set of rules and symbols used to operate a computer. Whatever command we give to computer, it is first converted in its own language.

- A computer language is also known as Programming Language. There are various types of programming languages. These languages are used to write programs to tell the computer what to do.
- A flowchart is a graphic representation of how a process works, showing, at a minimum, the sequence of steps.
- Algorithm is a finite sequence of instructions, which can be carried out to solve a particular problem in order to obtain the desired result.
- The sequence of instructions must possess the following characteristics:
    1. The instructions must be precise and unambiguous.
    2. Every instruction should be performed in finite time.
    3. The algorithm should ultimately terminate (the instructions should not repeat infinitely).
    4. The desired results (i.e. one or more outputs) should be obtained after the algorithm terminates.
- Software is a collection of instructions that enables a user to interact with the computer or have the computer that performs specific tasks for them.
- Without any software the computer would be useless. For example, you would not be able to interact with the computer without a software operating system.

5.2 Algorithm

- A sequence of instructions is called an algorithm.
- An algorithm is a procedure or formula for solving a problem.
- An algorithm is a set of instructions, sometimes called a procedure or a function, that is used to perform a certain task.
- An algorithm is a step-by-step problem-solving procedure, especially an established, recursive computational procedure for solving a problem in a finite number of steps.
- An algorithm is a definite list of well-defined instructions for completing a task; that given an initial state will proceed through a well-defined series of successive states, eventually terminating in an end-state.

Good Qualities of Algorithms:
1. Algorithms are correct for clearly defined solutions.
2. Algorithms are well documented.
3. Algorithms are economical in the use of computer time, storage and peripherals.
4. Algorithms are machine independent.
5. Algorithms are able to be used as a subprogram for other problems.
6. Algorithms can be easily modified, if necessary.
7. Algorithms are simple but powerful and general solutions.
8. Algorithms can be easily understood by others.

5.2.1 Definition
- An algorithm is set of instructions for solving a problem.
                     OR
- An algorithm is a step-by-step solution to a problem.
                     OR
- An algorithm is a sequence of instructions to be carried out in order to solve a specific problem.

5.2.2 Characteristics
1. **Finiteness:** An algorithm must terminate after a finite number of steps and further each steps must be executable in finite amount of time.
2. Each step of an algorithm must be precisely defined; the action to be carried out must be rigorously and unambiguously specified for each case.
3. **Input:** An algorithm has zero or more, but only finite number of inputs example: ASCII chart of 0-255.
4. **Output:** An algorithm has one or more output.
5. **Effectiveness:** An algorithm should be effective that means each of the operation to be performed in an algorithm must be sufficiently basic that it can, in principle, be done exactly and in a finite length of time, by a person using pencil and paper and should be computer programming language independent.

5.2.3 Advantages
1. Algorithm gives language independent layout of the program.
2. Using the basic layout, the program can be developed in any desired language.
3. Representation is in simple english language so it is very easy to understand.
4. Facilitates easy coding.

5.2.4 Examples

Ex. 1: Write an algorithm to check if the given number is a Palindrome. A palindrome is a number that reads same forward and backwards. e.g. 12321, 5445.

Sol.: Step 1: Read number

Step 2: Let temp = number and mirror = 0

Step 3: Repeat steps 4 and 5 until temp is not equal to 0

Step 4: Calculate mirror = temp mod 10 + mirror * 10

Step 5: Calculate temp = temp div 10

Step 6: If number = mirror then print "number is palindrome"

Step 7: If number is not = mirror then print "number is not palindrome"

Step 8: Stop.

Ex. 2: Write an algorithm to check whether a given number is prime number or not.

Sol.: Step 1: Read N
Step 2: Let counter = 0 and no = 2
Step 3: Let j = 1
Step 4: If j mod no ≠ 0 then Goto 9
Step 5: Add 1 to no
Step 6: If no not equal to j then goto step 4
Step 7: Add 1 to j
Step 8: If j is not equal to N then goto step 4
Step 9: Print j
Step 10: Stop

Ex. 3: Develop an algorithm to find sum of positive numbers and sum of negative numbers in a set of 10 numbers.

Sol.: Step 1: Set of sum of +ve numbers to zero
Step 2: Set of sum of –ve numbers to zero
Step 3: Set ctr equal to 1
Step 4: Repeat steps 5, 6, 7 and 8 until ctr is less than or equal to 10
Step 5: Read a number x
Step 6: If x is greater than zero add it in the sum of +ve numbers
Step 7: If x is less than zero add it in the sum of –ve numbers
Step 8: Add 1 in the ctr
Step 9: Print sum of +ve numbers and sum of –ve numbers
Step 10: Stop.

Ex. 4: Develop an algorithm to find sum of all divisors of an integer n.

Sol.: Step 1: Read n
Step 2: Sum = 1 and Counter = 2
Step 3: if (n mod counter = 0)
    sum = sum + counter
Step 4: Counter = Counter + 1
Step 5: Repeat steps 3 and 4 until counter is less than or equal to n.
Step 6: Stop

5.3 Flowchart

- Flowcharts are used in designing and documenting complex processes or programs.
- A flowchart is a graphical or symbolic representation of a process.
- The flowchart is a means of visually presenting the flow of data, the operations performed and the sequence in which they are performed to solve a problem.
- A flowchart is a diagrammatic representation that represents the sequence of operations to be performed to get the solution of a problem.

- A flow chart can be used to:
    1. Define and analyze processes.
    2. Build a step-by-step picture of the process for analysis, discussion, or communication.
    3. Define, standardize or find areas for improvement in a process.
- The most common **flowchart symbols** are:
    1. **Terminator** : An oval flowchart shape indicating the start or end of the process.
    2. **Process** : A rectangular flowchart shape indicating a normal process flow step.
    3. **Decision** : A diamond flowchart shape indication a branch in the process flow.
    4. **Connector** : A small, labeled, circular flow chart shape used to indicate a jump in the process flow. (Shown as the circle with the letter "A", in Fig. 5.1.)
    5. **Data** : A parallelogram that indicates data input or output (I/O) for a process.
    6. **Document** : Used to indicate a document or report.
    7. **Arrow** : Used to indicate the process flow.
- Fig. 5.1 shows symbols of flowchart.

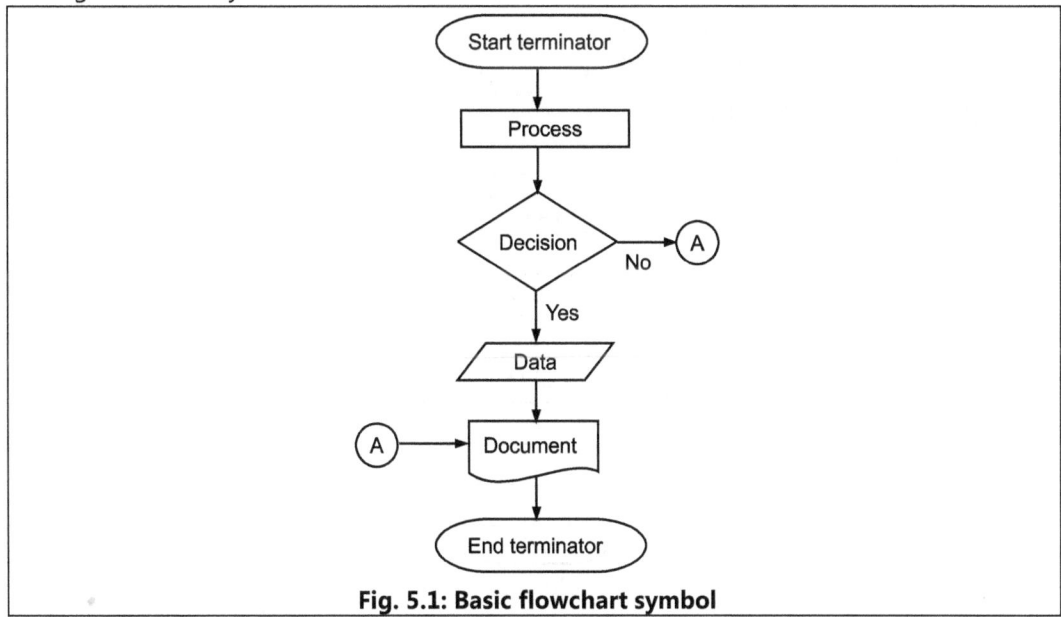

Fig. 5.1: Basic flowchart symbol

- Flowcharts are generally drawn in the early stages of formulating computer solutions.
- The purpose of a flow chart is to provide people with a common language or reference point when dealing with a project or process.

5.3.1 Definition

- A flowchart is a formalized graphic representation of a logic sequence, work or manufacturing process, organization chart, or similar formalized structure.

OR

- A flowchart is a diagram that describes a process or operation.

OR

- A flowchart visually displays the sequence of activities in a process and who is responsible for those activities.

5.3.2 Principles

1. Pictorial representation makes it a convenient method of communication.
2. It promotes logical accuracy and is a key to correct programming.
3. Takes care that no path is left incomplete without any action being taken.
4. Helps to develop program logic and serves as documentation.
5. It is an important tool for planning and designing a new system.

5.3.3 Examples

Ex. 1: Algorithm to convert temperature in celcius to fahrenheit.

Sol.:

Step 1: Read temperature in celcius as C

Step 2: Calculate F = (9 * C)/5 + 32

Step 3: Print the value of F

Step 4: End.

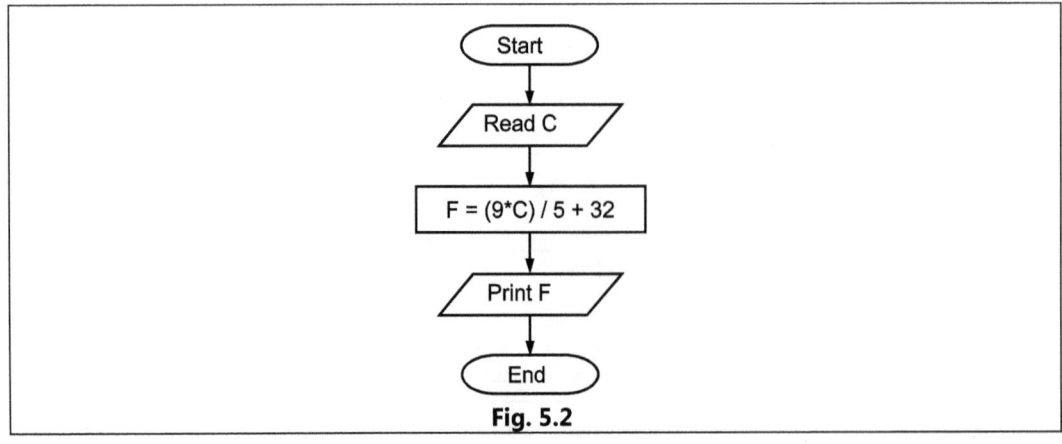

Fig. 5.2

Ex. 2: Display 1 through 100 numbers.
Sol.: 1. Start
2. A = 1
3. Display A
4. A = A + 1
5. If A ≤ 100, Go to Step 3
6. End.

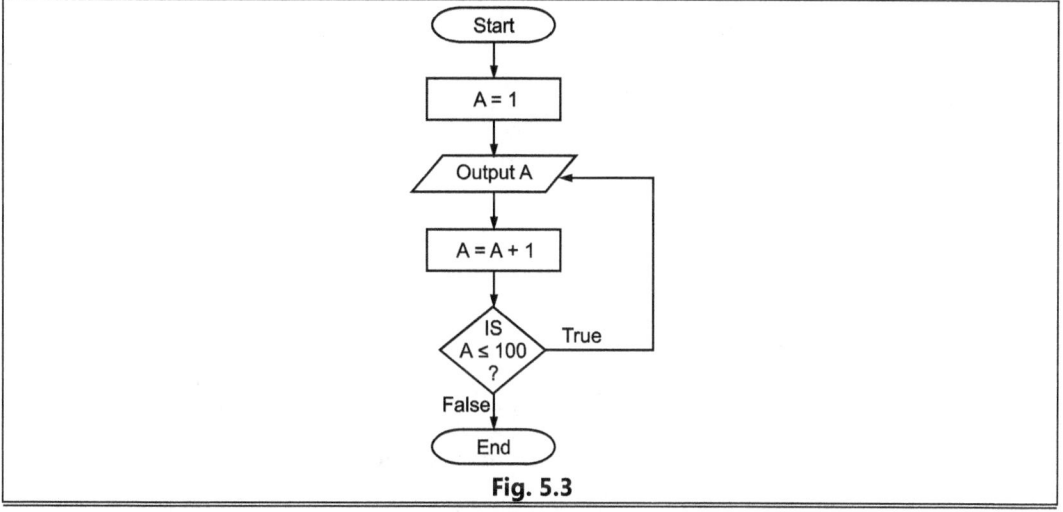
Fig. 5.3

Ex. 3: Print all odd numbers between 1 and 100.
Sol.: 1. A = 1
2. Display A
3. A = A + 2
4. If A < 100, Go to Step 2
5. End.

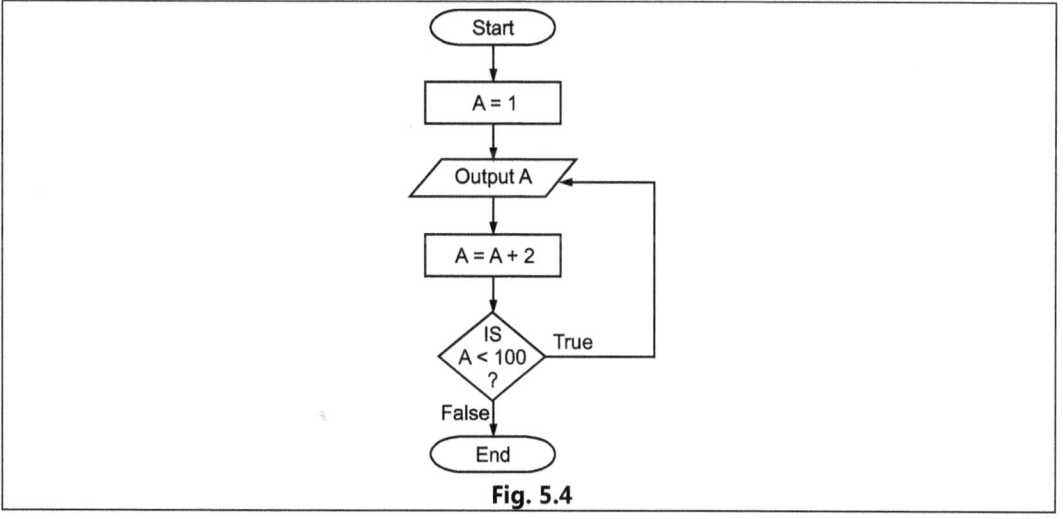
Fig. 5.4

Ex. 4: Display squares of all whole numbers from 1 through 10.
Sol.:
1. A = 1
2. Display A * A
3. A = A + 1
4. If A < 10, Go to Step 2
5. End.

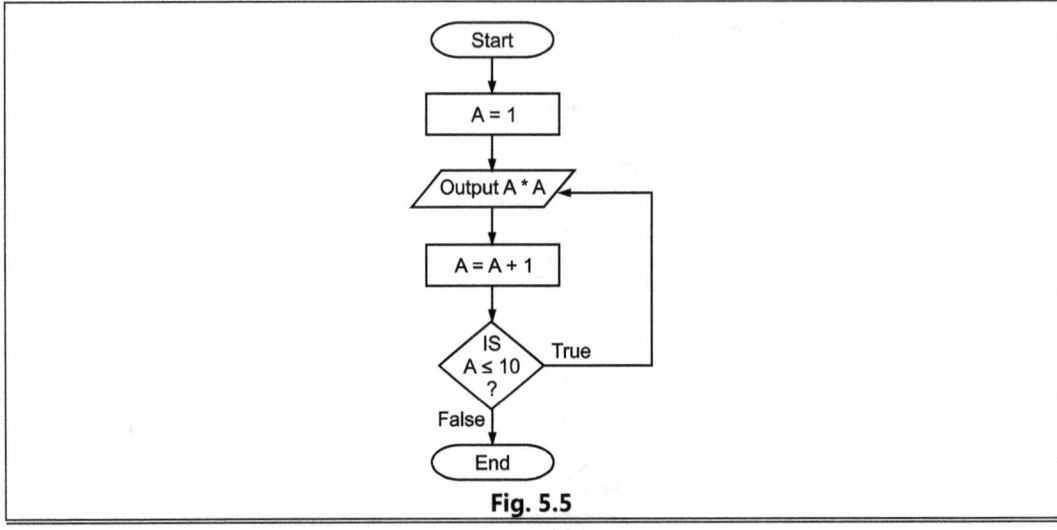

Fig. 5.5

Ex. 5: Draw a flowchart to find the sum of first 50 natural numbers.
Sol.:

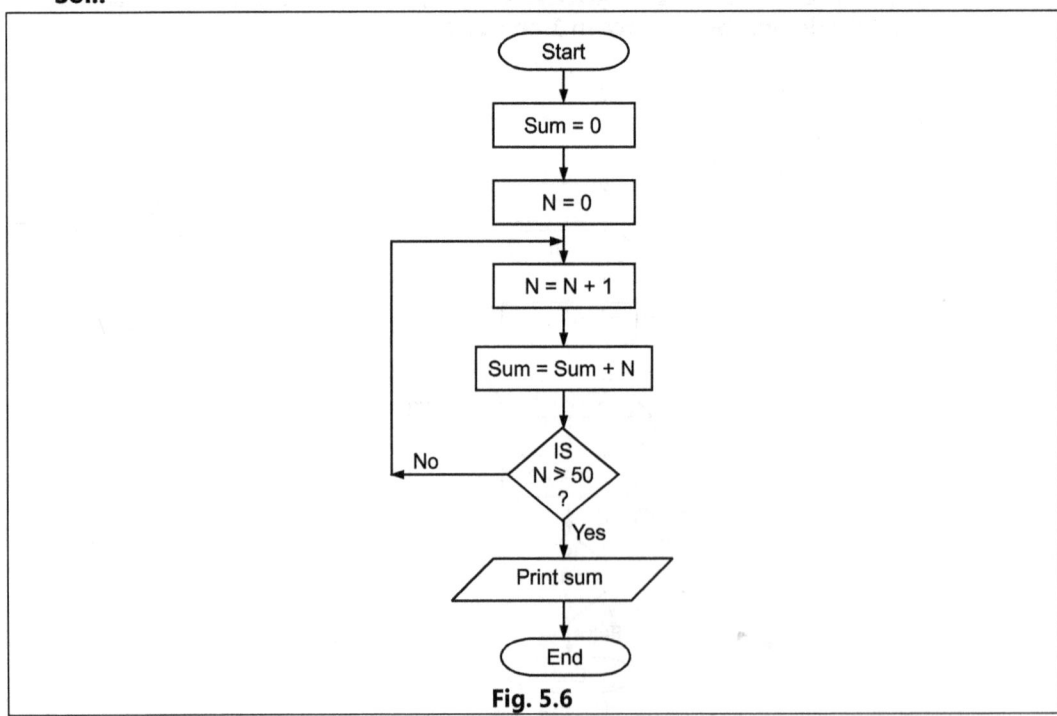

Fig. 5.6

Ex. 6: Draw a flowchart to find the largest of three numbers A, B and C.
Sol.:

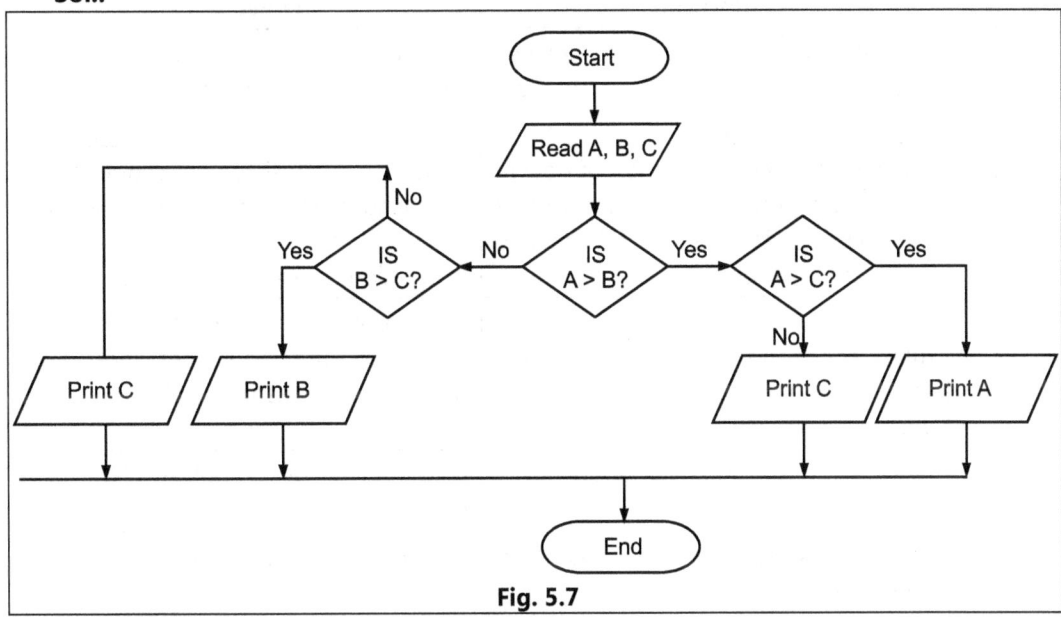

Fig. 5.7

5.3.4 Advantages and Disadvantages

Advantages:
1. **Proper Documentation:** Program flowcharts serve as a good program documentation, which is needed for various purposes.
2. **Efficient Coding:** The flowcharts act as a guide or blueprint during the systems analysis and program development phase.
3. **Efficient Program Maintenance:** The maintenance of operating program becomes easy with the help of flowchart. It helps the programmer to put efforts more efficiently on that part.
4. **Proper Debugging:** The flowchart helps in debugging process.
5. **Communication:** Flowcharts are better way of communicating the logic of a system to all concerned.
6. **Effective Analysis:** With the help of flowchart, problem can be analysed in more effective way.

Disadvantages:
1. **Loss of technical details:** The essentials of what is done can easily be lost in the technical details of how it is done.
2. **Complex logic:** Sometimes, the program logic is quite complicated. In that case, flowchart becomes complex and clumsy.
3. **Alterations and Modifications:** If alterations are required, the flowchart may require redrawing completely.
4. **Reproduction:** As the flowchart symbols cannot be typed, reproduction of flowchart becomes a problem.

Comparison between Algorithm and Flowchart:

Sr. No.	Algorithm	Flowchart
1.	An algorithm is just a detailed sequence of a simple steps that are needed to solve a problem.	A flowchart is a graphical representation of an algorithm.
2.	An algorithm is a description of how to carry out a process. An algorithm lists the steps those must be followed to complete the process.	A flowchart consists of a sequence of instructions linked together by arrows to show the order in which the instructions must be carried out.
3.	An algorithm is a precise rule (or set of rules) specifying how to solve some problem. Algorithm is stepwise analysis of the work to be done.	Each instruction is put into a box. The boxes are different shapes depending upon what the instruction is.
4.	Algorithm gives language independent layout of the program.	Flowchart gives logical flow of program.
5.	Less time is required as compared to flowchart.	Time consuming to write.
6.	Easy to update.	Difficult to update.

5.4 Computer Languages

- A language is a source of communication. With the help of computer language the programmer tells the computer what he/she wants it to do.
- Computer language has its own set of symbols, each symbol tell the computer to perform a specific task.
- Each and every problem solved by the computer has to be broken down into logical steps which has the following basic operations – Input data, Process data and Output data.
- Computer languages are classified into following categories:
    1. Machine language,
    2. Assembly language, and
    3. High-level language.

5.4.1 Machine Language

- The most elementary and first type of computer language, which was invented, was machine language.
- Sometimes machine language is referred to as machine code or object code. Machine language is a collection of binary digits or bits that the computer reads and interprets.
- Machine language is the only language a computer is capable of understanding.
- Machine language was machine dependent.

- A program written in machine language cannot be run on another type of computer without significant alterations. Machine language is sometimes also referred as the binary language i.e., the language of 0 and 1 where 0 stands for the absence of electric pulse and 1 stands for the presence of electric pulse.
- Machine languages are sometimes referred to as 1st generation programming languages.
- The popular binary coding systems ASCII and EBCDIC use 8-bits. The 'Unicode' is new system, uses 16-bits.
    1. **ASCII:** ASCII stands for "American Standard Code for Information Interchange". This binary coded system is widely used for microcomputers. The ASCII character set values are fixed to 0 to 9 numbers, A to Z and a to z alphabets and other symbols like +, – etc.
    2. **EBCDIC:** It is "Extended Binary Coded Decimal Interchange Code". It is developed by IBM company for main frame computers.
    3. **UNICODE:** It is 16-bit binary coding system. It is designed for Chinese and Japanese languages. These languages use many symbols and 8-bits are not sufficient for all the symbols in it. Hence, apple corporation, IBM and Microsoft developed this Unicode by their combined efforts.

Advantages of Machine Language:
1. It makes fast and efficient use of the computer.
2. It requires no translator to translate the code that is directly understood by the computer.
3. The performance and efficiency of CPU increases if instructions are given in machine language.

Disadvantages of Machine Language:
1. All operation codes have to be remembered.
2. All memory addresses have to be remembered.
3. It is hard to amend or find errors in a program written in the machine language.
4. These languages are machine dependent i.e. a particular machine language can be used on only one type of computer.
5. Many days are required to complete the program coding so it is time consuming.

5.4.2 Assembly Language

- As computer became more popular, it became quite apparent that machine language programming was simply too slow, tedious for most programmers.
- Sometimes, assembly language referred to as assembly or ASL. Assembly language is a low-level programming language used to interface with computer hardware.
- Assembly language uses structured commands as substitutions for numbers allowing humans to read the code easier than looking at binary. Although easier to read than binary, assembly language is a difficult language and is usually substituted for a higher language such as C.

- Assembly languages are also called as low level language instead of using the string of members programmers began using English like abbreviation to represent the elementary operation. The language provided an opportunity to the programmers to use English like words that were called MNEMONICS.
- It is low level programming language in which the sequence of 0s and 1s are replaced by mnemonic (ni-monic) codes. Typical instruction for addition and subtraction. Example: ADD for addition, SUB for subtraction etc.
- Since, our system only understand the language of 0s and 1s, therefore a system program is known as assembler.

Advantages Assembly Language:
1. **Easy to understand:** As compared to the machine language it is easier to understand.
2. **Easy to remove errors:** Because of the codes use English alphabets, its easy to locate and correct errors in an assembly language program.
3. **Easy to modify:** As the program written in assembly language is easy to understand, it is easy to modify this program as compared to the machine language program.
4. It saves time and reduces work.

Disadvantages Assembly Language:
1. Like machine language it is also machine dependent.
2. Since, it is machine dependent, the programmer should have the knowledge of the hardware also.
3. Coding is time consuming.

5.4.3 High Level Language

- The syntax that means rules and words used are close to English language. The research in computing field developed new types of assembler and translators.
- Initially for one command of the source programme, one instruction of machine language was developed. The advance assemblers can write more lines of code in machine level language.
- The required set of instructions can be stored and used whenever requested for it. This facility is used in higher level languages which saves time.
- High level languages are the computer languages in which it is much easier to write a program than the low level language.
- A program written in high level language is just like giving instruction to person in daily life.
- A high-level language is an advanced computer programming language that isn't limited by the computer, designed for a specific job, and is easier to understand.
- Today, there are dozens of high-level languages; some examples include BASIC, C, FORTRAN, Java, and Pascal.

Advantages:
1. High level languages require less time to write.
2. High level languages use words and symbols like English language, hence it is easier to learn it as compared to assembly level language.
3. Language is machine independent but programming is for the problem, hence can be used on any computer.
4. The length of programme i.e. lines of code are less than the assembly language code, hence less time is required.
5. Maintenance is easier.
6. Documentation is good as compared to other languages.
7. Machine independent languages.

Disadvantages:
1. The language processors required for these languages are of bigger size as these languages use many words.
2. The internal memory required is more due to bigger size.
3. During compilation, more time is required to find a match for word from big list.

5.5 Assembler

- An assembler is a program that takes basic computer instructions and converts them into a pattern of bits that the computer's processor can use to perform its basic operations.
- In other words, assembler is a program that translates assembly language into machine code.
- Assembly language is a low-level programming language in which a mnemonic is used to represent each of the machine language instructions.
- Assembly languages were developed to make programming easy, and simple.
- Since, the computer cannot understand assembly language, however, a program called assembler is used to convert assembly language programs into machine code.
- The assembler is a software utility that takes an assembly program as input and produces object code as output.
- Fig. 5.8 shows assembly process.

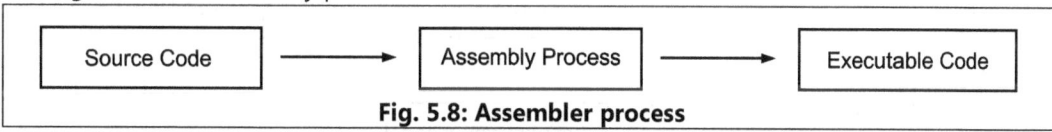

Fig. 5.8: Assembler process

5.6 Compiler

- The high-level languages are English like and easy to learn and program.
- A compiler is a program that translates a high level language into machine code.
- The Visual Basic compiler, for example, translates a program written in VB into machine code that can be run on a PC.

- A compiler is a computer program (or set of programs) that transforms source code written in a programming language (the source language) into another computer language (the target language, often having a binary form known as object code).
- Fig. 5.9 shows compilation process.

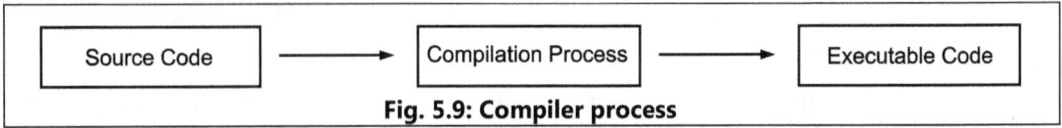

Fig. 5.9: Compiler process

Advantages:
1. Fast in execution.
2. The object/executable code produced by a compiler can be distributed or executed without having to have the compiler present.
3. The object program can be used whenever required without the need of recompilation.

Disadvantages:
1. Debugging (correcting errors) a program is much harder. Therefore, not so good at finding errors.
2. When an error is found, the whole program has to be re-compiled.

5.7 Interpreter

- An interpreter is also a program that translates high-level source code into executable code.
- However, the difference between a compiler and an interpreter is that an interpreter translates one line at a time and then executes it, no object code is produced and so the program has to be interpreted each time, it is to be run. If the program performs a section code 1000 times, then the section is translated into machine code 1000 times since each line is interpreted and then executed.
- Fig. 5.10 shows interpreter process.

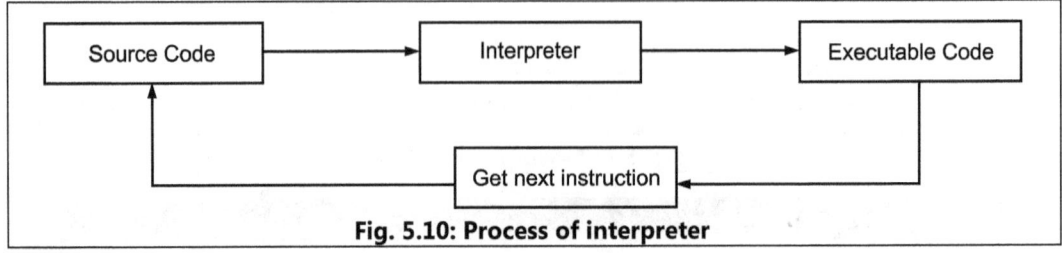

Fig. 5.10: Process of interpreter

Advantages:
1. Good at locating errors in programs
2. Debugging is easier since the interpreter stops when it encounters an error.
3. Cannot retain object code.

Disadvantages:
1. Slow in process.
2. No object code is produced, so a translation has to be done every time the program is running.
3. For the program to run, the interpreter must be present.

Comparison between Compiler and Interpreter:

Compiler	Interpreter
1. Translates the entire source code into machine code in one go when all the syntax errors are removed, execution takes place.	1. Translates the source cede line by line, indicated errors at each step every line is checked for syntax error and then converted to equivalent machine code.
2. Has capability to store compiled code for future usage.	2. Cannot retain object code.
3. More useful for commercial purposes.	3. More useful for learning purpose.
4. Execution time is less.	4. Execution time is more.
5. Slow for debugging (removal of mistakes from a program).	5. Good for fast debugging.

5.8 Characteristics of a Good Language

- There might be many reasons for the success of a language, but one obvious reason is the characteristics of the language.
- Several characteristics believed to be important for making a programming language good are:
    1. **Simplicity:** A good programming language must be simple and easy to learn and use. It should provide a programmer with a clear, simple and unified set of concepts, which can be easily grasped. The overall simplicity of a programming language strongly affects the readability of the programs written in that language, and programs, which are easier to read and understand, are also easier to maintain. It is also easy to develop and implement a compiler or an interpreter for a programming language, which is simple. However, the power needed for the language should not be sacrificed for simplicity.
    2. **Naturalness:** A good language should be natural for the application area, for which it has been designed. That is, it should provide appropriate operators, data structures, control structures, and a natural syntax to facilitate the users to code their problem easily and efficiently.

3. **Abstraction:** Abstraction means the ability to define and then use complicated structures or operations in ways that allow many of the details to be ignored. The degree of abstraction allowed by a programming language directly effects its write ability. Object oriented language support high degree of abstraction. Hence, writing programs in object oriented language is much easier. Object oriented language also support re usability of program segments due to this features.

4. **Efficiency:** Programs written in a good programming language are efficiently translated into machine code, are efficiently executed, and acquire as little space in the memory as possible. That is a good programming language is supported with a good language translator which gives due consideration to space and time efficiency.

5. **Structured:** Structured means that the language should have necessary features to allow its users to write their programs based on the concepts of structured programming. This property moreover, forces a programmer to look at a problem in a logical way, so that fewer errors are created while writing a program for the problem.

6. **Compactness:** In a good programming language, programmers should be able to express intended operations concisely. A verbose language is generally not liked by programmers, because they need to write too much.

7. **Locality:** A good programming language should be such that while writing a programmer concentrates almost solely on the part of the program around the statement currently being worked with.

5.9 Software

- Software, is any set of machine-readable instructions (most often in the form of a computer program) that directs a computer's processor to perform specific operations.
- Software is a set of programs, procedures, algorithms and its documentation concerned with the operation of a data processing system.
- Software is a general term for the various kinds of programs used to operate computers and related devices.
- Software can be grouped into following categories:
  1. **System software** is the basic software needed for a computer to operate (most notably the operating system).
  2. **Application software** is the software that uses the computer system to perform useful work beyond the operation of the computer itself.

3. **Embedded software** resides as firmware within embedded systems, devices dedicated to a single use. In that context there is no clear distinction between the system and application software.

5.9.1 System Software

- System software helps to run the computer hardware and computer system. It includes operating systems, devices drivers, diagnostic tools, servers, windowing systems, utilities and more.
- The purpose of systems software is to insulate the applications program as much as possible from the details of the particular complex being used, especially memory and other hardware features and such as accessory devices as communications, printers, readers, displays, keyboards, etc.
- System software is a set of one or more programs, used to control the operation and extend the processing capability of a computer system.

Functions of System Software:

- System software performs one or more of the following functions:
    1. Monitors the effective use of various hardware resources, such as CPU, memory, peripherals etc.
    2. Supports the development of other application of software.
    3. Supports the execution of other application software.
- System software makes the operation of a computer system more effective and efficient. Programs in a system software package are called system programs, and the programmers who prepare system software are referred to a system programmers.

Types of System Software:

1. **Communication software:** In a network environment, communications software enables transfer of data and programs from one computer system to another.
2. **Operating Systems:** Every computer system has an operating system software, which takes care of the effective and efficient utilization of all the hardware and software components of the computer system.
3. **Utility Programs:** Utility programs also known as utilities. Utility programs are a set of programs, which help users in system maintenance tasks, and in performing tasks of routine nature. Some of the tasks commonly performed by utility programs include formatting of hard disks or floppy disks, taking backup of files stored in hard disk on to a tape or floppy disk.
4. **Programming Language Translators:** Programming language translators are system software, which transform the instructions prepared by programmers in a programming language, into a form, which can be interpreted and executed by a computer system.

5.9.2 Application Software

- Application software allows end users to accomplish one or more specific (non-computer related) tasks. Typical applications include industrial automation, business software, educational software, medical software, databases and computer games.
- Businesses are probably the biggest users of application software, but almost every field of human activity now uses some form application software.
- Application software is a set of one or more programs, used to solve a specific problem.
- The program in an application software package are called application programs and the programmers who prepare application software are referred to as application programmers.
- There are millions of application softwares available for a wide range of applications, ranging from simple applications, such as word processing, inventory management, preparation of tax returns, banking, hospital administration, insurance, publishing, to complex scientific and engineering applications.

Types of Application Software:

1. **Personal Assistance Software:** A personal assistance software allows us to use personal computers for storing and retrieving our personal information and planning and managing our schedules, contacts, financial and inventory of important items.

2. **Graphics Software:** A graphics software enables user to use a computer system for creating, editing, viewing, storing, retrieving and printing designs, drawings, pictures, graphs and anything else that can be drawn in the traditional manner.

3. **Education Software:** Education software allows a computer system to be used as a teaching and learning tool.

4. **Word Processing Software:** A word-processing software enables user to make use of a computer system for creating, editing, viewing, formatting, storing, retrieving and printing documents.

5. **Database Software:** A database is a collection of related data stored and treated as a unit for information retrieval purposes. A database software is a set of one or more programs, which enable us to create a database, maintain it, organize its data in desired fashion and to selectively retrieve useful information from it.

6. **Spreadsheet Software:** A spreadsheet software is a numeric data analysis tool. It allows user to create a kind of computerized ledger.

7. **Entertainment Software:** Entertainment software allows a computer system to be used as an entertainment tool.

Difference between System and Application Softwares:

System software	Application software
1. System software is a set of programs that controls operation of a computer system.	1. Application software is a set of programs that accomplishes user specific tasks.
2. We can define System software as "it is computer software designed to operate the computer hardware and to provide a platform for running application software."	2. We can define Application software as "it is computer software designed to help the user to perform specific tasks."
3. System software is written to perform a several task.	3. Application software is written to perform a specific task.
4. Generally users do not interact with system software.	4. Generally users interact with application software.
5. System software runs independently.	5. Application cannot run without the present of the system software.
6. System software is not specific purpose software.	6. Application software is specific purpose software.
7. Operating system, Text editor, Compiler are examples of system softwares.	7. Word, Excel, PowerPoint, Paint are examples of application softwares.

Questions

1. What is an algorithm? State its advantages.
2. Define computer language.
3. Draw and explain flowchart symbols in detail.
4. What is software? What are its types?
5. Enlist characteristics of good language.
6. What is machine language? State its advantages and disadvantages.
7. Explain uses of algorithm.
8. Write short note on: assembly language.
9. What are the types of application software?
10. With the help of diagram describe compiler.

11. What is system software? Explain its types.
12. What is interpreter? Explain its working diagrammatically.
13. Distinguish between application software and system software.
14. Explain the term assembler in detail.
15. Compare algorithm and flowchart.
16. Draw an algorithm to print first N numbers.
17. Define:
    (i) Algorithm,
    (ii) Flowchart, and
    (iii) Software.
18. Draw a flowchart to calculate average of n numbers.
19. Describe characteristics of algorithm.

Chapter 6...

Operating System

Contents ...

6.1 Introduction to Operating System
    6.1.1 Definition
    6.1.2 Objectives
    6.1.3 Characteristics
    6.1.4 Features
    6.1.5 Need
    6.1.6 Advantages
    6.1.7 Disadvantages
6.2 Evolution of Operating System
6.3 Functions of Operating System
6.4 Types of Operating Systems
6.5 Windows Operating System
6.6 Linux
    6.6.1 Features
    • Questions

6.1 Introduction to Operating System

- An Operating System (OS) is a software program that enables the computer hardware to communicate and operate with the computer software.
- Without a computer operating system, a computer and software programs would be useless.
- An operating system is a layer of software which takes care of technical aspects of a computer's operation.
- An operating system is a program that acts as an interface between the software and the computer hardware.
- An operating system is low-level software that enables a user and higher-level application software to interact with a computer's hardware and the data and other programs stored on the computer.
- OS is an integration set of specialised programs that are used to manage overall resources and operations of the computer.

- An operating system is a collection of software that manages computer hardware resources and provides common services for computer programs.
- Most popular operating systems are Windows 7, Windows XP, Windows 8, Macintosh OSX, Linux, Unix, Windows Vista, Debian, Xandros Linux, Android, Solaris, etc.

6.1.1 Definition

- An operating system is a computer program that manages the resources of a computer.

  OR

- An operating system is software that communicates with the hardware and allows other programs to run.

  OR

- An operating system is the program that, after being initially loaded into the computer by a boot program, manages all the other programs in a computer.

  OR

- An operating system is a program that controls the execution of application programs and acts as an interface between the user of a computer and the computer hardware. In other words" The software that controls the hardware".

6.1.2 Objectives

- Objectives of operating system are listed below:
    1. To provide users a convenient interface to use the computer system.
    2. Manage the resources of a computer system.
    3. Making a computer system convenient to use in an efficient manner.
    4. The efficient and fair sharing of resources among users and programs.
    5. To hide the details of the hardware resources from the users.
    6. Keep the track of who is using which resource, granting resource requests, according to resource using and mediating conflicting requests from different programs and users.
    7. To act as an intermediary between the hardware and its users and making it easier for the users to access and use other resources.

6.1.3 Characteristics

- The operating system have the following characteristics:
    1. Operating system is a collection of programs those are responsible for the execution of other programs.
    2. Operating system is that which is responsible for controlling all the input and output devices those are connected to the system.
    3. Operating system is that which is responsible for running all the application software's.
    4. Operating system is that which provides scheduling to the various processes means allocates the memory to various process those want to execute.

5. Operating system is that which provides the communication between the user and the system.
6. Operating system is stored into the BIOS means in the Basic Input and Output System means when a user starts his system then this will read all the instructions those are necessary for executing the system means for running the operating system, operating system must be loaded into the computer this will use the floppy or hard disks which stores the operating system.

6.1.4 Features

- Some of the features of operating systems are detailed here:
    1. **Software and hardware management:** The operating system is the bridge between computer hardware and software and makes the communication between them possible. Also communication between different softwares in the computer is also taken care by operating system.
    2. **Constant API:** Application Program Interface (API) is a software that allows different applications that run on a computer to work on other computers also. But they should have same operating system. So it is very vital to have consistent API in the operating system.
    3. **Execution of programs:** Programs running in the computer are completely dependent on the operating system. But program execution is a tough process. The multitasking and multithreading features of the operating system are dependent upon the type of program execution feature of operating system.
    4. **Interruptions:** Interruption may happen at any time while using the computers. So the operating system should allow and handle many numbers of interrupts. Whenever, an interruption occurs, the operating system should respond to it by saving and stopping the current execution and work on the new execution. This is the most hard-hitting process for the operating system.
    5. **Managing memory:** The operating system provides the memory for the programs those are executed at any moment. So the operating system should have good memory allocation facility to execute the programs smoothly. The prioritization and allocation of memory to the applications running should be taken care by the operating systems.
    6. **Networking:** Today computers are nothing without internet connection or some network connection. This is the age of networking. So if computers are connected to a network, the there should be definitely communication between one computer and another. So the operating system is what makes it possible for one computer to communicate with other computers.
    7. **Security:** Security is the important feature that should be looked for in an operating system. An operating system in the computer takes care of all security issues of computer and data in it. Log in passwords, firewall settings, and every such aspect related to security depends on the ability of the operating system. Some of the computers in network may involve in file sharing, and other data sharing. So it is important in such cases to have powerful secured operating systems.

6.1.5 Need

- An operating system is an essential component of a computer system. The primary objectives of an operating system are to make computer system convenient to use and utilizes computer hardware in an efficient manner.
- An operating system is a large collection of software which manages resources of the computer system, such as memory, processor, rite system and input/output devices.
- Operating system keeps track of the status of each resource and decides who will have a control over computer resources, for how long and when.
- The main objective of operating system is to execute multiple programs in interleaved fashion or different time cycle is called multiple programming systems.
- Some of the **important reasons why do we need an operating system** are as follows:
  1. Operating system provides an environment for running user programs.
  2. Operating system provides an interface to the user to communicate with the system.
  3. User interacts with the computer through operating system in order to accomplish his/her task since it is his primary interface with a computer.
  4. It helps the user in understand the inner functions of a computer very closely.
  5. Operating system executes user programs and to make solving user problems easier.
  6. Operating system provides an overall control to the system.
  7. Many concepts and techniques found in operating system have general applicability in other applications.
  8. Operating system manages the computer resources in an efficient manner.
  9. Operating system uses hardware of the system in efficient manner.
- The positioning of operating system in overall computer system is shown in Fig. 6.1.

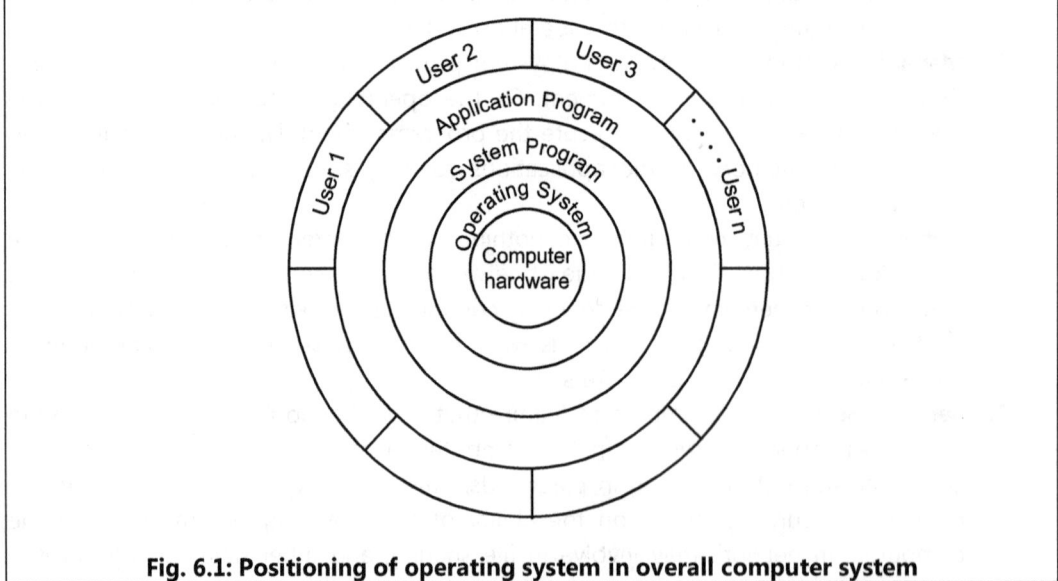

Fig. 6.1: Positioning of operating system in overall computer system

6.1.6 Advantages

- Operating system consists of following advantages:
  1. Operating system provides direct Hardware access.
  2. Fast in speed because it provides direct access of computer hardware.
  3. Easy and complete memory use, and
  4. Efficiency use of computer hardware.

6.1.7 Disadvantages

- Disadvantages of operating systems are given below:
  1. No back-up available.
  2. Unrestricted access.
  3. Deadlock problems, and
  4. Problems of memory data loss.

6.2 Evolution of Operating System

- First operating systems were developed in the early 1950's for the IBM 701 computers. This operating system was elementary in nature and was not so powerful as the operating system of today's computers, lot of research work has been carried out in this direction.
- Today there are more powerful operating systems which are machine independent and can execute several jobs at a time on the same system.
- The main aim of development in operating system was to minimize the idle time of the system and to use the computer system in the most efficient and economical way.
- The primary goal of some operating systems is convenience for the user, efficient operation of the computer system. The design of an operating system is a complex task.
- Designers face many tradeoffs' in the design and implementations and many people are involved not only in bringing an operating system to fruition, but also constantly revising and updating it.
- Today's operating system is very sophisticated and does more than what developed over the past 50 years.
- The evolution of operating system went through seven major phases. Six of them significantly changed the ways in which users accessed computers through the open shop, batch processing, multiprogramming, time sharing, personal computing and distributed systems.
- In the seventh phase the foundations of concurrent programming were developed and demonstrated in model operating system.

Table 6.1: Classic operating system and Fundamental ideas

No.	Major Phase	Operating Systems	Technical Innovations
1.	Open shop	IBM 701 open shop (1954)	The idea of Operating System.
2.	Batch Processing	BKS systems (1961)	Tape Batching, First-In-First-Out scheduling.
3.	Multiprogramming	Atlas Supervisor (1961) B5000 system (1964) Exec II system (1966) Egdon system (1966)	Processor Multiplexing, Indivisible operations, Demand Paging, Input/output spooling, Remote Job Entry.
4.	Time Sharing	CTSS (1962) Multics File System (1965) Titan File System (1972) Unix (1974)	Simultaneous user interaction, Online File systems.
5.	Concurrent programming	THE system (1968) RC 4000 system (1969) Venus System (1972) Boss 2 system (1975) Solo System (1976) Solo Program Text (1976)	Hierarchical Systems, Extensible Kernels, Parallel Programming concepts, Secure Parallel Languages.
6.	Personal Computing	OS 6 (1972) Alto system (1979) Pilot system (1980) Star User Interface (1982)	Graphics User Interfaces.
7.	Distributed Systems	WFS file server (1979) Unix United RPC (1982) Unix United System (1982) Amoeba system (1990)	Remote Servers.

6.3 Functions of Operating System

- Fig. 6.2 shows various functions of operating system.
    1. **Process Management:** The process management activities handled by the OS are:
        (i) Controlled access to shared resources like file, memory, I/O and CPU,
        (ii) Controlled execution of applications,
        (iii) Create, execute and delete a process (system process or user process),

(iv) Cancel or resume a process,
(v) Schedule a process, and
(vi) Synchronization, communication and deadlock handling for processes.

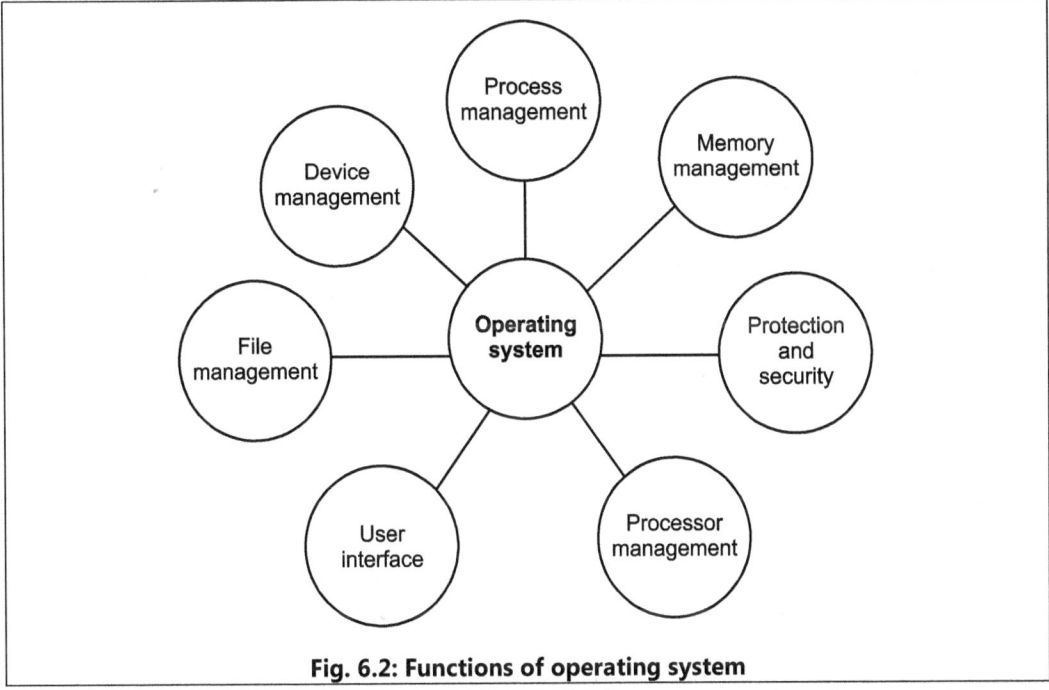

Fig. 6.2: Functions of operating system

2. **Memory Management:** It keeps tracks of primary memory i.e. what part of it are in use by whom, what part are not in use etc. Allocates the memory when the process or program request it. The activities of memory management handled by OS are:
   (i) Allocate memory,
   (ii) Free memory,
   (iii) Re-allocate memory to a program when a used block is freed, and
   (iv) Keep track of memory usage.
3. **File Management:** Allocates the resources. De-allocates the resource. Decides who gets the resources. The file management tasks include:
   (i) Create and delete both files and directories,
   (ii) Provide access to files,
   (iii) Allocate space for files,
   (iv) Keep back-up of files, and
   (v) Secure files.
4. **Device Management:** Keep tracks of all devices. This is also called I/O controller. Decides which process gets the device when and for how much time. The device management tasks handled by OS are:
   (i) Open, close and write device drivers, and
   (ii) Communicate, control and monitor the device driver.

5. **Protection and Security:** OS protects the resources of system. User authentication, file attributes like read, write, encryption, and back-up of data are used by OS to provide basic protection. By means of passwords and similar other techniques, preventing unauthorized access to programs and data.
6. **User Interface or Command Interpreter:** Operating system provides an interface between the computer user and the computer hardware. The user interface is a set of commands or a graphical user interface via which the user interacts with the applications and the hardware.
7. **Processor Management:** Allocate the processor (CPU) to a process. Deallocate processor when processor is no longer required.

6.4 Types of Operating Systems

1. **Batch Operating System:**
- In old days the computers were large systems run from a console. The common input devices were card readers and tape drives and output devices were line printers, tape drives and card punches.
- The computer system did not directly interact with the users instead the computer users used to prepare a format that consisted of the programs, the data and some control information about the nature of the job and submitted it to the computer operator.
- The job was usually in the form of punch cards. The process as a whole took a lot of time and was slow. To speed up the processing jobs with similiar needs were batched together and were run through the computer as a group.
- Fig. 6.3 shows the memory layout for a simple batch system.

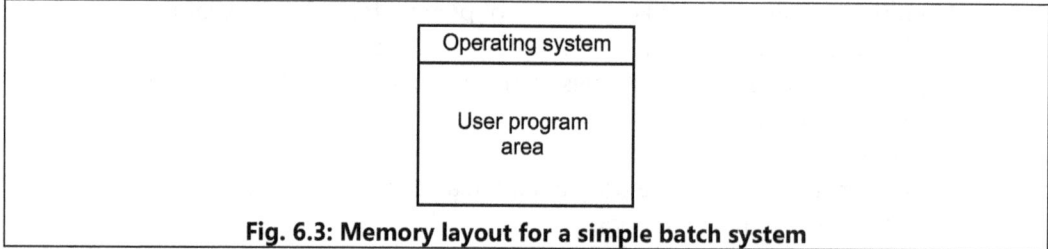

Fig. 6.3: Memory layout for a simple batch system

- A batch operating system, normally reads a stream of separate jobs, each with its own control cards that predefine what the job does. When the job is complete, its output is usually printed.
- The important feature of a batch system is lack of interaction between the user and the job while that job is being executed. The job is prepared and submitted and at some later time, the output appears.
- In a batch processing system, a job is described by a sequence of control statements stored in a machine-readable form.
- The operating system can read and execute a series of such jobs without human intervention except for such functions as tape and disk mounting. The order in which the jobs are selected and executed can be scheduled using appropriate algorithms.

- A batch is a sequence of user jobs.
- Batch processing came into vogue at a time when punched cards were used to record user jobs.
- Processing of a job involved physical actions by the system operator, e.g. loading a deck of cards into the card reader, pressing switches on the computers console to initiate a job, etc., all of which wasted a lot of computer time. This wastage could be reduced by automating the processing of a batch of jobs.
- A computer operator forms a batch by arranging user jobs in a sequence and inserting special markers to indicate the start and end of the batch.
- After forming a batch, the operator submits it for processing. The primary function of the batch processing system is to implement the processing of a batch of jobs without requiring any intervention of the operator.
- The operating system achieves this by making an automatic transition from the execution of one job to that of the next job in the batch.
- Batch processing is implemented by locating a component of the batch processing operating system, called the batch monitor (or batch supervisor), permanently in one part of the computer's main memory.
- The remaining part of the memory is used to process a user job i.e. the current job in the batch.
- The batch monitor is responsible for:
    o accepting command from the system operator,
    o initiate the processing of a batch,
    o sets up the processing of the first job,
    o at end of the job, terminates process and initiate execution of the next job,
    o at end of the batch, terminates batch and awaits initiation of the next batch by the operator.
- Fig. 6.4 depicts the schematic of a batch processing system.

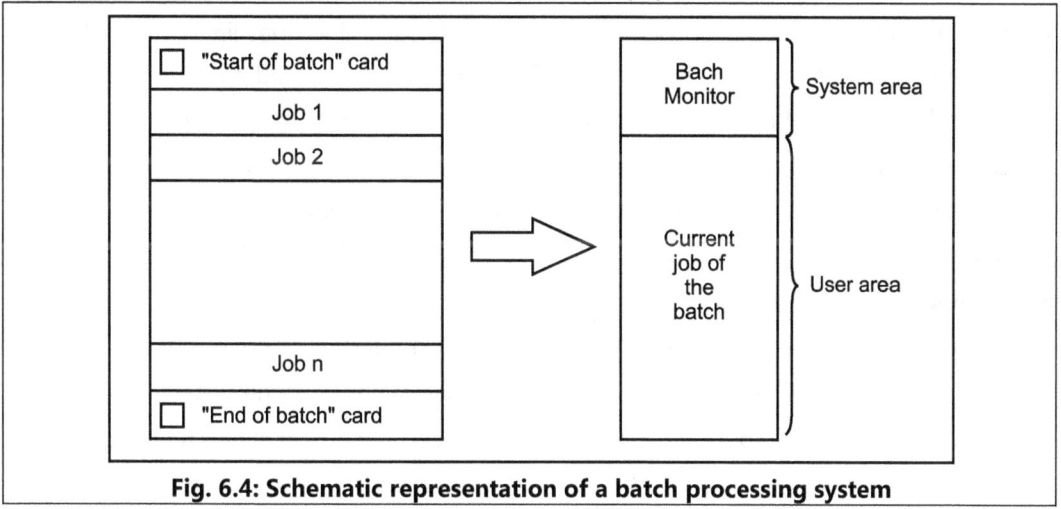

Fig. 6.4: Schematic representation of a batch processing system

Advantages of batch operating system:
   (i) Move much of the work of the operator to the computer.
   (ii) Increased performance since it was possible for job to start as soon as the previous job finished.

Disadvantages of batch operating system:
   (i) Turn around time can be large from user standpoint.
   (ii) Difficult to debug program.
   (iii) Due to lack of protection scheme, one batch job can affect pending jobs.
   (iv) A job could corrupt the monitor, thus affecting pending jobs.
   (v) A job could enter an infinite loop.

Spooling Technique:
- In the batch operating system execution environment, the CPU is often idle. This idleness occurs because the speeds of the mechanical I/O devices are slower than those of electronic devices.
- As time passed, improvements in technology resulted in faster I/O devices and CPU speeds increased even faster, so the problem was not only unsolved but also increased.
- In the disk technology rather than the cards being read from the card reader directly into memory, and then the job being processed, cards are read directly from the card reader onto the disk.
- The location of the card images is recorded in a table kept by the operating system. When a job is executed, the operating system satisfied its request for card reader input by reading from the disk.
- Similarly, when the job requests the printer to output a line, that line is copied into a system buffer and is written to the disk. When the job is completed, the output is actually printed. This form of processing is called spooling as shown in Fig. 6.5.
- Spooling is used for data processing of remote sites. The CPU sends the data via communication paths to a remote printer. The remote processing is done at its own speed, with no CPU intervention.

Advantages of spooling:
   (i) Spooling overlaps the I/O of one job with the computation of other jobs.
   (ii) Spooling has a direct beneficial effect on the performance of the system.
   (iii) Spooling can keep both the CPU and the I/O devices working at much higher rates.
   (iv) Spooling operating uses a disk as a very large buffer.

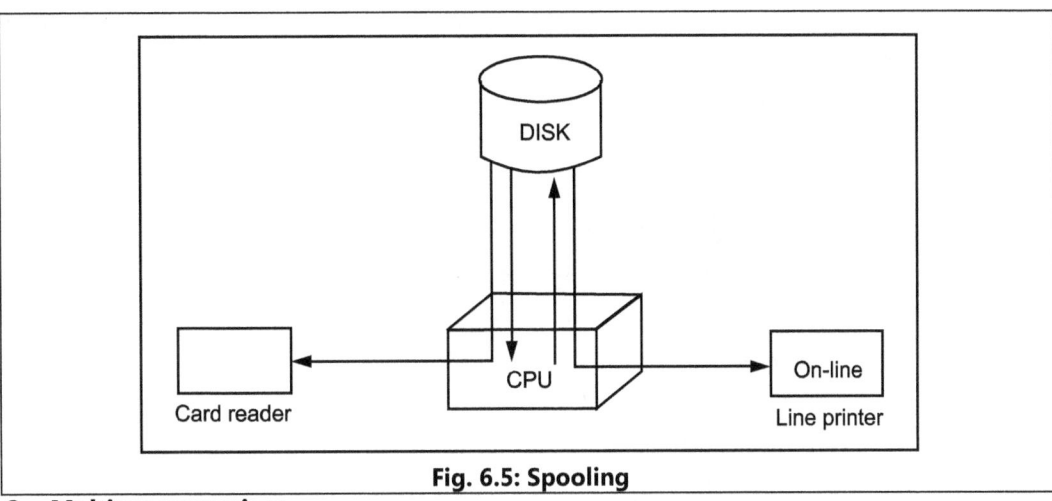

Fig. 6.5: Spooling

2. Multiprogramming:

- Multiprogramming is a technique to execute number of programs simultaneously by a single processor.
- In multiprogramming number of processes reside is main memory at a time and the operating system picks and begins executing one of the jobs in the main memory.
- The Fig. 6.6 and Fig. 6.7 shows the layout of the multiprogramming system, which consists of 5 jobs.

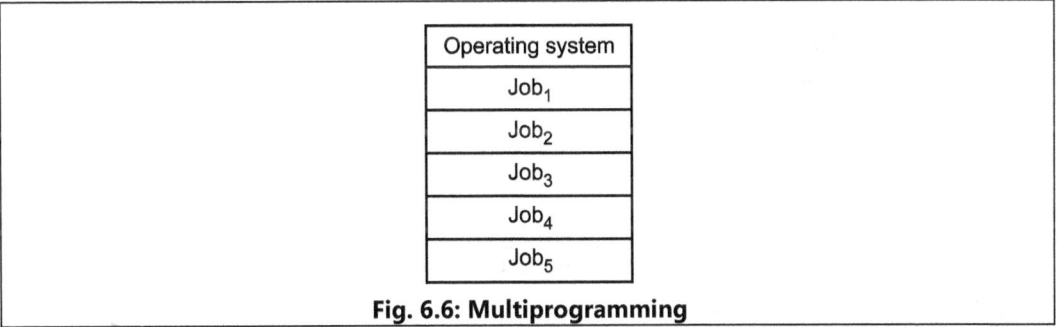

Fig. 6.6: Multiprogramming

- In non-multiprogramming system, the CPU can execute only one program at a time, if the running program waiting for any I/O device, the CPU sits idle, this will effect the performance of the CPU.
- But in case of multiprogramming environment any I/O wait by a process, will switch the CPU from that job to another job in the job pool eliminating the CPU idle time.
- This type of system permits several user jobs to be executed concurrently. The operating system takes care of switching the CPU among the various user jobs. It also provides a suitable run-time environment and other support functions, so the jobs do not interfere with each other.
- The goal of multiprogramming is to improve the system utilization by exploiting the concurrency between the CPU and the IO subsystem.
- The basic premise of multiprogramming is that while the IO subsystem is busy with an IO operation for an user job, the CPU can execute another user job.
- This requires the presence of multiple user jobs simultaneously in the computer's memory.

- Fig. 6.7 illustrates the schematic of a multiprogramming OS. The processor and IO channel are busy with different user jobs residing in the memory. Thus, they access different areas of memory.

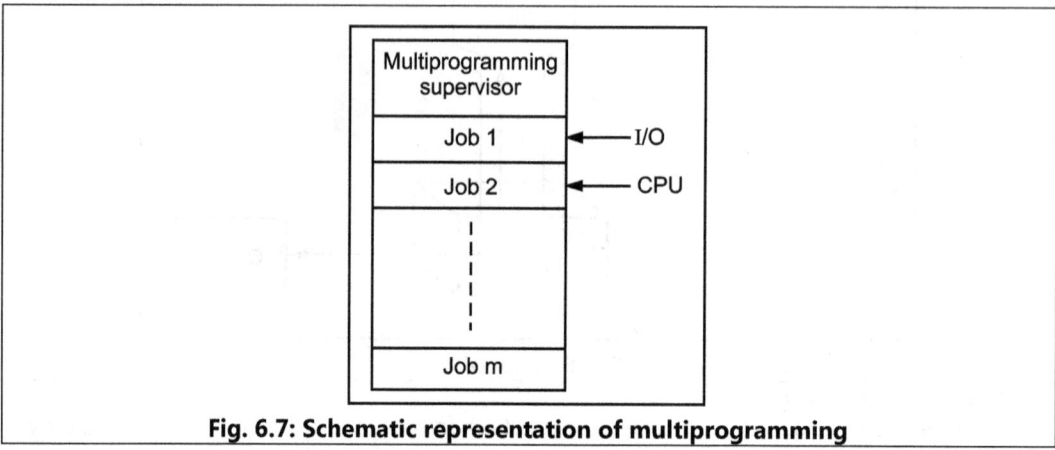

Fig. 6.7: Schematic representation of multiprogramming

- This ensures that their activities would not interfere with one another.
- One part of the main memory is occupied by the supervisor and it consists of a permanently resident part and a transient part which is loaded whenever required.
- The architectural (or hardware) features essential for multiprogramming are:
  - IO channels and the interrupt hardware,
  - Memory protection, and
  - Privileged mode of CPU operation.

Advantages of multiprogramming are:

(i) Efficient memory utilization.

(ii) CPU never sits idle, so it increases the CPU performance.

(iii) Throughput of the CPU increases.

(iv) In non-multiprogramming environment (mono programming) the user/ program has to wait for CPU much time. But waiting time is limited in multiprogramming.

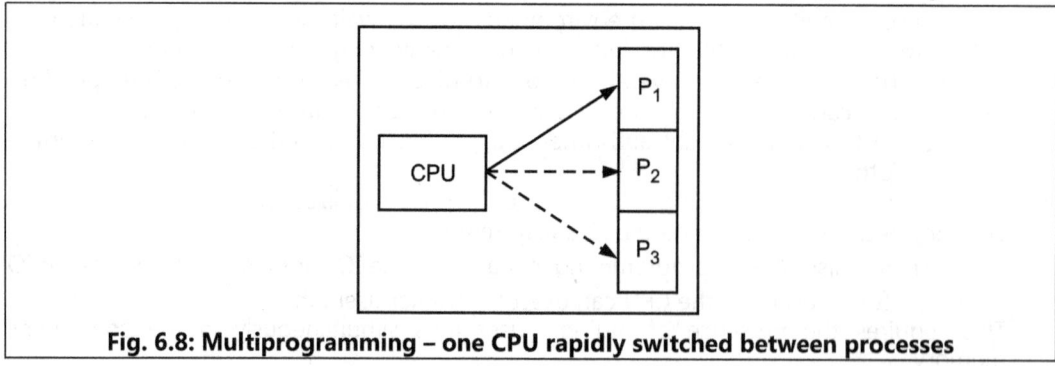

Fig. 6.8: Multiprogramming – one CPU rapidly switched between processes

3. Multiprocessing (Multiprocessor) System:

- Multiprogramming allows running a program on more than one CPU simultaneously.
- This system is similar to multiprogramming system, except that there is more than one CPU available.
- In most multiprocessor systems, the processors share a common memory. Thus, the user can view the system as if it were a powerful single processor.
- Fig. 6.9 depicts the manner in which multiple processors may be used for multiprogramming. Usually, we visualize several separate processes as being in memory.
- In actuality, a process is often paged so that only part of it is in memory at one time; this allows the number of processes active in the system to be very large.

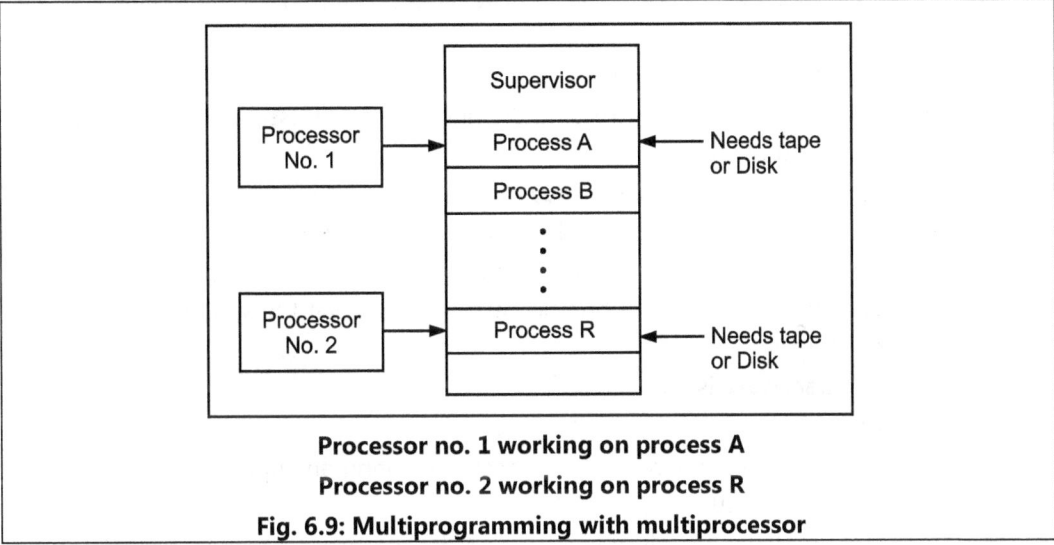

Processor no. 1 working on process A
Processor no. 2 working on process R
Fig. 6.9: Multiprogramming with multiprocessor

- A processor is assigned to a task and operates on it until it is blocked. When a task is blocked, the processor selects another task and continues processing.
- After the blocking condition has been satisfied, a processor will eventually be assigned to the process; it need not be the same physical processor as before.
- Multiprocessing is the use of two or more Central Processing Units (CPUs) within a single computer system.
- The term also refers to the ability of a system to support more than one processor and/or the ability to allocate tasks between them.
- There are many variations on this basic theme, and the definition of multiprocessing can vary with context, mostly as a function of how CPUs are defined (multiple cores on one die, multiple chips in one package, multiple packages in one system unit, etc.).
- Multiprocessing sometimes refers to the execution of multiple concurrent software processes in a system as opposed to a single process at any one instant.
- However, the term multiprogramming is more appropriate to describe this concept, which is implemented mostly in software, whereas multiprocessing is more appropriate to describe the use of multiple hardware CPUs.

- A system can be both multiprocessing and multiprogramming, only one of the two, or neither of the two.
- Below are some examples of multiprocessing operating systems.
  - Linux,
  - Unix, and
  - Windows 2000.
- **Multiprocessor System (Parallel System):** Most systems in today's date are single processor i.e. they have only one main CPU. Some systems have more than one processor in close communication, sharing the computer bus, the clock and sometimes memory and peripheral devices. These systems are referred to as Tightly Coupled Systems.

Advantages of multiprocessor systems:
  (i) **Increases throughput:** by increasing the number of processors, more work done in a shorter period of time.
  (ii) Multiprocessors can also **save money** compared to multiple single systems, because the processors can share peripherals, cabinets and power supplies.
  (iii) It **increases reliability:** if functions can be distributed properly among several processors, then the failure of one processor will not halt the system, but rather will only slow it down.
  (iv) **Minimum hardware** is required.

4. **Multithreading:**
- Multithreading is a technique in which a process executing an application is divided into threads that can run concurrently.
  (i) **Thread:** A dispatchable unit of work. It includes a processor context (which includes the program counter and stack pointer) and its own data area for stack.(to enable subroutine branching). A thread executes sequentially and is interruptable so that the processor can turn to another thread.
  (ii) **Process:** A collection of one or more threads and associated system resources. (Such as memory containing both code and data, open files and devices).
- Multithreading is useful for applications that perform a number of essentially independent tasks that do not need to be serialized.
- An example is a database server that listens for and processes numerous client requests. Threads are also useful for structuring processes that are part of the operating system's kernel.
- Operating systems allow different parts of a software program to run concurrently.
- Operating systems that would fall into this category are:
  - Linux
  - Unix
  - Windows 2000.

- Multithreading refers to the ability of an operating system to support multiple threads of execution per process. The traditional approach of a single thread of execution per process is referred to as a single threaded approach.
- MS-DOS is an example of an operating system that supports a single user process and a single thread.

Advantages of multithreading:
   (i) The efficiency of multithreading system is evident in multiprocessor system where parallel processing of thread is possible.
   (ii) Thread switching is faster than process switching.
   (iii) Threads are also useful for structuring processes that are part of the kernel.

Disadvantages of multithreading:
   (i) Multithreading is a complicated concept due to which operating system maintainability and designing are time consuming and expensive.
   (ii) It is still evolving and requires multiprocessor machines, increased machine speed, high speed network attachments and increased size and variety of memory storage devices.

5. **Multitasking or Time Sharing:**
- Time sharing or multitasking, is a logical extension of multiprogramming. Multiple jobs are executed by the CPU switching between them, but the switches occur so frequently that the users may interact with each program while running.
- Time sharing systems were developed to provide interactive use of a computer at reasonable cost.
- A time shared operating system uses CPU scheduling and multiprogramming to provide each user with a small portion of a time-shared computer. Each user has atleast one separate program in memory.
- A program that is loaded into memory and is being executed is commonly referred to as a process.
- Below are some examples of multitasking operating systems.
   o Unix
   o Windows 2000.
- A time shared operating system allows many uses to share the computer simultaneously. Since each action or command in, in a time-shared system tends to be short, only a little CPU time is needed for each user.
- Time sharing operating systems are even more complex than a multiprogrammed operating systems.
- As in multiprogramming several jobs must be kept simultaneously in memory, which require some form of memory management and protection.
- If a reasonable time can be obtained, jobs may have to be snapped in and out of main memory to the disk that now serves as a backing store for main memory.
- A common method for achieving this goal is virtual memory, which is a technique that allows the execution of a job that may not be completely in memory.

- A time sharing system provides an interactive or conversational access to a number of users. The operating system executes commands as they are entered, attempting to provide each user with a reasonably short response time to each command.
- Development of time sharing systems was motivated by the desire to provide fast response times to interactive users of a computer system.
- The response time is the time since the submission of a computational request by a user till its results are reported to the user.
- Emphasis on good response times, rather than good utilization efficiency or throughput, requires certain basic changes in the design of the operating system. These changes mainly concern the scheduling and memory management components of the time sharing supervisor.

6. **Distributed Systems:**
- A distributed system is a collection of processors that do not share memory or a clock. Instead, each processor has its own local memory, and the processors communicate with each other through various communication lines.
- A distributed system is shown in the Fig. 6.10.

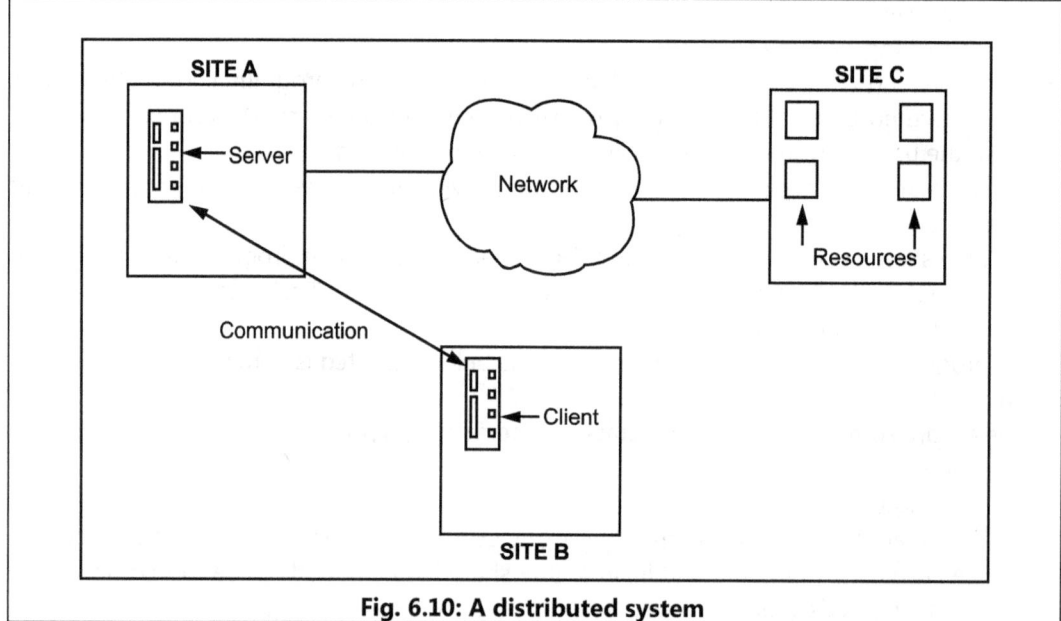

Fig. 6.10: A distributed system

- The processors in a distributed system vary in size and function.
- They may include small microprocessors, workstations, minicomputers and large general purpose computer systems.
- From the point of view of a specific processor in a distributed system, the rest of the processors and their respective resources are remote, whereas its own resources are local.
- The purpose of distributed system is to provide an efficient and convenient environment for this type of sharing of resources.

- Two general categories of network oriented operating systems are:
  - **(i) Network Operating Systems:** A network operating system provides an environment in which users, who are aware of the multiplicity of machines, can access remote resources by either logging into the appropriate remote machine or transferring data from the remote machine to their own machines.
  - **(ii) Distributed Operating System:** In a distributed operating system, the users access remote resources in the same manner as they do local resources. Data and process migration from one site to another are under the control of the distributed operating system.
- A distributed operating system allows a more complex type of network organization. This kind of operating system manages hardware and software resources, so that the user views the entire network as a simple system.
- The user is unaware of which machine on the network is actually running a program or storing data.

Advantages of distributed systems are:
  (i) Resource sharing,
  (ii) Reliability,
  (iii) Computation speed-up,
  (iv) Communication, and
  (v) Incremental growth.

7. Real Time Operating System (RTOS):
- Real Time Operating Systems are used to control machinery, scientific instruments and industrial systems.
- An RTOS typically has very little user-interface capability, and no end-user utilities, since the system will be a sealed box when delivered for use.
- A very important part of an RTOS is managing the resources of the computer so that a particular operation executes in precisely the same amount of time, every time it occurs.
- In a complex machine, having a part move more quickly just because system resources are available may be just as catastrophic as having it not move at all because the system is busy.

6.5 Windows Operating System

- Windows is a personal computer operating system from Microsoft that, together with some commonly used business applications such as Microsoft Word and Excel, has become a de facto standard for individual users in most corporations as well as in most homes.
- The original 1985 version of Windows introduced to home and business PC users many of the Graphical User Interface (GUI) ideas that were developed at an experimental lab at Xerox and introduced commercially by Apple's Lisa and Macintosh computers.

- Some of the well-known versions of Windows have included: Windows 286, Windows 386, Windows 3.0 and 3.11, Windows 95, Windows 98, Windows NT, Windows 2000, Windows CE, Windows Me, Windows XP, Windows Vista, Windows 7, Windows 8.

Note: We consider Windows 7 for this book.

Windows history:

Year	Event
1983	Bill Gates announces Microsoft Windows November 1983.
1985	Microsoft Windows 1.0 is introduced in November 1985.
1987	Microsoft Windows 2.0 was released December 1987. Microsoft Windows/386 or Windows 386 is introduced December 1987.
1988	Microsoft Windows/286 or Windows 286 is introduced June, 1988.
1990	Microsoft Windows 3.0 was released May 1990.
1991	Following its decision not to develop operating systems cooperatively with IBM, Microsoft changes the name of OS/2 to Windows NT. Microsoft Windows 3.0 or Windows 3.0a with multimedia was released October, 1991.
1992	Microsoft Windows 3.1 was released April, 1992. Microsoft Windows for Workgroups 3.1 was released October, 1992.
1993	Microsoft Windows NT 3.1 was released July, 1993. Microsoft Windows 3.11, an update to Windows 3.1 is released December 1993. The number of licensed users of Microsoft Windows now totals more than 25 Million.
1994	Microsoft Windows for Workgroups 3.11 was released February, 1994. Microsoft Windows NT 3.5 was released September 1994.
1995	Microsoft Windows NT 3.51 was released May 1995. Microsoft Windows 95 was released August 1995. Microsoft Windows 95 Service Pack 1 is released February 1996.
1996	Microsoft Windows NT 4.0 was released July 1996. Microsoft Windows 95 (4.00.950B) aka OSR2 with FAT32 and MMX support is released August 1996. Microsoft Windows CE 1.0 was released November, 1996.
1997	Microsoft Windows CE 2.0 was released November, 1997. Microsoft Windows 95 (4.00.950C) aka OSR2.5 is released November 1997.
1998	Microsoft Windows 98 was released June, 1998. Microsoft Windows CE 2.1 was released July, 1998. In October of 1998 Microsoft announced that future releases of Windows NT would no longer have the initials of NT and that the next edition would be Windows 2000.
1999	Microsoft Windows 98 SE (Second Edition) was released May 1999.

contd. ...

1999	Microsoft Windows CE 3.0 was released 1999.
2000	On January 4th at CES Bill Gates announces the new version of Windows CE will be called Pocket PC. Microsoft Windows 2000 was released February 2000. Microsoft Windows ME (Millennium) released June 2000.
2001	Microsoft Windows XP is released October 2001. Microsoft Windows XP 64-Bit Edition (Version 2002) for Itanium systems is released March 2003.
2003	Microsoft Windows Server 2003 is released March 2003. Microsoft Windows XP 64-Bit Edition (Version 2003) for Itanium 2 systems is released on March 2003. Microsoft Windows XP Media Center Edition 2003 is released on December 2003.
2004	Microsoft Windows XP Media Center Edition 2005 is released on October 2004.
2005	Microsoft Windows XP Professional x64 Edition is released on April 2005. Microsoft announces it's next operating system, codenamed "Longhorn" will be named Windows Vista on July 2005.
2006	Microsoft releases Microsoft Windows Vista to corporations on November 2006.
2007	Microsoft releases Microsoft Windows Vista and Office 2007 to the general public January 2007.
2009	Microsoft releases Windows 7 October 2009.
2012	Microsoft releases Windows 8 October 2012.

1. **Windows Desktop:**
- The Desktop is the very first screen we see after Windows starts.
- There we find the folders: My Documents, My Computer, the Recycle Bin and any Shortcuts for applications and files that we have created.

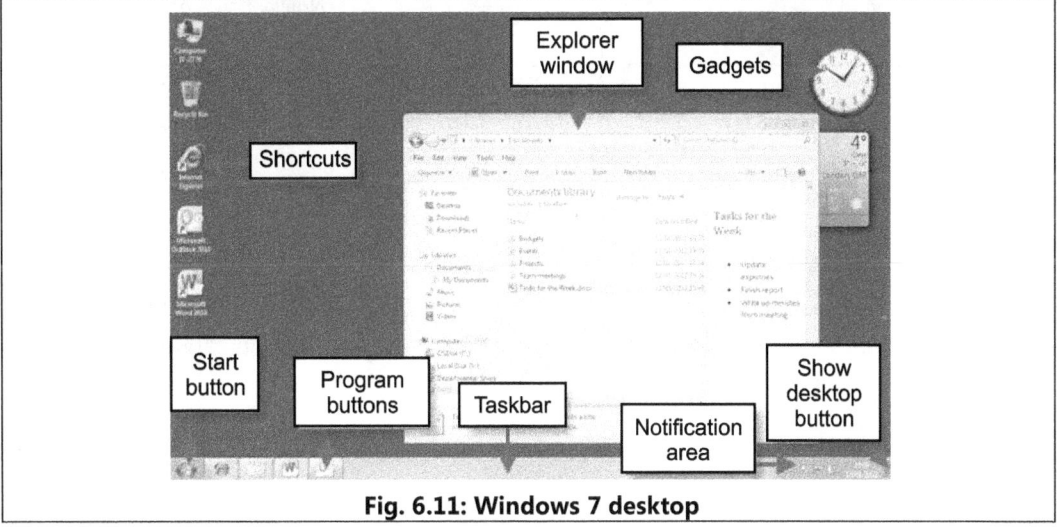

Fig. 6.11: Windows 7 desktop

- Following table shows feature of windows 7 desktop.

Windows 7 Features	Description
1. Start Button	The Start Button is located on the taskbar.
2. Program Buttons	Each open program appears as a button - even when multiple items for a program are open - but we can choose to change this view. We can pin programs to the taskbar.
3. Taskbar	The horizontal line at the bottom of your screen is the taskbar.
4. Show Desktop Button	This button will minimise all open windows to display the desktop.
5. Explorer Window	In the Explorer Window we can manage your files and folders. We can use the back and forward buttons to navigate around.
6. Gadgets	Gadgets can be placed anywhere on your desktop. They offer information - such as the time or the weather - at a quick glance.
7. Notification Area	The notification area displays the time, the date and any program related icons. We can click an icon to display a window of options.
8. Shortcuts	Shortcuts allow we to open a program without having to search for it in the Start Menu.

2. Windows 7 Taskbar:
- The taskbar is the thin strip that runs across the bottom of your screen.
- It is split into a number of different areas: a round Start button, Quick Launch icons, a notification area, and a clock.
- All other areas are the Taskbar itself. The Fig. 6.12 shows where the different areas of taskbar.

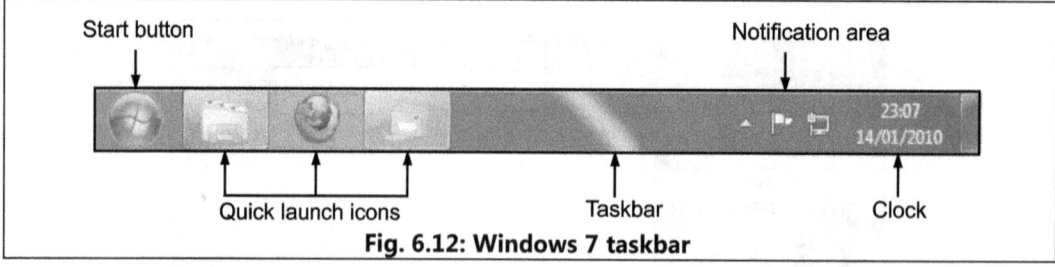

Fig. 6.12: Windows 7 taskbar

3. Windows 7 Start Button:
- Arguably, the most important part of the Taskbar is the Start button. The Start button is where a lot of the action takes place in Windows 7. The Start button can be found in the bottom left of the screen, and looks like this:

Fig. 6.13: Windows 7 start button

- Click the Start button once with the left mouse button and we will see a menu appear:

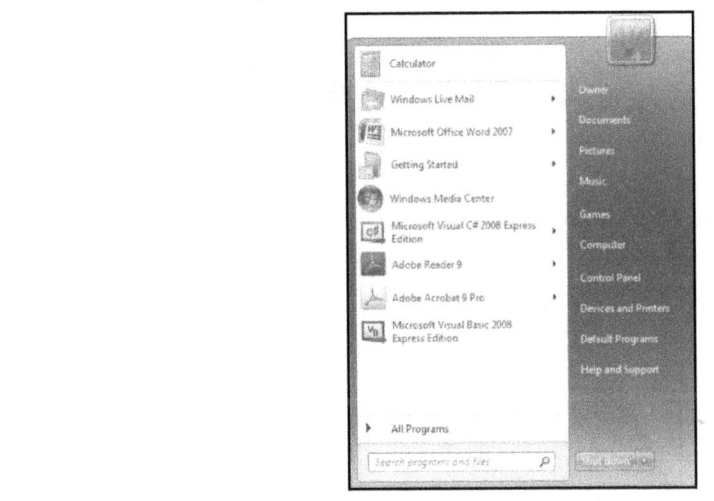

Fig. 6.14: Start menu

- The Start menu is split into two different areas. The white area on the left is for software programmes that have been installed on the computer. But these are the programmes have been recently used. If an entry has a black arrow it means that documents can be opened by clicking the shortcut.
- The other area is the darker strip on the right. These are shortcuts for locations on the computer. We will explore these options in later sections, especially the Control Panel and Computer options. But one more thing to notice in the dark area on the right of the Start menu is the Shut down button. Clicking this will obviously Shut down the computer, but click the arrow to the right of the Shutdown button to see the following options:

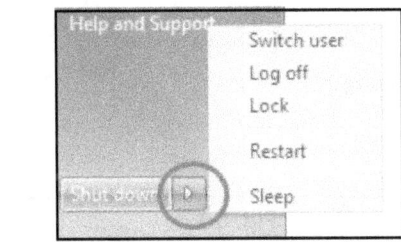

Fig. 6.15: Logging menus

- As we can see, there are five options in the menu. The first is useful if we share the computer with others, and have set up multiple accounts. Click Switch user to see other account names. A user can then enter login details without the need to shutdown the computer and start again.
- The Log Off option logs us out of the account. Again, the computer doesn't shut down. Instead, we can see a screen where we or others can log back in again.

- The Lock option prevents others from using the computer until we enter your password again.
- The final two options are Restart and Sleep. The Restart is self-explanatory. But the Sleep option is useful if we are not going to use the computer for a while. It powers down the hardware, saving the energy.

4. **Toolbars in Windows 7:**
- We can add Toolbars to the taskbar area. A toolbar is a list of shortcuts to favourite areas of the computers.
- Right click the Taskbar to see the following menu.

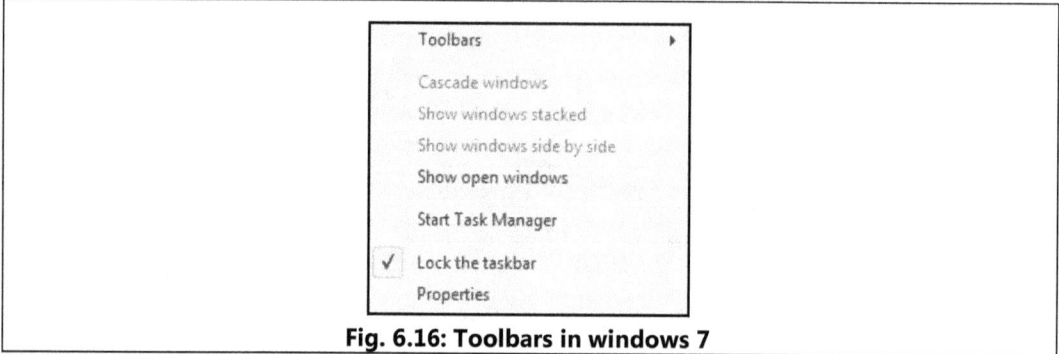

Fig. 6.16: Toolbars in windows 7

- Select Toolbars to see the built-in Windows 7 ones:

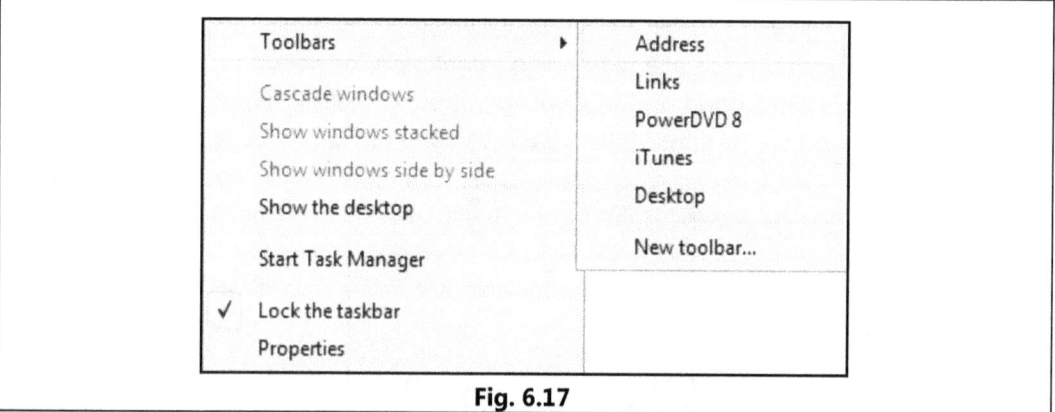

Fig. 6.17

- As we can see, there are entries for Address, Links, PowerDVD 8, Desktop, and New toolbar.

5. **Windows Explorer:**
- Windows Explorer is the main tool that we use to interact with Windows 7. We will need to use the Windows Explorer to view the libraries, files, and folders.
- We can access Windows Explorer by clicking the Start menu and then clicking either Computer or one of your many folders, such as Documents, Pictures, or Music.

- When we open a folder or library, we can see it in a window. The various parts of this window are designed to help us navigate around Windows or work with files, folders, and libraries more easily. Here's a typical window and each of its parts:

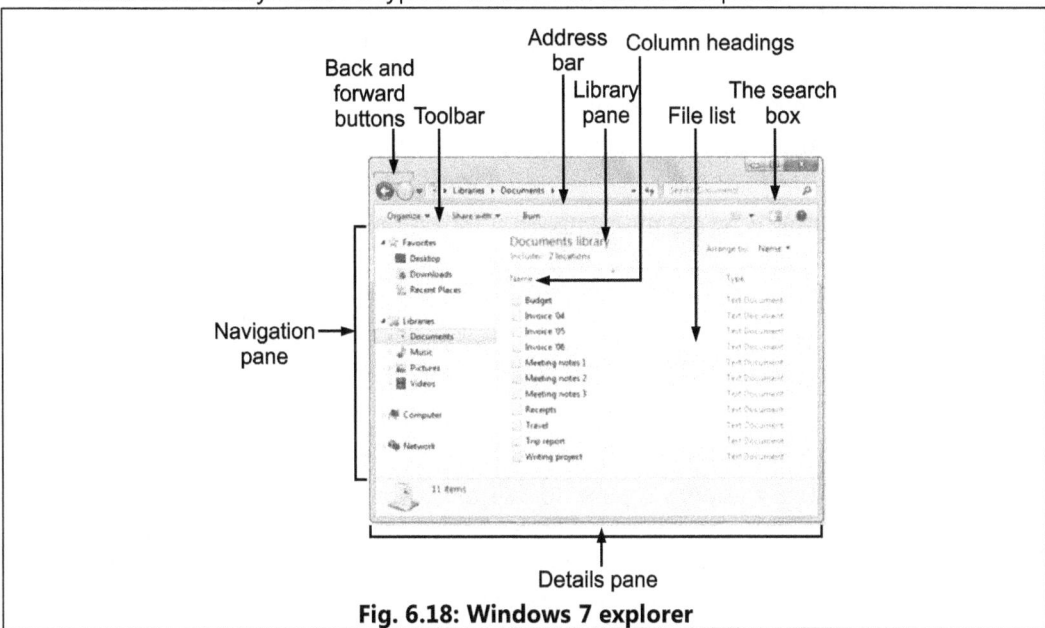

Fig. 6.18: Windows 7 explorer

- Following table shows various parts of Windows 7 explorer.

Window part	What it's useful for
1. Navigation pane	Use the navigation pane to access libraries, folders, saved searches, and even entire hard disks. Use the Favorites section to open the most commonly used folders and searches; use the Libraries section to access your libraries. We can also expand Computer to browse folders and subfolders.
2. Back and Forward buttons	Use the Back button and the Forward button to navigate to other folders or libraries we have already opened without closing the current window. These buttons work together with the address bar; after we use the address bar to change folders, for example, we can use the Back button to return to the previous folder.
3. Toolbar	Use the toolbar to perform common tasks, such as changing the appearance of the files and folders, burning files to a CD, or starting a digital picture slide show. The toolbar's buttons change to show only the tasks that are relevant. For example, if we click a picture file, the toolbar shows different buttons than it would if we clicked a music file.
4. Address bar	Use the address bar to navigate to a different folder or library or to go back to a previous one.

contd. ...

5.	Library pane	The library pane appears only when we are in a library (such as the Documents library). Use the library pane to customize the library or to arrange the files by different properties.
6.	Column headings	Use the column headings to change how the files in the file list are organized. For example, we can click the left side of a column heading to change the order the files and folders are displayed in, or we can click the right side to filter the files in different ways. (Note that column headings are available only in Details view.
7.	File list	This is where the contents of the current folder or library are displayed. If we type in the search box to find a file, only the files that match the current view (including files in subfolders) will appear.
8.	Search box	Type a word or phrase in the search box to look for an item in the current folder or library. The search begins as soon as we begin typing—so if we type "B," for example, all the files with names starting with the letter B will appear in the file list.
9.	Details pane	Use the details pane to see the most common properties associated with the selected file. File properties are information about a file, such as the author, the date we last changed the file, and any descriptive tags we might have added to the file. For more information, see Change the properties for a file.
10.	Preview pane	Use the preview pane to see the contents of most files. If we select an e-mail message, text file, or picture, for example, we can see its contents without opening it in a program. If we don't see the preview pane, click the Preview pane button in the toolbar to turn it on.

6. File, Folders and Icons:

- A file is an item that contains information—for example, text or images or music.
- When opened, a file can look very much like a text document or a picture that we might find on someone's desk or in a filing cabinet. On the computer, files are represented with icons; this makes it easy to recognize a type of file by looking at its icon.
- Fig. 6.19 shows are some common file icons.

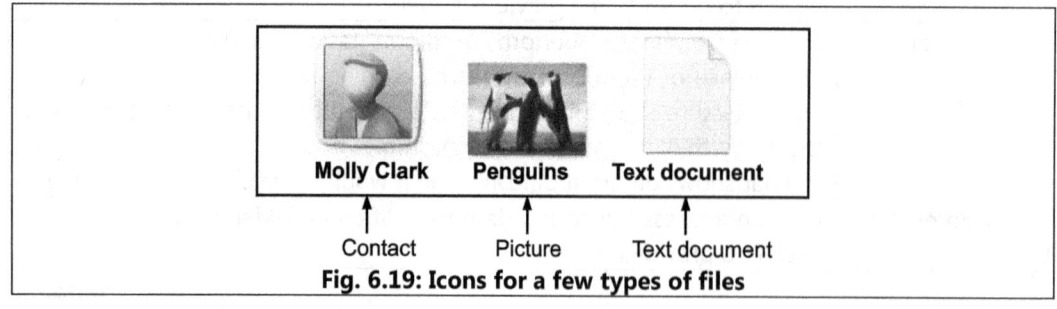

Fig. 6.19: Icons for a few types of files

- A folder is a container we can use to store files in. If we had thousands of paper files on the desk, it would be nearly impossible to find any particular file when we needed it.
- That's why people often store paper files in folders inside a filing cabinet. On the computer, folders work the same way. Here are some typical folder icons:

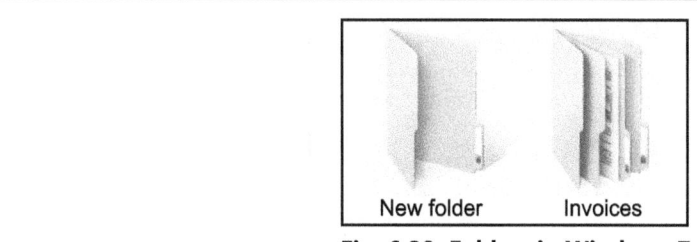

Fig. 6.20: Folders in Windows 7

- An empty folder (left); a folder containing files (right).
- Folders can also store other folders. A folder within a folder is usually called a subfolder. We can create any number of subfolders, and each can hold any number of files and additional subfolders.

7. **Control Panel:**
- The control panel is a part of the Microsoft Windows Graphical User Interface (GUI) which allows users to view and manipulate basic system settings and controls via applets, such as adding hardware, adding and removing software, controlling user accounts, and changing accessibility options.

Add/Remove Programs in Windows 7:
1. Click on the Start button and we will notice Control Panel item in right pane (See Fig. 6.20).

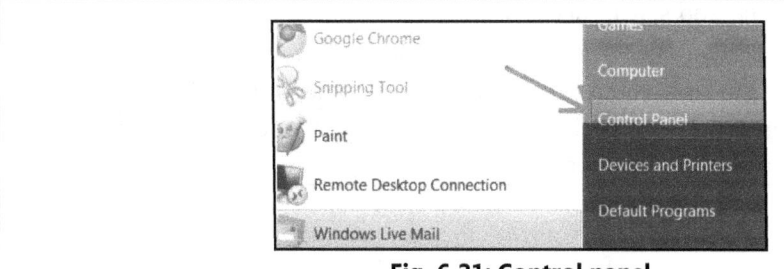

Fig. 6.21: Control panel

2. Click on Control Panel option and it will bring up new dialog box Adjust the computer's settings. There is a option named Programs. Click on it.

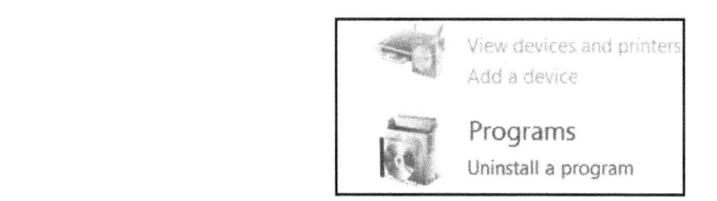

Fig. 6.22: Options in control panel

3. Clicking on Programs option will bring up new window that has section Programs and Features as shown below. We will notice that this section has few moe options to perform various tasks related to adding or removing programs.

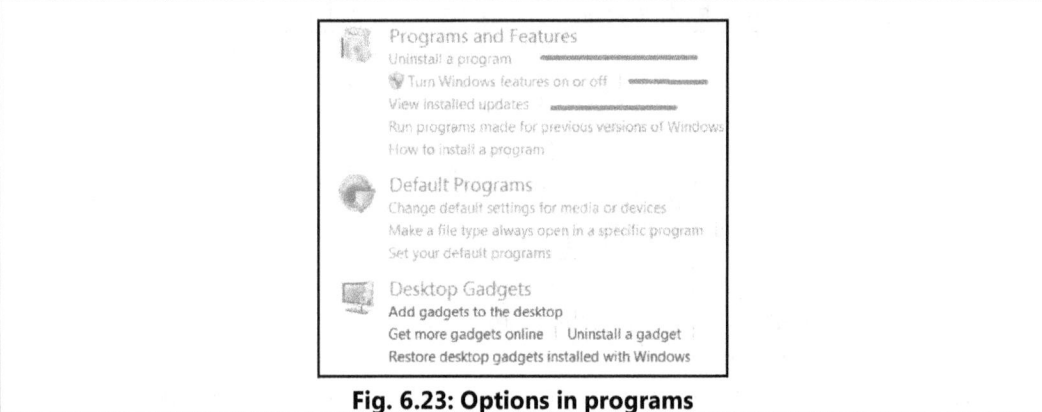

Fig. 6.23: Options in programs

Uninstall a program:
- Clicking on this option will bring up list of all programs that are currently installed on your machine. Click on the one that we want to uninstall or update, click on that program. And then click on Uninstall/Change link in the bar to perform the action.

8. Windows Accessories:

(i) Windows 7 Calculator:
- We can use Calculator to perform simple calculations such as addition, subtraction, multiplication, and division. Calculator also offers the advanced capabilities of a programming, scientific, and statistical calculator.
- We can perform calculations by clicking the calculator buttons, or we can type calculations by using the keyboard. We can also use the numeric keypad to type numbers and operators by pressing Num Lock. For more information about using the keyboard with Calculator, see Keyboard shortcuts.

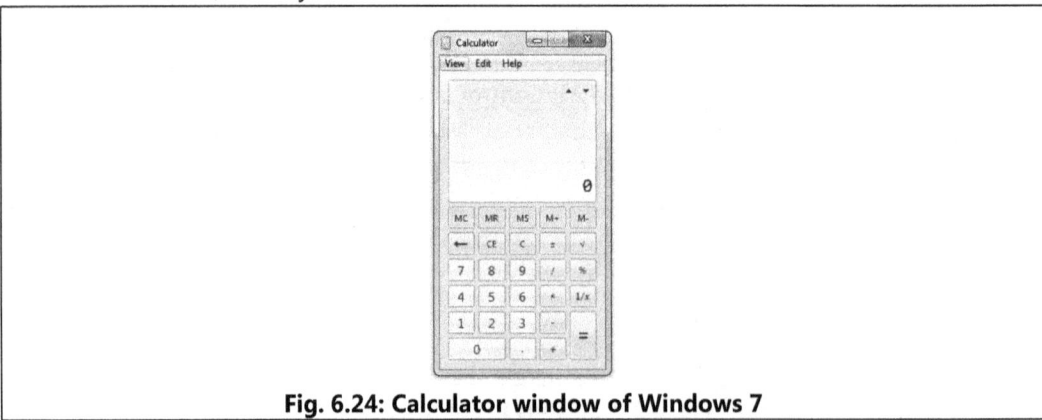

Fig. 6.24: Calculator window of Windows 7

Opening calculator windows:

1. Open Calculator by clicking the Start button. In the search box, type Calculator, and then, in the list of results, click Calculator.
2. Click the View menu, and then click the mode that we want. When we switch modes, the current calculation is cleared. Calculation history and numbers stored by the memory keys are retained.
3. Click the calculator keys to perform the required calculation.

(ii) WordPad:

- WordPad is a text-editing program we can use to create and edit documents. Unlike Notepad, WordPad documents can include rich formatting and graphics, and we can link to or embed objects, such as pictures or other documents.

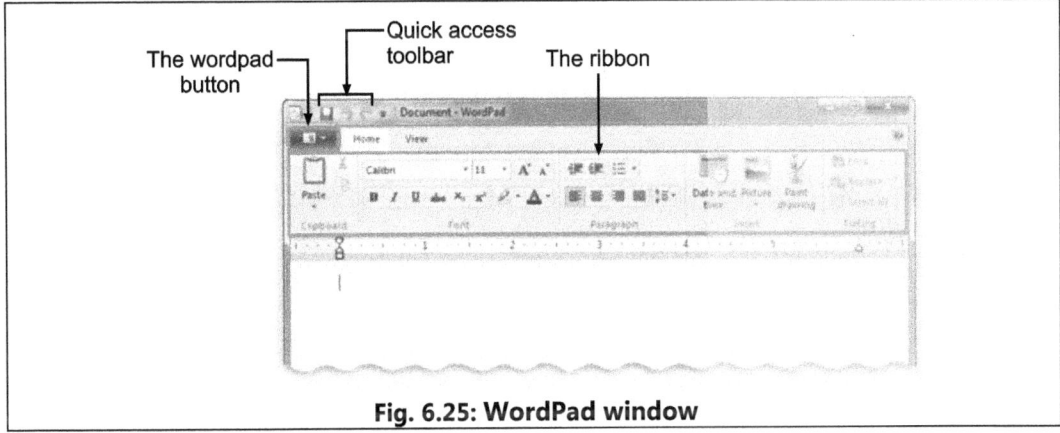

Fig. 6.25: WordPad window

Create, open, and save documents:

1. Open WordPad by clicking the Start button. In the search box, type WordPad, and then, in the list of results, click WordPad.
2. Use the following commands to create, open, or save documents:

To	Do this
Create a new document	Click the WordPad menu button, and then click New.
Open a document	Click the WordPad menu button, and then click Open.
Save a document	Click the WordPad menu button, and then click Save.
Save a document with a new name or format	Click the WordPad menu button, point to Save as, and then click the format we want to save the document in.

(iii) Notepad:

- The inbuilt Notepad in Windows is a basic text editor we can use for simple documents or for creating Web pages.
- Although there are a few basic Notepad tips to help we get the best out of it, if we are looking for a more jazzed up or a feature-rich Notepad replacement, we may want to check out some of these freeware Notepad replacements for the Windows.

1. Click on the Start button to open the Start menu. If we are lucky we will already have the notepad on it.

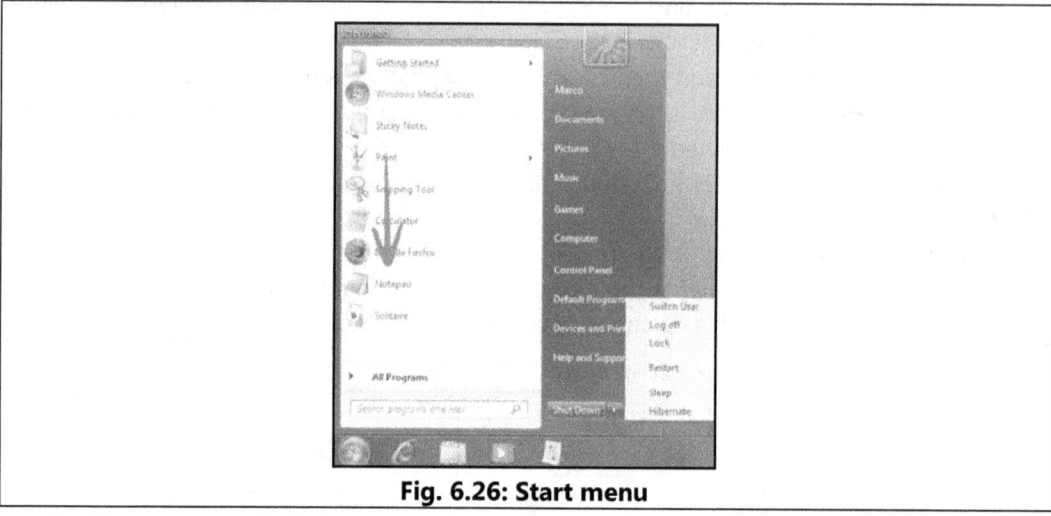

Fig. 6.26: Start menu

2. If we cannot find the notepad on the Start menu, we will have to click on All programs.
3. A list of programs appears, click on Accessories and then on Notepad.

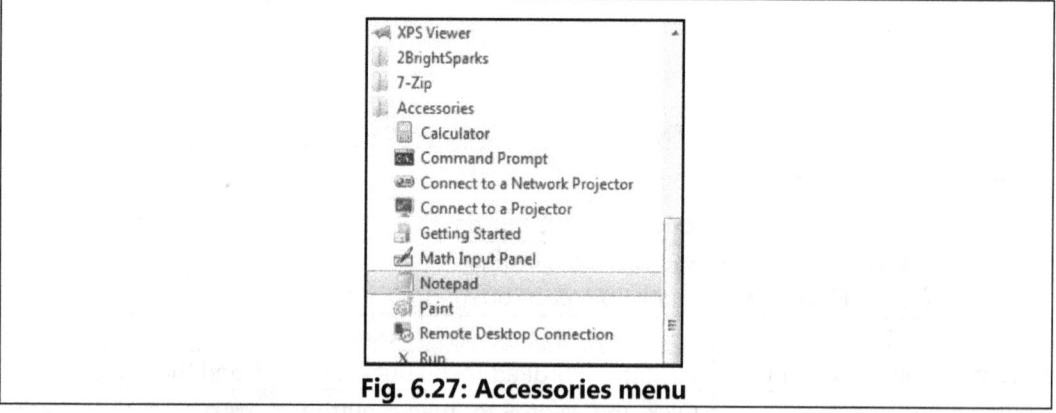

Fig. 6.27: Accessories menu

6.6 Linux

- Linux is an operating system that is evolved from a kernel created by Linus Torvalds when he was a student at the University of Helsinki.
- Generally, it is obvious most people know what Linux is. However, both for political and practical reasons, it needs to be explained further.
- To say that Linux is an operating system means that it's meant to be used as an alternative to other operating systems, Windows, Mac OS, MS-DOS, Solaris and others.
- Linux is not a program like a word processor and is not a set of programs like an office suite. Linux is an interface between computer/server hardware, and the programs which run on it.

6.6.1 Features

- Linux has evolved to have the following features as an outstanding operating system which is strong in security and networking.
  1. **Multitasking:** Several programs can run at the same time.
  2. **Multiuser:** Several users can logon to the same machine at the same time There is no need to have separate user licenses.
  3. **Multiplatform:** Linux runs on many different CPUs, that means it supports multiprocessor machine.
  4. **Multithreading:** Linux has native kernel support for multiple independent threads of control within a single process memory space.
  5. **Crash proof:** Linux has memory protection between processes, so that one program can't bring the whole system down.
  6. **Demand loads executables:** Linux only reads from those parts of a program that are actually used on the disk.
  7. **Shared copy-on-write pages among executables:** This means that multiple processes can use the same memory to run in. When one tries to write to that memory, that page (with 4KB piece of memory) is copied somewhere else. Copy-on-write has two benefits that is increasing speed and decreasing memory use.
  8. **Virtual memory uses paging (not swapping whole processes)** to disk to a separate partition or a file in the file system, or both, with the possibility of adding more swapping areas during runtime. A total of 16 of these 128 MB (2GB in recent kernels) swapping areas can be used at the same time, for a theoretical total of 2 GB of usable swap space. It is simple to increase this if necessary, by changing a few lines of source code.
  9. **Linux has a unified memory pool** for user programs and disk cache, so that all free memory can be used for caching, and the cache can be reduced when running large programs.
  10. Linux does **core dumps for post-mortem analysis**, allowing the use of a debugger on a program not only while it is running but also after it has crashed.
  11. Linux is mostly **compatible with POSIX**, System V, and BSD at the source level.
  12. **Free and Open source code for all:** All source code of Linux is available, including the whole kernel and all drivers, the development tools and all user programs; also, all of it is freely distributable. Plenty of commercial programs are being provided for Linux without source, but everything that has been free, including the entire base operating system, is still free.
  13. **Linux supports pseudoterminals (pty's) and multiple virtual consoles:** By several independent login sessions through the console, we can switch between by pressing a hot-key combination. These are dynamically allocated; we can use up to 64.

14. **Support several common file systems:** Linux supports several common file systems, including minix, Xenix, and all the common system V file systems, and has an advanced file system of its own, which offers file systems of up to 4 TB, and names up to 255 characters long.
15. Linux has a **transparent access to MS-DOS partitions** (or OS/2 FAT partitions) via a special file system.
16. Linux has **CD-ROM file system** which reads all standard formats of CD-ROMs.
17. Linux performs well with TCP/IP networking, including ftp, telnet, NFS, etc.
18. Linux is userfriendly as Netware client and server.
19. Linux also runs as LAN Manager/Windows Native (SMB) client and server.
20. **It integrates many networking protocols:** The base protocols available in the latest development kernels include TCP, IPv4, IPv6, AX.25, X.25, IPX, DDP (Appletalk), Netrom, and others. Stable network protocols included in the stable kernels currently include TCP, IPv4, IPX, DDP, and AX.25.

Questions

1. What is operating system?
2. Explain objectives of operating system.
3. What are the features of operating system?
4. Describe evolution of operating system in detail.
5. State advantages and disadvantages of operating system.
6. With the help of diagram describe:
   (i) Batch processing, and
   (ii) Multitasking.
7. Give the history of windows operating system.
8. What are the types of operating system? Explain two of them in detail.
9. Write short note on Linux.
10. With the help of diagram describe functions of operating system.
11. Explain RTOS in brief.
12. Compare multitasking and multiprogramming.
13. Enlist various features of Linux.
14. Describe windows operating system in detail.
15. Distinguish between Windows and Linux operating systems.
16. Explain the following windows component:
    (i) Control panel.
    (ii) Windows explorer.
    (iii) Windows toolbar.
    (iv) Taskbar.

Chapter 7...

Networking

Contents ...

7.1 Introduction
7.2 Network Concepts
    7.2.1 Definition
    7.2.2 How does a Computer Network Works?
    7.2.3 Advantages
    7.2.4 Disadvantages
7.3 Basic elements of a Communication System
7.4 Data Transmission Media
7.5 LAN (Local Area Network)
7.6 MAN (Metropolitan Area Network)
7.7 WAN (Wide Area Network)
7.8 Internet
7.9 Topologies
    7.9.1 Bus Topology
    7.9.2 Ring Topology
    7.9.3 Star Topology
    7.9.4 Mesh Topology
    7.9.5 Tree Topology
    7.9.6 Hybrid Topology
    • Questions

7.1 Introduction

- A computer network, or simply a network, is a collection of computers and other hardware interconnected by communication channels that allow sharing of resources and information.
- When one process in one device is able to send/receive data to/from one process residing in a remote device, the two devices are said to be networked.
- A network is a group of devices connected to each other.
- Networks may be classified into a wide variety of characteristics: the medium used to transport the data, communications protocol used, scale, topology, benefit, and organisational scope.

- Two or more computers connected together through a communication media form a computer network. The computers are connected in a network to exchange information and data.

Need of Computer Networks:
- Computer networks help users on the network to share the resources and in communication.
- The following are the important benefits of a computer network:
  1. **File sharing:** Networking of computers helps the users to share data files.
  2. **Hardware sharing:** Users can share devices such as printers, scanners, CD-ROM drives, hard drives etc.
  3. **Application sharing:** Applications can be shared over the network, and this allows to implement client/server applications
  4. **User communication:** Networks allow users to communicate using e-mail, newsgroups, and video conferencing etc.

7.2 Network Concepts

- A network is a group of computers or computer like devices connected together to share the resources like file, printer, services etc.
- A computer network is a collection of computers and devices connected by communication channels that facilitate communication among users and allow users share resources with other users.
- A network is nothing more than two or more computers connected by a cable or by a wireless connection so that they can communicate and exchange information or data.
- In other words "Network means a collection of interconnected computer network of stand-alone computers".
- A computer network is interconnection of various computer systems located at different places.
- In computer network two or more computers are linked together with a medium and data communication devices for the purpose of communication data and sharing resources.

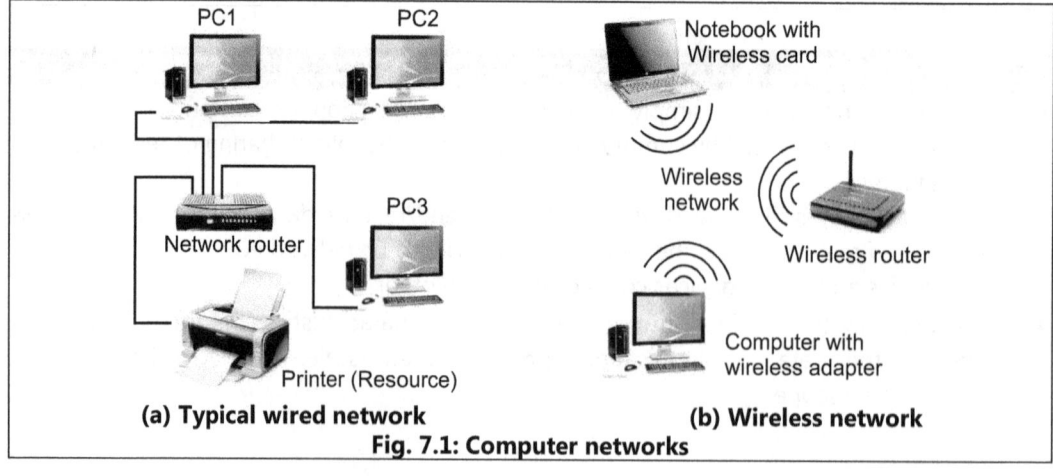

Fig. 7.1: Computer networks

- The computer that provides resources to other computers on a network is known as Server.
- In the network the individual computers, which access shared network resources, are known as Nodes.
- The computers on a network may be linked through cables, telephone lines, radio waves, satellites, or infrared light beams.

Network Services:
1. **File services:** This includes file transfer, storage, data migration, file update, synchronization and achieving.
2. **Printing services:** This service produces shared access to valuable printing derives.
3. **Message services:** This service facilitates e-mail, voice mails and coordinate object oriented applications.
4. **Application services:** This services allows to centralize high profile applications to increase performance and scalability.
5. **Database services:** This involves co-ordination of distributed data and replication.

7.2.1 Definition of Computer Network

- Computer networks is a group of computers connected in same fashion in order to share resources.

OR

- Computer networks is a collection of autonomous computers interconnected by a single technology. Two computers are said to be interconnected if they are able to exchange information.
- Network is a group of computers and associated peripheral devices connected by a communications channel capable of sharing files and other resources among several users.
- The purpose of a computer network is to link two or more clients together in order to exchange information.

7.2.2 How does a Computer Network Works?

- How does one computer send information to another? It is rather simple. Fig. 7.2 below shows a simple network.

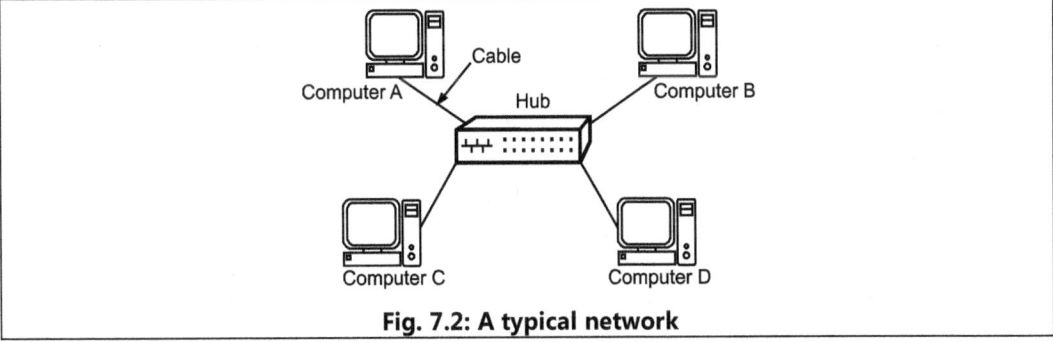

Fig. 7.2: A typical network

- If computer A wants to send a file to Computer B, the following procedure would take place:
    1. Based on a protocol that both computers use, the NIC (Network Interface Card), in Computer A translates the file, (which consists of binary data 1's and 0's) into pulses of electricity.
    2. The pulses of electricity pass through the cable with a minimum (hopefully) of resistance.
    3. The hub takes in the electric pulses and shoots them out to all of the other cables.
    4. Computer B's NIC interprets the pulses and decides if the message is for it or not. In this case, it is, so Computer B's NIC translates the pulses back into the 1's and 0's that make up the file.
- If Computer A sends the message to the network using NetBEUI (NetBIOS Extended User Interface), a Microsoft protocol, but Computer B only understands the TCP/IP protocol, it will not understand the message; no matter how many times Computer A sends it.
- Computer B also would not get the message if the cable is getting interference from the fluorescent lights or if the network card has decided not to turn on today etc.

Logical Classification of Network:
- A network can be divided into two categories:

1. Peer-to-Peer:
- A Peer-to-Peer network has no dedicated servers. Here a number of workstations are connected together for the purpose of sharing information or devices.
- All the workstations are considered as equal. Any one computer can act as client or server at any instance.
- This network is ideal for small networks where there is no need for dedicated servers, like home network or small business establishments or shops.

2. Client-Server:
- The client/server model consists of high-end servers serving clients continuously on a network, by providing them with specific services upon request.

Computer Network Components:
- There are different components of a network. Following are the basic components of network.
    1. **Server:** Powerful computers that provide services to the other computers on the network.
    2. **Client:** Computer that uses the services that a server provides. The client is less powerful than server.
    3. **Media:** A physical connection between the devices on a network.
    4. **Network Adapter:** Network adapter or Network Interface Card (NIC) is a circuit board with the components necessary for sending and receiving data. It is plugged into one of the available slots on the Pc and transmission cable is attached to the connector on the NIC.

5. **Resources:** Any thing available to a client on the network is considered a resource. Printers, data, fax devices and other network devices and information are resources.
6. **User:** Any person that uses a client to access resources on the network.
7. **Protocols:** These are written rules used for communications. They are the languages that computers use to talk to each other on a network.

7.2.3 Advantages

1. Networking provides the advantage of centralization of data from all the user systems to one system where it can be managed in an easy and better way.
2. Using networking peripherals such as printers can be shared amongst many different users.
3. Communication across the network is cheap and fast.
4. Networking terminals are cheaper than standalone PCs.
5. Using networking software can be shared amongst different users.
6. Networking provides a flexible networking environment. Employees can work at home by connecting through networks into the computer at office.
7. Networking also provides the function of back-up.
8. Networking supports increased storage capacity since there is one or more computers which can easily share files.

7.2.4 Disadvantages

1. Proper maintenance of a network requires considerable time and expertise.
2. Security threats are always problems with large networks. There are hackers who are trying to steal valuable data of large companies for their own benefit.
3. One major disadvantages of networking is the breakdown of the whole network due to an issue to the server, therefore once established it is vital to maintain it properly to prevent such disastrous breakdowns.
4. Security measures are needed to restrict access to the network.
5. Computer networks are expensive to set up.
6. Since most networks have client/server architecture, the client users lack any freedom, as centralized decision making sometimes hinder how a client wants to use his computer.
7. Networks need efficient handlers that is any user with just the basic skills cannot operate/administer a computer network.

7.3 Basic Elements of a Communication System

- The main purpose of communication system is to exchange data between two points by electric means.
- Fig. 7.3 shows components of communication system.

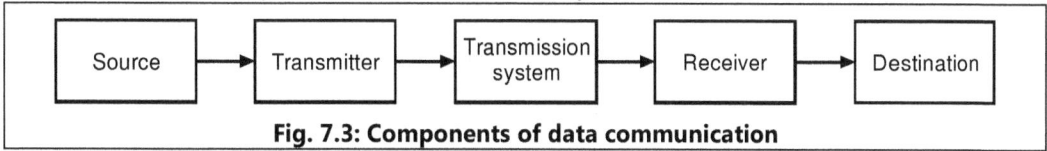

Fig. 7.3: Components of data communication

- Following are the different blocks of communication system:
  1. **Source:** Source generates the data which is to be transmitted.
     Examples: 1. Terminal, 2. Computer, 3. Mainframe, 4. Telephone.
  2. **Transmitter:** Data from the source are not transmitted in the same form which are generated by source, transmitter converts and encodes the data so as to produce electromagnetic signals.
     Modem is used to convert incoming data stream into analog signals that can be handled by telephone network.
  3. **Transmission System:** It is a single transmission line or network connecting source and destination.
     Examples: 1. Cabling, 2. Microwave, 3. Fiber optics, 4. Infrared.
  4. **Receiver:** Function of the receiver is to accept the information from transmission line or network and converting it into digital data in the form of stream so that destination computer can handle the data.
     Example: Printer terminal.
  5. **Destination:** Destination is a device like computer that receives the data.

7.4 Data Transmission Media

- Transmission media can be divided into two broad categories: Guided and Unguided.
- Fig. 7.4 shows various types of transmission media.

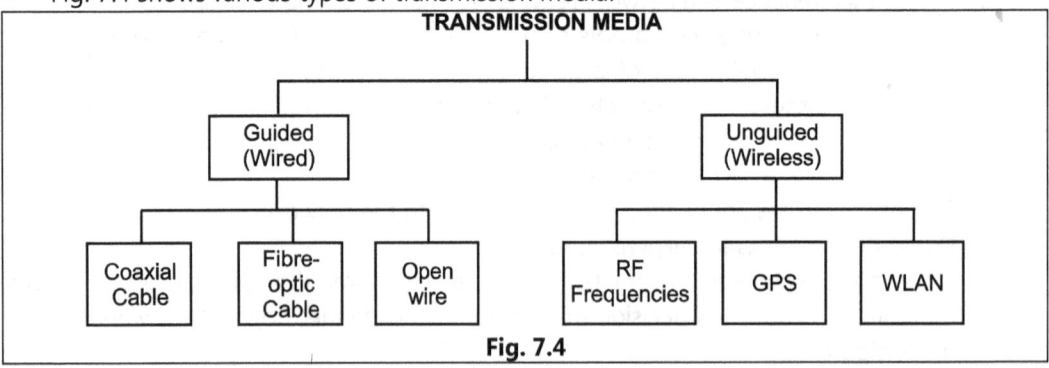

Fig. 7.4

1. **Guided Media:**
- Guided media are the physical links through which signals are confined to narrow path.
- Guided media is also known as bounded media or wired media or wired communication.
- Guided media are great for use because they offer high speed, good security and low cost. However, some cannot be used for distant (long distance) communication.
- Guided transmission media uses a cabling system that guides the data signals along a specific path.
- In other words the data signals are bound by the cabling system.
- In guided media cable is the medium through which information usually moves from one network device to another.

- Twisted pair cable and coaxial cable use metallic (copper) conductors that accept and transport signals in the form of electric current.
- Fiber optic cable is a glass or plastic cable that accepts and transports signals in the form of light.

Types of Guided Media:

(i) Twisted-Pair (TP) Cable:

- Twisted-pair cable is least expensive and most widely used.
- The wires in twisted pair cabling are twisted together in pairs. Each pair would consist of a wire used for the +ve data signal and a wire for the –ve data signal.
- Any noise that appears on one wire of the pair would occur on the other wire. Because the wires are of opposite polarities, they are 180 degrees out of phase.
- When the noise appears on both wires, it cancels or nulls itself out at the receiving end.
- Twisted-pair cables are most effectively used in systems that use a balanced line method of transmission: polar line coding (Manchester Encoding) as opposed to unipolar line coding (TTL logic).

Physical Description:

- In TP two insulated copper wires are arranged in regular spiral pattern.
- Number of pairs are bundled together in a cable.
- Twisting decreases the crosstalk interference between adjacent pairs in the cable, by using different twist length for neighboring pairs.
- A twisted pair consists of two conductors (normally copper), each with its own plastic insulation, twisted together.

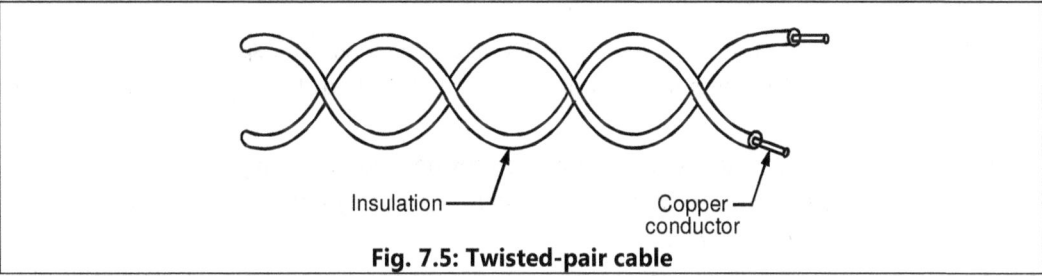

Fig. 7.5: Twisted-pair cable

(ii) Coaxial Cable:

- A form of network cabling used primarily in older Ethernet networks and in electrically noisy industrial environments.
- The name coax comes from its two-conductor construction in which the conductors run *concentrically* with each other along the *ax*is of the cable.

Physical Description:

- Fig. 7.6 shows the construction of basic coaxial cable.
- Coaxial cable consists of two conductors with construction that allows it to operate over a wider range of frequencies compared to twisted pair. Hollow, outer cylindrical conductor surrounding a single inner wire conductor.

- Inner conductor held in place by regularly spaced insulating rings or solid dielectrical material. Outer conductor covered with a jacket or shield. Diameter from 1 to 2.5 cm.
- Shielded concentric construction reduces interference and crosstalk. Coaxial cable can be used over longer distances and support more stations on a shared line than twisted pair.

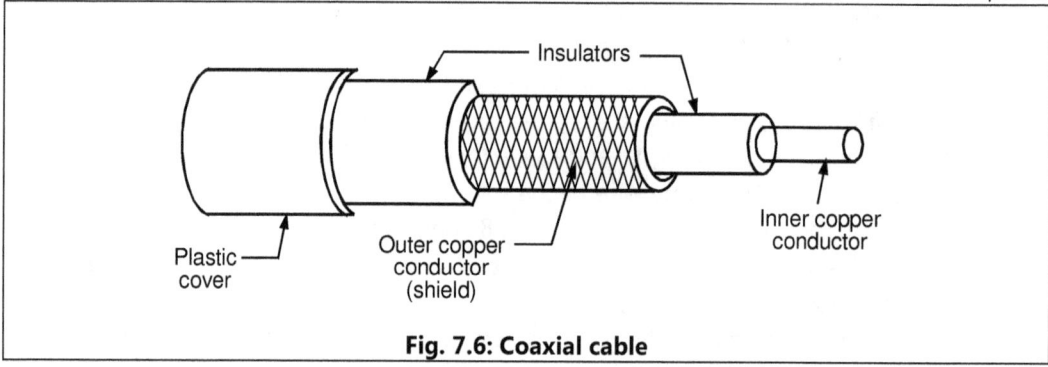

Fig. 7.6: Coaxial cable

(iii) Fiber Optics:
- Fiber optics is a glass cabling media that sends network signals using light.
- Fiber optics cabling has higher bandwidth capacity than copper cabling and is used mainly for high-speed network Asynchronous Transfer Mode (ATM) or Fiber Distributed Data Interface (FDDI) backbones, long cable runs and connections to high-performance workstations.
- A fiber optic cable is made of glass or plastic and transmits signals in the form of light. Light is a form of electromagnetic energy.
- It travels at its fastest in a vacuum: 3,00,000 kilometers/sec. The speed of light depends on the density of the medium through which it is traveling (the higher the density, the slower the speed).
- Light travels in a straight line as long as it is moving through a single uniform substance. If a ray of light traveling through one substance suddenly enters another (more or less dense), the ray changes direction.
- A main purpose of a fiber optic cable is to protect the fiber core inside the cable that carries the light signal transmission.

Physical Description:
- Fig. 7.7 shows the construction of a fiber optic cable.

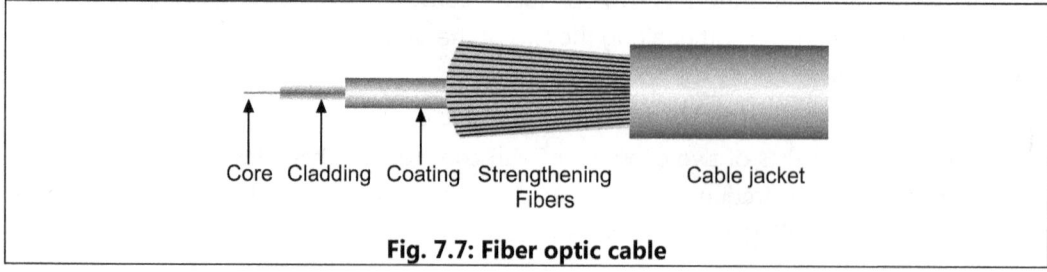

Fig. 7.7: Fiber optic cable

- Parts of fiber optic cables are described below:
  1. **Core:** The fiber core is made of silica glass and is the central part of the fiber optic cable that carries the light signal. They are hair-thin in size and the diameter of the fiber core is typically 8 microns for single mode fiber, and 50 microns or 62.5 microns for multi mode fiber.
  2. **Cladding:** The cladding is also made of glass, and is the layer that surrounds the fiber core. Together, they form a single solid fiber of glass that is used for the light transmission. The diameter of the cladding is typically 125 microns.
  3. **Primary coating:** After the cladding, there is the primary coating that is also known as the primary buffer. This layer provides protection to the fiber core and cladding. They are made of plastic and only provide mechanical protection. They do not interfere with the light transmission of the core and the cladding.
  4. **Strengthening fibers:** The next layer is strengthening fibres. They are strands of aramid yarn, or better known as Kevlar. They are added to the fiber optic cable to prevent the breakage of the fiber glass during installation. When fiber is pulled through a duct, the outer cover would stretch and the pulling load would be rested on the fiber. The strength members prevent this as their material is designed to take the strain.
  5. **Cable jacket:** The last layer is the cable jacket, which are comprised of different materials depending on the choice of the end user and the application in use. Like the primary coating, they serve only as a mechanical protection to the fiber core and cladding inside. Common types of fiber optic cable jacket ratings are:
     (i) **OFNP:** OFNP (Optical Fiber, Nonconductive, Plenum) are used in plenum applications.
     (ii) **OFNR:** OFNR (Optical Fiber, Nonconductive, Riser) are used in riser applications.
     (iii) **LSZH:** LSZH (Low Smoke Zero Halogen) cable jackets are composed of fire retardant materials that reduces the amount of smoke emitted when combusted.
- Fig. 7.8 shows fiber optics propagation modes.

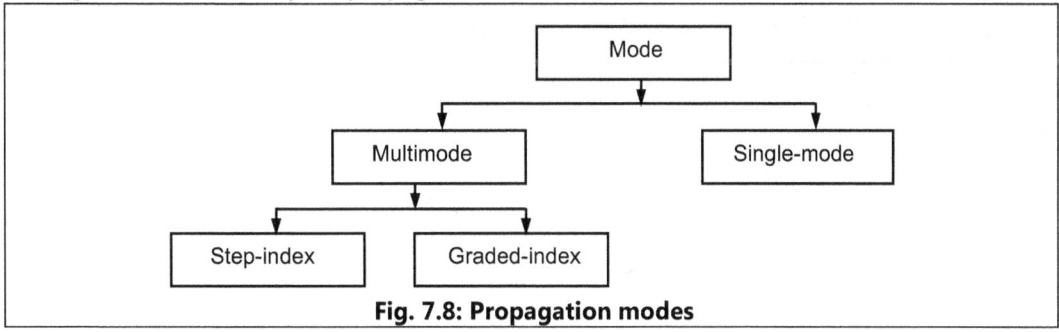

Fig. 7.8: Propagation modes

2. Unguided Media:

- In unguided media the data signals are transferred through air.
- Unguided media, also known as wireless communication or unbounded media and it transports electromagnetic waves without using a physical connection.
- Unguided transmission media consists of a means for the data signals to travel but nothing to guide them along a specific path.
- The data signals are not bound to a cabling media.
- Signals are broadcasted through air and thus are available to anyone who has a device capable of receiving them.
- In wireless communication, transmission and reception are achieved using an antenna.
- Transmitter sends out the electromagnetic signal into the medium. Receiver picks up the signal from the surrounding medium.
- Wireless transmission can be divided into three groups: radiowaves, microwave, and infrared waves.

Types of Unguided Media:

(i) Radio Transmission

- Radio waves are widely used for both indoor and outdoor communication because they are easy to generate, can travel over long distances, and can penetrate buildings easily.
- Because they travel in all directions from the transmitter (i.e. they are omni directional), the transmitter and receiver do not need to be carefully aligned.
- The properties of radio waves are dependent on frequency.

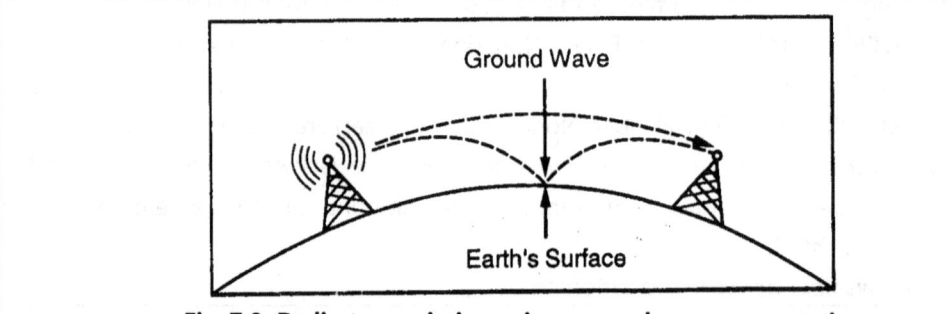

Fig. 7.9: Radio transmission using ground wave propagation

(ii) Microwave Transmission:

- Microwave transmission is weather and frequency dependent. The frequency band of 10 GHz is in the routine use.
- Microwave communication is widely used for long distance telephone communication, cellular telephones, television distribution and other uses that a severe shortage of spectrum has developed.
- Fig. 7.10 shows typical example of microwave link using dish antenna and satellite.

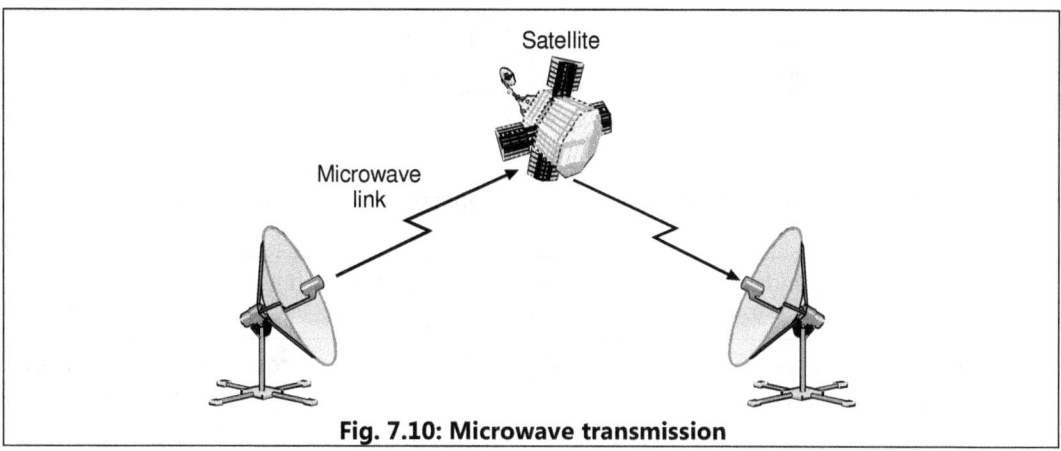
Fig. 7.10: Microwave transmission

Types of microwave transmission:

(i) Terrestrial Microwave Transmission:
- Terrestrial microwave transmission systems transmit tightly focused beams of radio frequencies from one ground-based microwave antenna to anther.
- Terrestrial microwave systems typically use directional parabolic antennas to send and receive signals in the lower gigahertz (GHz) range.
- The signals are highly focused and the physical path must be line-of-sight. Relay towers are used to extend signals. Terrestrial microwave systems are typically used when using cabling is cost-prohibitive.

(ii) Satellite Microwave Transmission:
- In satellite microwave, the signals are transmitted from a ground station to a satellite and then after amplifying, from the satellite to some other ground station.
- It covers large geographical areas than terrestrial microwaves.
- Satellite microwave systems transmit signals between directional parabolic antennas. Like terrestrial microwave systems, they use low gigahertz (GHz) frequencies and must be in line of sight.
- The main difference with satellite systems is that one antenna is on a satellite in geosynchronous orbit about 36,000 kilometers (22,300 miles) above the equator. Because of this, satellite microwave systems can reach the most remote places on earth and communicate with mobile devices.

Comparison between Guided Media and Unguided Media:

Guided Media	Unguided Media
1. Guided media also called bounded or wired media.	1. Unguided media also called unbounded or wireless media.
2. Twisted pair wires, coaxial cable, fiber optic cables are the examples of wired media.	2. Radio microwave and infrared light are the examples of wireless media.

contd. ...

3. Additional transmission capacity can be obtained by adding more wires.	3. It is not possible to obtain additional capacity.
4. Wired media lead to discrete network topologies.	4. Wireless media leads to continuous network topologies.
5. Installation is costly, time-consuming and complicated.	5. Installation needs less time and money.
6. Attenuation depends exponentially on the distance.	6. Attenuation is proportional to square of the distance.
7. The signal energy is contained and guided within a solid medium.	7. The signal energy propagates in the form of unguided electromagnetic waves.
8. Used for point-to-point communication.	8. Used for radio broadcasting in all directions.

7.5 LAN (Local Area Network)

- LAN is a group of computers and associated peripheral devices connected by a communications channel, capable of sharing files and other resources among several users.
- A LAN is a high-speed data network that covers a relatively small geographic area (less than 1 km).

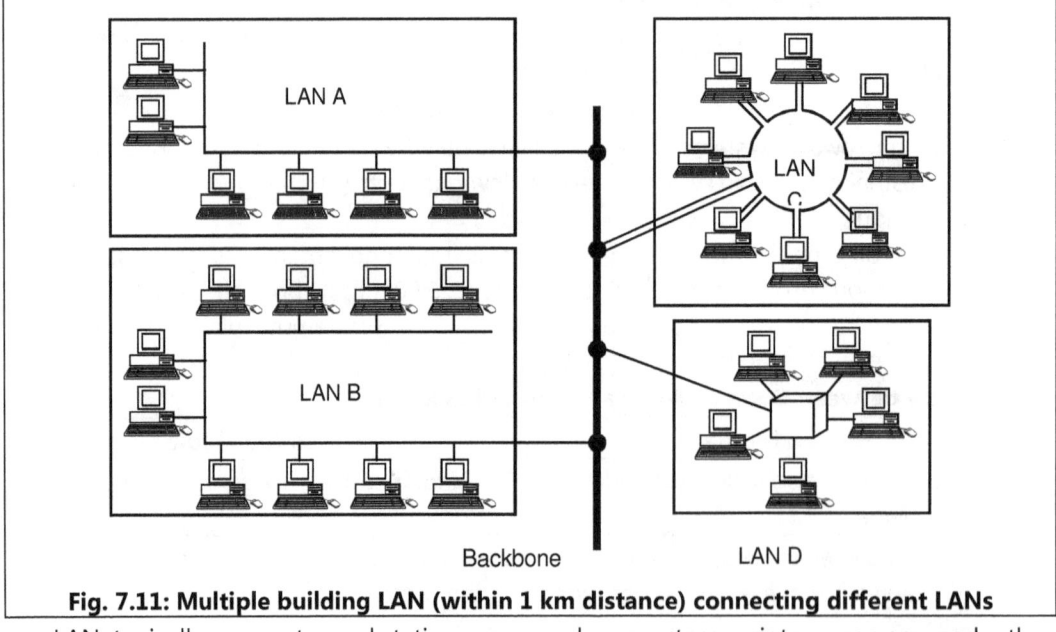

Fig. 7.11: Multiple building LAN (within 1 km distance) connecting different LANs

- LAN typically connects workstations, personal computers, printers, servers, and other devices.

- LAN is usually privately owned and links the devices in a single office, building or campus.
- LAN is a group of computes and associated devices that share a common communications line or wireless link.
- LANs are capable of transmitting data at very fast rates, much faster than data can be transmitted over a telephone line; but the distances are limited, and there is also a limit on the number of computers that can be attached to a single LAN.
- LAN have data rate 10 to 100 Mbps.

Components of a LAN:
1. **Network devices** such as Workstations, printers, file servers which are normally accessed by all other computers.
2. **Network Communication Devices** such as hubs, routers, switches etc. used for network connectivity.
3. **Network Interface Cards (NICs)** for each network device required to access the network. It is the interface between the machine and the physical network.
4. **Cable** as a physical transmission medium.
5. **Network Operating System** software applications required to control the use of network operation and administration.

Characteristics of LAN:
1. Every computer has the potential to communicate with any other computers of the network.
2. High degree of interconnection between computers.
3. Easy physical connection of computers in a network.
4. Inexpensive medium of data transmission.
5. High data transmission rate.

Advantages of LAN:
1. Expensive hardware can be shared e.g. laser printers.
2. Network software is cheaper than buying individual packages.
3. Users can access the same files.
4. Messages can be sent between users.
5. A single internet connection can be shared among many users.

Disadvantages of LAN:
1. Quite expensive to set up and maintain.
2. A virus can be easily spread to all the computers on the network.
3. More prone to hacking because of multiple points of access.
4. If the file server goes down, the entire network may go down (star network).
5. Distance and number of computers in a LAN is limited.

Uses of LAN:
1. File transfers and access.
2. Word and text processing.

3. Electronic message handling.
4. Remote database access.
5. Personal computing.
6. Digital voice transmission and storage.

7.6 MAN (Metropolitan Area Network)

- Large computer networks that typically span a large city or campus are called Metropolitan Area Networks (MAN).
- MANs geographic scope falls between WAN and LAN. A MAN is smaller than a Wide Area Network (WAN) but larger than a Local Area Network (LAN).
- MANs provide internet connectivity for LANs in a metropolitan region and connect them to wider area networks like the internet.
- MAN is a public, high-speed network, capable of voice and data transmission over a distance of up to 80 kilometers (50 miles).
- MAN is designed to extend over an entire city. Multiple local area networks MLANs that are connected on a campus or industrial complex using a high-speed backbone.
- Multiple networks that are connected within the same city to form a citywide network for a specific government or industry.
- Fiber Distributed Data Interface (FDDI) is a good network technology for building a Metropolitan Area Network (MAN).
- A MAN may be wholly owned and operated by a private company. Number of LANs connected so that resources may be shared LAN-to-LAN as well as device-to-device. For example: Cable television network.

Characteristics of MAN:
1. It generally covers towns and cities (50 kms).
2. Communication medium used for MAN are optical fibers, cables etc.
3. Data rates adequate for distributed computing applications.

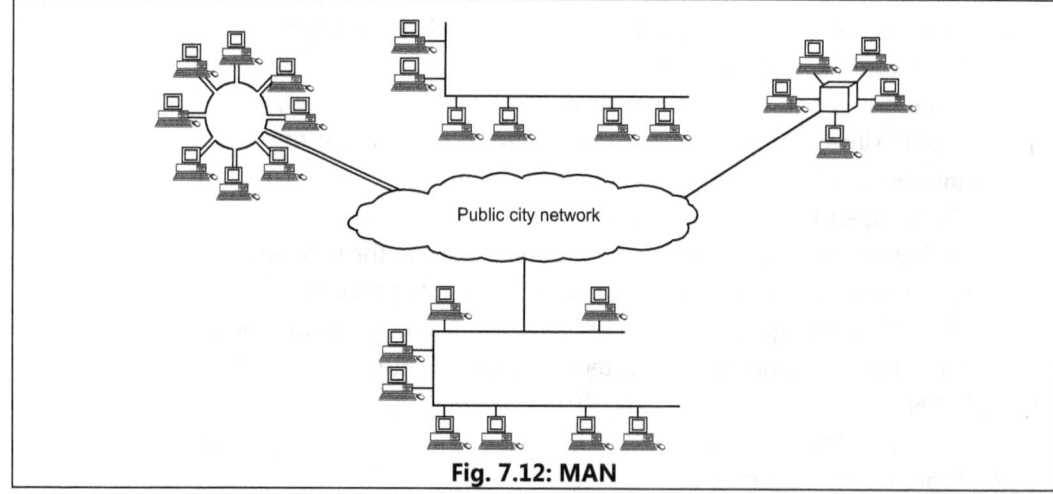

Fig. 7.12: MAN

Advantages:
1. MAN spans large geographical area than LAN.
2. MAN falls in between the LAN and WAN therefore, increases the efficiency of handling data. While at the same time saves the cost attached to establish a wide area network.
3. MAN offers centralized management of data. It enables we to connect many fast LANs together.

7.7 WAN (Wide Area Network)

- WAN is a network that connects users across large distances, often crossing the geographical boundaries of cities or states.
- A WAN provides long-distance transmission of data, voice, image, and video information over large geographical areas that may comprise a country, or even whole world.
- A geographically distributed network composed of local area networks (LANs) joined into a single large network using services provided by common carriers.
- Wide area networks are commonly implemented in enterprise networking environments in which company offices are in different cities, states, or countries or on different continents.
- WANs often connect multiple smaller networks, such as Local Area Networks (LANs) or Metropolitian Area Networks (MANs).

Characteristics of WAN:
1. It generally covers large distances (states, countries, continents).
2. Communication medium used are satellite, public telephone networks which are connected by routers.
3. Routers forward packets from one to another, through a route from the sender to the receiver.

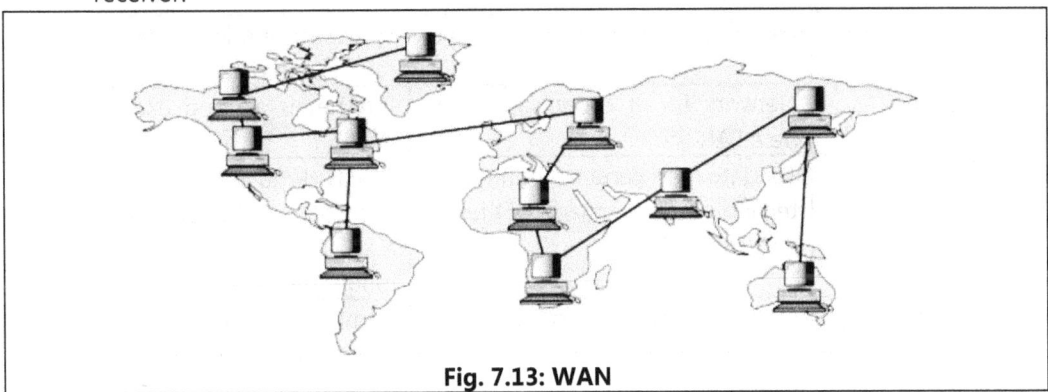

Fig. 7.13: WAN

Advantages:
1. WAN covers a large geographical area so long distance businesses can connect on the one network.
2. WAN shares software and resources with connecting workstations.

3. Messages can be sent very quickly to anyone else on the network. These messages can have pictures, sounds, or data included with them (called attachments).
4. Expensive things (such as printers or phone lines to the internet) can be shared by all the computers on the network without having to buy a different peripheral for each computer.
5. Everyone on the network can uses the same data. This avoids problems where some users may have older information than others.

Disadvantages:
1. WANs are expensive and generally slow.
2. WANs need a good firewall to restrict outsiders from entering and disrupting the network.
3. Setting up a network can be an expensive and complicated experience. The bigger the network the more expensive it is.
4. Security is a real issue when many different people have the ability to use information from other computers. Protection against hackers and viruses adds more complexity and expense.

Difference between LAN and WAN:

Terms	LAN	WAN
1. Definition	LAN (Local Area Network) is a computer network covering a small geographic area, like a home, office, schools, or group of buildings.	WAN (Wide Area Network) is a computer network that covers a broad area (For example, any network whose communications links cross metropolitan, regional, or national boundaries over a long distance).
2. Speed	High speed (1000 mbps).	Less speed (150 mbps).
3. Data transfer rates	LANs have a high data transfer rate.	WANs have a lower data transfer rate as compared to LANs.
4. Example	Network in an organisation can be a LAN.	Internet is a good example of a WAN.
5. Technology	Tend to use certain connectivity technologies, primarily Ethernet and Token Ring.	WANs tend to use technology like MPLS, ATM, Frame Relay and X.25 for connectivity over the longer distances.
6. Connection	One LAN can be connected to other LANs over any distance via telephone lines and radio waves.	Computers connected to a wide-area network are often connected through public networks, such as the telephone system. They can also be connected through leased lines or satellites.

contd. ...

7.	Components	Layer 2 devices like switches, bridges. Layer 1 devices like hubs, repeaters.	Layers 3 devices like routers, multi-layer switches and technology specific devices like ATM or Frame-relay switches etc.
8.	Fault tolerance	LANs tend to have fewer problems associated with them, as there are a smaller amount of systems to deal with.	WANs tend to be less fault tolerant. As it consists of a large amount of systems there is a lower amount of fault tolerance.
9.	Data transmission error	Experiences fewer data transmission errors.	Experiences more data transmission errors as compared to LAN.
10.	Ownership	Typically owned, controlled, and managed by a single person or organisation.	WANs (like the Internet) are not owned by any one organisation but rather exist under collective or distributed ownership and management over long distances.
11.	Set-up costs	If there is a need to set-up a couple of extra devices on the network, it is not very expensive to do that.	In this case since networks in remote areas have to be connected hence the set-up costs are higher. However WANs using public networks can be setup very cheaply, just software (VPN etc.).
12.	Geographical spread	Have a small geographical range and do not need any leased telecommunication lines.	Have a large geographical range generally spreading across boundaries and need leased telecommunication lines.
13.	Maintenance costs	Because it covers a relatively small geographical area, LAN is easier to maintain at relatively low costs.	Maintaining WAN is difficult because of its wider geographical coverage and higher maintenance costs.
14.	Bandwidth	High bandwidth is available for transmission.	Low bandwidth is available for transmission.
15.	Geographical area	LAN covers 100 m.	Wan covers more than 100 m.

7.8 Internet

- The internet is a worldwide, publicly accessible network of interconnected computer networks that transmit data using the standard internet protocol.
- The internet is a global system of interconnected computer networks that use the standard Internet protocol suite (TCP/IP) to serve billions of users worldwide.

- Internet is a network of networks that consists of millions of private, public, academic, business, and government networks, of local to global scope, that are linked by a broad array of electronic, wireless and optical networking technologies.
- The internet carries an extensive range of information resources and services, such as the inter-linked hypertext documents of the World Wide Web (WWW) and the infrastructure to support email.
- The internet is a network of the interlinked computer networking worldwide, which is accessible to the general public. These interconnected computers work by transmitting data through a special type of packet switching which is known as the IP (Internet Protocol).

Advantages:
1. **Faster Communication:** The foremost target of internet has always been speedy communication and it has excelled way beyond the expectations. Newer innovations are only going to make it faster and more reliable. Now, we can communicate in a fraction of second with a person who is sitting in the other part of the world. For more personal and interactive communication, we can avail the facilities of chat services, video conferencing and so on.
2. **Information Resources:** Information is probably the biggest advantage that internet offers. Internet is a virtual treasure trove of information. Any kind of information on any topic under the sun is available on the internet. The search engines like Google, Yahoo are at our service on the internet. There is a huge amount of information available on the Internet for just about every subject known to man, ranging from government law and services, trade fairs and conferences, market information, new ideas and technical support, the list is simply endless.
3. **Entertainment:** Entertainment is another popular reason why many people prefer to surf the internet. In fact, the internet has become quite successful in trapping the multifaceted entertainment industry. Downloading games or just surfing the celebrity websites are some of the uses people have discovered. Even celebrities are using the internet effectively for promotional campaigns. Besides, there are numerous games that can be downloaded for free. The industry of online gaming has tasted dramatic and phenomenal attention by game lovers.
4. **Social Networking:** One cannot imagine an online life without Facebook or Twitter. Social networking has become so popular amongst youth that it might one day replace physical networking. It has evolved as a great medium to connect with millions of people with similar interests. Apart from finding long-lost friends, we can also look for job, business opportunities on forums, communities etc. Besides, there are chat rooms where users can meet new and interesting people. Some of them may even end up finding their life partners.
5. **Online Services:** The internet has made life very convenient. With numerous online services we can now perform all the transactions online. We can book tickets for a movie, transfer funds, pay utility bills, taxes etc., right from our home. Some travel websites even plan an Itinerary as per our preferences and take care of airline tickets, hotel reservations etc.

6. **E-Commerce:** The concept of e-commerce is used for any type of commercial maneuvering or business deals that involves the transfer of information across the globe via internet. It has become a phenomenon associated with any kind of shopping, business deal etc. We name a service, and e-commerce with its giant tentacles engulfing every single product and service will make it available at the doorstep. Websites such as eBay allow us to even bid for homes, buy, sell or auction stuff online.

Disadvantages:
1. **Theft of Personal Information:** If we use the internet for online banking, social networking or other services, we may risk a theft to the personal information such as name, address, credit card number etc. Unscrupulous people can access this information through unsecured connections or by planting software and then use the personal details for their benefit. Needless to say, this may land us in serious trouble.
2. **Spamming:** Spamming refers to sending unwanted e-mails in bulk, which provide no purpose and needlessly obstruct the entire system. Such illegal activities can be very frustrating for us as it makes the internet slower and less reliable.
3. **Virus Threat:** Internet users are often plagued by virus attacks on their systems. Virus programs are inconspicuous and may get activated if we click a seemingly harmless link. Computers connected to the internet are very prone to targeted virus attacks and may end up crashing.
4. **Social Disconnect:** Thanks to the internet, people now only meet on social networks. More and more people are getting engulfed in virtual world and drifting apart from their friends and family. Even children prefer to play online games rather than going out and mingling with other kids. This may hamper a healthy social development in children.
5. **Pornography:** Pornography is perhaps the biggest disadvantage of the internet. Internet allows us to access and download millions of pornographic photos, videos and other X-rated stuff. Such unrestricted access to porn can be detrimental for children and teenagers. It can even play a havoc in marital and social lives of adults.

7.9 Topologies

- Topologies are the geometric arrangement of a computer system.
- Topology is the map of a network. Two or more devices connect to a link; two or more links form a topology.
- The physical topology of a network refers to the configuration of cables, computers and other peripherals.
- Network topology is the layout pattern of interconnection of the various systems.
- A topology is essential and stable geometric arrangement of computers in a network.
- The topology of a network is the geometric representation of the relationship of all the links and linking devices (usually called nodes) to one another.
- Topology defines the physical or logical arrangement of links or nodes in a network.

- A topology defines how nodes/stations are connected.
- **Physical topology** describes where the cables are run and where the workstations, nodes, routers, and gateways are located. Networks are usually configured in bus, ring, star, or mesh topologies.
- The physical topology of a network refers to the configuration of cables, computers, and other peripherals.
- The way that the workstations are connected to the network through the actual cables that transmit data, forming physical structure of the network is called the physical topology.
- **Logical topology** refers to the paths that messages take to get from one user on the network to another.
- Topology can be understood as the shape or structure of network.
- The logical topology is also called as signal topology.
- The logical topology is the way that the signals act on the network media, or the way that the data passes through the network from one device to the next without regard to the physical interconnection of the devices.
- Logical topologies are bound to the network protocols that direct how the data moves across a network.
- Physical topology should not be confused with logical topology which is the method used to pass information between workstations.

> In short, topology is the physical layout of computers, cables, switches, routers, and other components of a network. This term can also refer to the underlying network architecture, such as Ethernet or Token Ring. The word topology comes from topos, a Greek word for "place."

- Fig. 7.14 shows different categories of topologies in computer network.

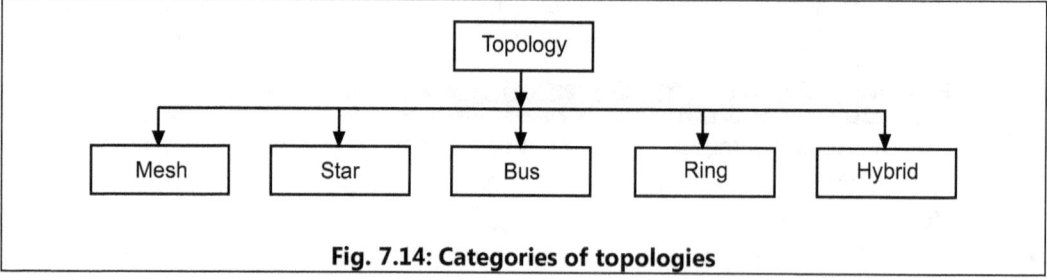

Fig. 7.14: Categories of topologies

7.9.1 Bus Topology

- A topology that allows all network nodes to receive the same message through the network cable at the same time is called as bus topology.
- In bus topology all the devices are connected to a central cable, called the bus or backbone.

- The bus pattern connects the computer to the same communications line. In bus topology all nodes/stations are connected to common link/medium. In bus topology communications goes in both directions along the line. It is a multipoint configuration.
- Bus topology, more completely called a common bus multipoint topology.
- Bus topology is a network where basically one single network cable is used from one end of the network to the other with different network devices connected to the cable at different locations.

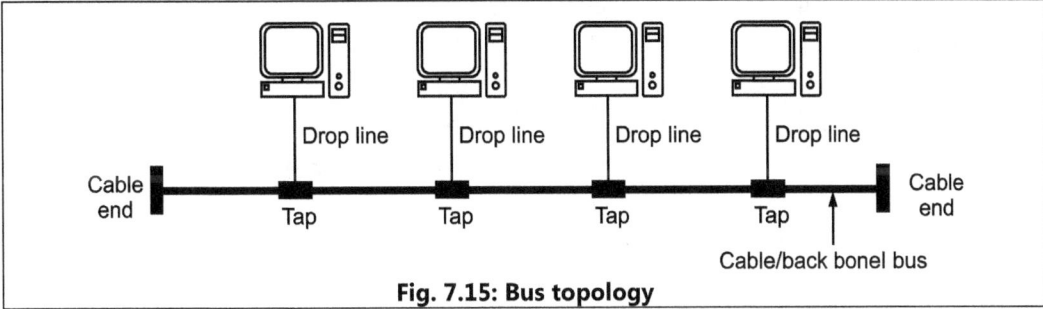

Fig. 7.15: Bus topology

- In bus topology one long cable acts as a backbone to link all the devices in a network. Nodes are connected to the bus by drop lines and tap.
- A drop line is a connection running between a device and the main cable.
- A signal from the source travels in both direction to all machines connected to bus cable until it finds the intended recipients.
- A tap is a connector that either splices into the main cable or punctures the sheathing of a cable to create a contact with the metallic core.
- A bus topology consists of a main run of cable with a terminator at each end. All nodes (file server, workstations and peripherals) are connected to the linear cable.
- Ethernet and LocalTalk networks use a linear bus topology.
- A network that uses a bus topology is referred to as a Bus Network. Fig. 7.16 shows a bus network.

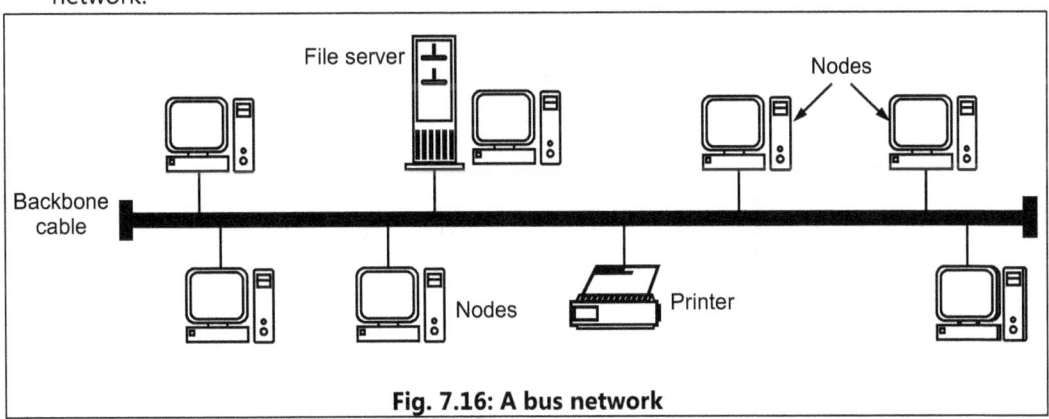

Fig. 7.16: A bus network

Advantages:
1. Easy to install.
2. It is very easy to connect a computer or peripheral to a bus.
3. Requires less cabling length so cheaper.
4. Any one computer or device being down does not affect the others.
5. Fast as compare to ring topology.
6. Sufficient for small network.
7. Cabling cost is less than other topologies.

Disadvantages:
1. Can not connect a large number of computers.
2. Difficult faulty isolation. A fault or break in the bus cable stops all transmission. Difficult to identify the problem if the entire network shuts down.
3. Collision may occur.
4. Signal reflection at the taps can cause degradation in quality.
5. Entire network shuts down if there is a break in the main cable.
6. Terminators are required at both ends of the backbone cable.
7. Not meant to be used as a stand-alone solution in a large building.

7.9.2 Ring Topology

- Ring topology is a network topology in the form of a closed loop or circle, with each node in the network connected to the next. Messages move in one direction around the system.
- Each device in ring topology has a dedicated point-to-point line configuration only with the two devices on either side of it, (dedicated means that the link carries traffic only between the two devices that it connects.)
- Nodes form a ring by point-to-point links to adjacent neighbours.
- A signal in ring topology is passed along the ring in one direction, from device to device, until it reaches its destination.
- Ring topology is a network topology that is set-up in circular fashion.

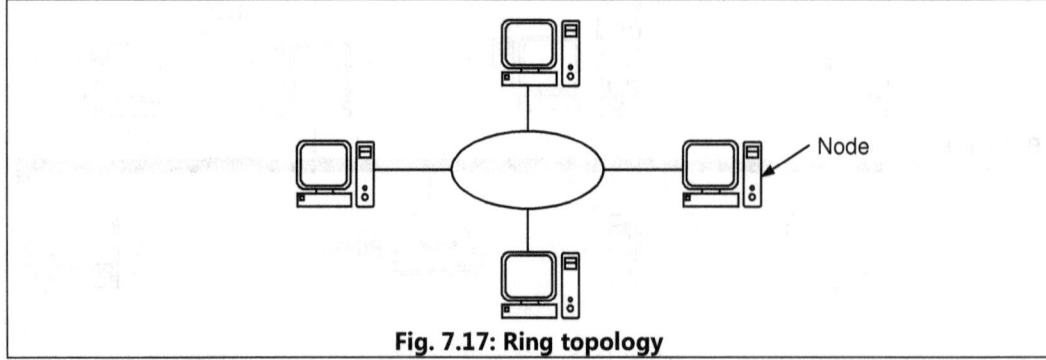

Fig. 7.17: Ring topology

- Ring topology is actually not a physical arrangement of a network cable.
- The ring network behaves like a ring where the network signal travels around the ring to each node in turn.
- Each device in the ring incorporates a repeater. When a device receives a signal intended for another device, its repeater regenerates the bits and passes them along.
- A network that uses a ring topology is referred as Ring network. Fig. 7.18 shows a ring network.
- Ring topology usually seen in a Token Ring or FDDI (Fiber Distributed Data Interface) network.

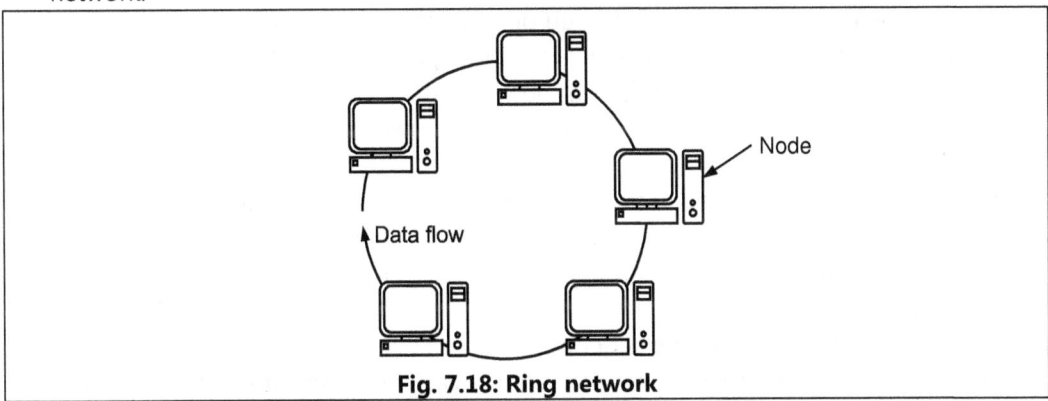

Fig. 7.18: Ring network

Advantages:
1. Requires less cabling.
2. Less expensive.
3. Fault isolation is simplified.

Disadvantages:
1. Traffic is unidirectional.
2. If one node goes down, it takes down the whole network.
3. Slow in speed.
4. Reconfiguration to add one node, whole network must be down first.
5. Difficult for troubleshooting the ring.

7.9.3 Star Topology
- Star topology is one topology in which a central unit called a hub or concentrator host a set of network cables that radiate out to each node on the network.
- The devices are not directly linked to one another in star topology. A star topology does not allow direct traffic between devices.
- Each device in star topology has a dedicated point-to-point link to central controller, usually called a hub or switch.
- The controller acts as an exchange: If one device wants to send data to another, it sends the data to the controller, which then relays the data to the other connected device. The hub act as signal repeater.

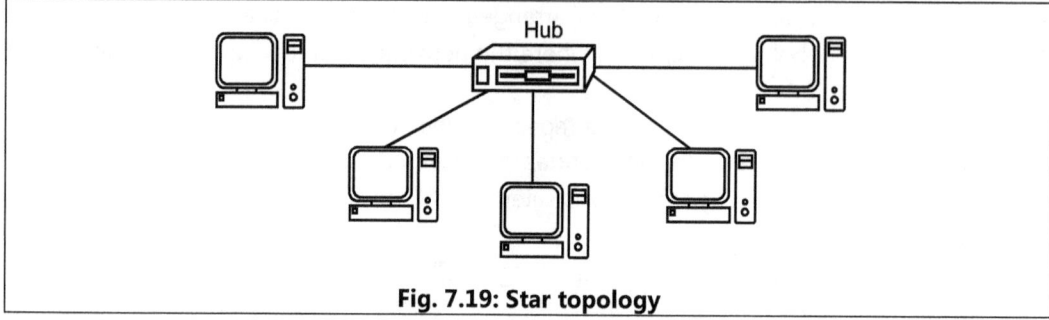

Fig. 7.19: Star topology

- At the center of the star is a wiring hub or concentrator and the nodes or workstations are arranged around the central point representing the points of the star.
- Wiring costs tend to be higher for star networks than for other configurations, because each node requires its own individual cable. Star networks do not follow any of the IEEE standards.
- A star topology is designed with each node, (file server, workstations and peripherals) connected directly to a central network hub or concentrator.
- Data on a star network passes through the hub or concentrator before continuing to its destination. The hub or concentrator manages and controls all functions of the network. It also acts as a repeater for the data flow.
- This configuration is common with twisted pair cable; however, it can also be used with coaxial cable or fiber optic cable.
- The protocols used with star configurations are usually Ethernet or LocalTalk. Computers are connected by cable segments to a centralized hub. Signal travels through the hub to all other computers.
- Fig. 7.20 shows a star network.

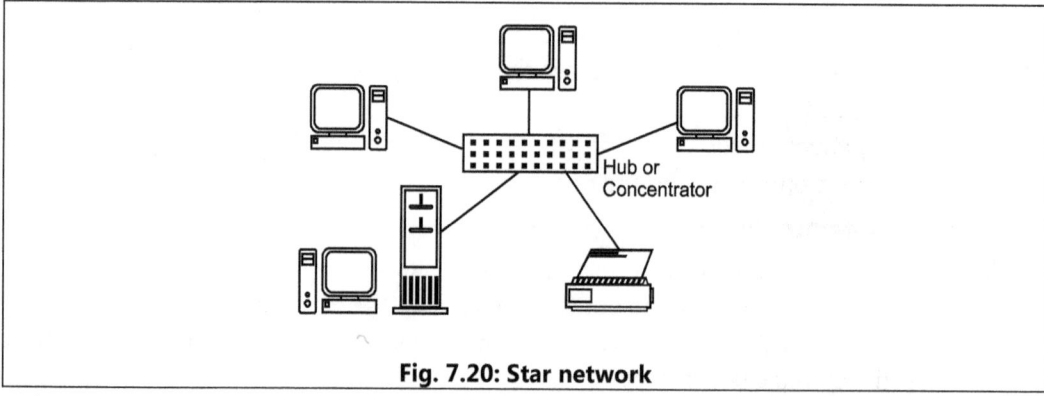

Fig. 7.20: Star network

Advantages:
1. Easy to install, reconfigure and wire.
2. Robustness: If one link fails, only that link is affected.
3. Fast as compare to ring topology.
4. Multiple devices can transfer data without collision.

5. Eliminates traffic problem.
6. No disruptions to the network then connecting or removing devices.
7. Easy to detect faults and to remove parts.
8. Supported by several hardware and software venders.

Disadvantages:
1. If central node (hub or switch) goes down then entire network goes down.
2. More cabling is required than bus topology.
3. More expensive than bus topologies because of the cost of the concentrators (hub or switch).

7.9.4 Mesh Topology

- Each device in mesh topology has a dedicated point-to-point link to every other device. The mesh topology connects each computer on the network to the others.
- Fully connected mesh network has n(n−1)/2 links for n devices. To accommodate n(n-1)/2 links, every device on the network must have n−1 input/output (I/O) ports.
- Mesh topology uses a significantly larger amount of network cabling than do the other network topologies, which makes it more expensive.

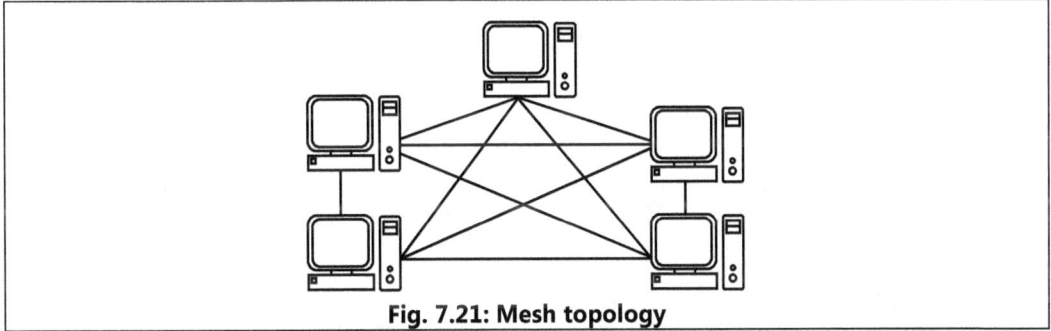

Fig. 7.21: Mesh topology

- The mesh topology is highly fault tolerant i.e. every computer has multiple possible connection paths to the other computers on the network, so a single cable break will not stop network communications between any two computers.
- Multiple links to each device are used to provide network link redundancy.
- In most practices networks that are based upon the particularly connected topology all of the data that is transmitted between nodes in network.

Advantages:
1. Each connection can carry its own data load due to dedicated link.
2. Eliminates traffic problem.
3. Mesh topology is robust. If one link becomes unusable, it does not affect other systems.
4. Privacy or security because of dedicated line.
5. Point-to-point link make fault identification easy.

Disadvantages:
1. More cables are required than other topologies.
2. n−1 input/output ports are required for n devices.
3. Installation and reconfiguration is very difficult because each device must be connected to every other device.
4. Expensive due to hardware requirements such as cables and input/output ports.

7.9.5 Tree Topology

- A tree topology is variation of a star topology. In tree topology not every device plugs to the central hub.
- The majority of devices connect to a secondary hub that in turn is connected to the central hub.
- A tree topology can also combine characteristics of linear bus and star topologies. It consists of groups of star-configured workstations connected to a linear bus backbone cable.
- Tree topologies allow for the expansion of an existing network and enable schools to configure a network to meet their needs.

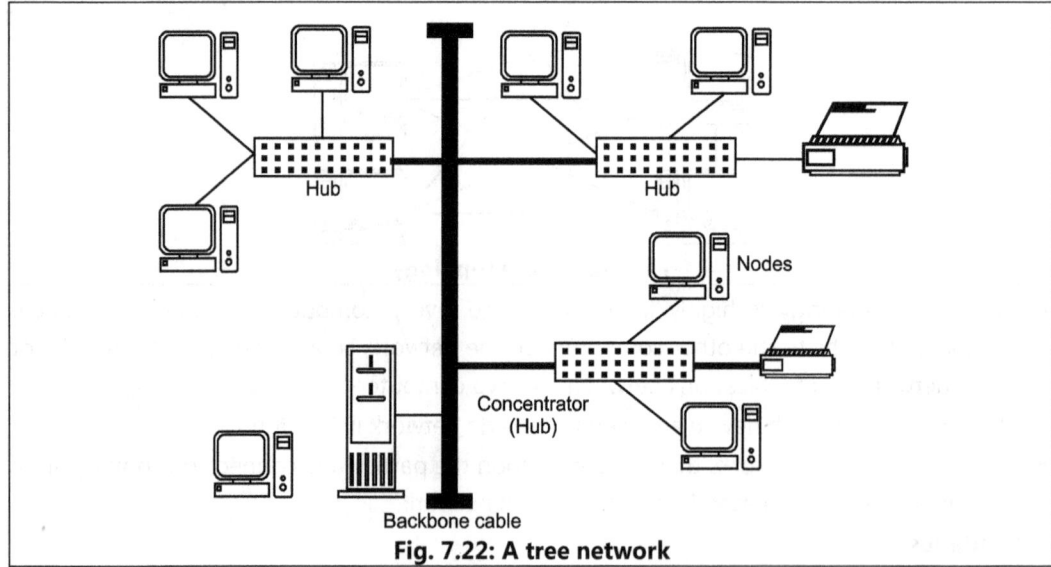

Fig. 7.22: A tree network

Advantages:
1. Easy to install and wire.
2. Fast as compare to other topologies.
3. Multiple devices can transfer data without collision.
4. Eliminates traffic problem.

5. No disruptions to the network by connecting or removing devices.
6. Easy to detect faults and to remove parts.
7. Supported by several hardware and software venders.

Disadvantages:
1. If central node (hub) goes down then entire network goes down.
2. Increases the distance of a signal can travel between network devices.
3. More expensive than bus topology because of the cost of the concentrators (hub or switch).
4. The cabling cost is more.

7.9.6 Hybrid Topology

- A hybrid topology is combination of two or more network topologies.
- Hybrid topology is a mixture or combination of topologies to implement a network.
- A very common and popular hybrid topology is star-bus topology in which a number of star topologies and bus topologies are connected by a central hub or switch.
- Fig. 7.23 shows a hybrid star and bus topologies.
- This topology is popular because the bus will connect hubs that are spread over distances.

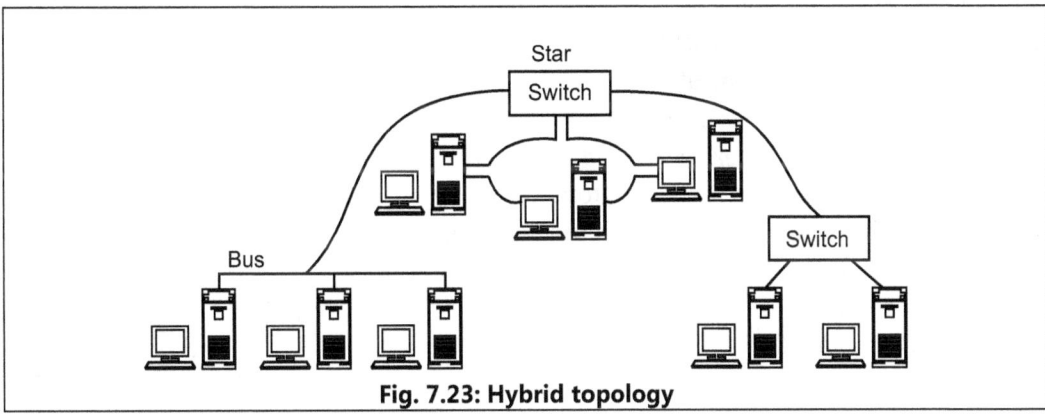

Fig. 7.23: Hybrid topology

- In star bus topology, if a computer fails, it will not affect the rest of the network. However, if the central component or hub, that attaches all computers in a star fails, then we have to face big problems since no computer will be able to communicate.

Advantages:
1. Network expansion is very simple in case of hybrid technology.
2. If one client fails, the entire network does not fail.

Disadvantage:
1. If one hub fails, all connections to that hub fail, although other hubs continue to function.

Questions

1. What is networking? How does a computer network works?
2. Enlist network services in detail.
3. Define computer network? List out various advantage and disadvantages of computer network.
4. With the help of diagram describe elements of communication.
5. Differentiate between LAN, WAN and MAN.
6. Enlist characteristics of LAN.
7. Define topology? What are its types.
8. Describe the term MAN in detail.
9. With the neat diagram explain star topology.
10. With the neat diagram describe bus topology. State its advantages and disadvantages.
11. With the neat diagram describe mesh topology.
12. With the neat diagram describe tree topology.
13. With the neat diagram describe ring topology.
14. Write short notes on Data transmission media.
15. What is internet? State its advantages and disadvantages.
16. Enlist disadvantages of LAN.
17. Enlist disadvantages of WAN.
18. Enlist various applications of LAN.
19. With the neat diagram explain WAN.
20. With the neat diagram explain hybrid topology.
21. Differentiate between star and ring topologies.
22. What are the components of a computer networks.
23. Explain in detail:
    (i) Guided media
    (ii) Unguided media.

■■■

Chapter 8...

MS-Office

Contents ...

8.1 Introduction to MS-Office
    8.1.1 Components
    8.1.2 Features
8.2 MS-Word
    8.2.1 Creating a Letter
    8.2.2 Tables
    8.2.3 Fonts
    8.2.4 Page Layout
    8.2.5 Formatting Documents
    8.2.6 Spell Check
    8.2.7 Print Preview
    8.2.8 Template
    8.2.9 Colours
    8.2.10 Mail Merge
    8.2.11 AutoText
    8.2.12 Inserting Picture
    8.2.13 WordArt
8.3 MS-Excel
    8.3.1 Introduction to Excel
    8.3.2 Sorting
    8.3.3 Queries
    8.3.4 Graphs/Charts
    8.3.5 Formulas and Functions
8.4 MS-PowerPoint
    8.4.1 Introduction to PowerPoint
    8.4.2 Creation of Slides
    8.4.3 Inserting Pictures
    8.4.4 Preparing Slide Show with Animation
8.5 MS-Access (Creation and Manipulation of Files)
- Questions

8.1 Introduction to MS-Office

- Microsoft Office is an office suite of desktop applications, servers and services for the Microsoft Windows and OS X operating systems, introduced by Microsoft on August 1989.
- Initially a marketing term for a bundled set of applications, the first version of Office contained Microsoft Word, Microsoft Excel, and Microsoft PowerPoint.
- Over the years, Office applications have grown substantially closer with shared features such as a common spell checker, OLE data integration and Microsoft Visual Basic for Applications scripting language.
- Microsoft also positions Office as a development platform for line-of-business software under the Office Business Applications brand. Office is reported to now be used by over a billion people worldwide.

8.1.1 Components

- MS-Office contains following components:

1. Word:

- Microsoft Word is a word processor and was previously considered the main program in Office.
- Its proprietary DOC format is considered a de facto standard, although Word 2007 can also use a new XML-based, Microsoft Office-optimized format called .DOCX, which has been standardized by Ecma International as Office Open XML and its SP2 update supports PDF and a limited ODF.
- Word is also available in some editions of microsoft works. It is available for the Windows and OS X platforms.
- The first version of Word, released in the autumn of 1983, was for the MS-DOS operating system and had the distinction of introducing the mouse to a broad population. Word 1.0 could be purchased with a bundled mouse, though none was required.

2. Excel:

- Microsoft Excel is a spreadsheet program that originally competed with the dominant Lotus 1-2-3, but eventually outsold it. It is available for the Windows and OS X platforms.
- Microsoft released the first version of Excel for the Mac OS in 1985, and the first Windows version in November 1987.

3. Outlook/Entourage:

- Microsoft Outlook is a personal information manager and e-mail communication software.
- The replacement for Windows Messaging, Microsoft Mail, and Schedule+ starting in Office 97, it includes an e-mail client, calendar, task manager and address book.
- On the Mac OS, Microsoft offered several versions of Outlook in the late 1990s, but only for use with Microsoft Exchange Server. In Office 2001, it introduced an alternative application with a slightly different feature set called Microsoft Entourage. It reintroduced Outlook in Office 2011, replacing Entourage.

4. PowerPoint:
- Microsoft PowerPoint is a presentation program for Windows and OS X.
- It is used to create slideshows, composed of text, graphics, and other objects, which can be displayed on-screen and shown by the presenter or printed out on transparencies or slides.
- Other desktop applications (Windows version only):
    1. **Microsoft Access:** Database manager.
    2. **Microsoft InfoPath:** An application to design rich XML-based forms.
    3. **Microsoft OneNote:** Note-taking software for use with both tablet and conventional PCs.
    4. **Microsoft Project:** Project Management software to keep track of events and to create network charts and Gantt charts (not bundled in any Office suite).
    5. **Microsoft Publisher:** Desktop Publishing (DTP) software mostly used for designing brochures, labels, calendars, greeting cards, business cards, newsletters, and postcards.
    6. **Microsoft Visio:** Diagram and flowcharting software (not bundled in any Office suite)

8.1.2 Features
- Microsoft Office 2010 offers flexible and powerful new ways to deliver the best work—at the office, at home, or at school.

1. **Express your ideas and create visual impact:**
- With improved picture and media editing features, it is easy to add creativity to the work and make the ideas stand out. Whether you are delivering a presentation to your colleagues or classmates, creating a company brochure or a personal invitation, Office 2010 empowers you to be your own graphic designer.
    (i) Edit your pictures right within select Office 2010 programs. Try an array of eye-catching artistic effects and new background removal tool to polish your images.
    (ii) Add flair to your text with new OpenType typography in Word 2010 and Publisher 2010. Use ligatures, stylistic sets, and other typography features available in many OpenType fonts.
    (iii) Easily edit your embedded videos right in PowerPoint 2010, with no additional software needed. Trim, add fades and effects, or even include bookmarks in your video to trigger animations.

2. **Boost your productivity with easy-to-use tools:**
- Enhancements in Office 2010 help you accomplish your work more intuitively, so you can focus on the task at hand and produce better results.
    (i) Office 2010 simplifies how you find and use features. The new Microsoft Office Backstage™ view replaces the traditional File menu to give you centralized and easy access to operations such as save, share, print, and publish. With the improved Ribbon, you can access more commands quickly and customize it to fit your work style.

(ii) Use the new Paste with Live Preview feature, available in many Office 2010 applications, to preview your Paste Options before you paste.

(iii) Store, organize, and track information in one place to stay connected to all of your thoughts and ideas with OneNote 2010. Enhanced navigation, search tools, new page versions, and wiki linking help you find and track your resources quickly. You can even take notes while working in Word 2010, PowerPoint 2010, or Internet Explorer, and link those notes automatically back to the source content.

(iv) Find what you need faster with the improved Navigation Pane in Word 2010. Quickly browse by headings or use the integrated Find tools to instantly search your document with all of your results highlighted.

3. **Bring new insights to your information and make better decisions:**
- From business financials to household budgets, Office 2010 makes it easier to manage and analyze your data and present it in meaningful ways.
    (i) Turn complexity into clarity with new visualization tools in Excel 2010. Add a visual summary of your analysis alongside your values with tiny charts called Sparklines. Use a Slicer to dynamically filter data in a PivotTable or PivotChart and display only the relevant details.

    (ii) Design your own database faster than before in Access 2010, even if you are not a database expert. With new features such as Application Parts, you can add prebuilt components to your database in just a few clicks. Use Access 2010 to design Navigation Forms for your frequently used forms and reports using drag-and-drop functionality.

4. **Break down location and communication barriers:**
- MS-Office 2010 offers innovative and flexible ways to bring people together. New technologies and improved features help you easily share your files and keep up with your communications.
    (i) With new co-authoring capabilities in Office 2010, you can edit your files simultaneously with people in different locations. Co-authoring is available in Word 2010, PowerPoint 2010, OneNote 2010, Excel Web App, and OneNote Web App.

    (ii) The new Broadcast Slide Show feature in PowerPoint 2010 lets you instantly broadcast your live presentation over the Web. Your remote audience can view your presentation in high fidelity, even if they do not have PowerPoint installed.

    (iii) Reduce information overload and manage your e-mail more efficiently in Outlook 2010. The improved Conversation View and new conversation management tools enable you to clean up redundant messages or ignore an e-mail discussion. The Ignore feature moves current and all future messages to your Deleted Items folder. With the new Quick Steps, you can perform multi-step tasks, such as reply and delete, all within a single click.

    (iv) With Microsoft Lync integrated throughout several Office 2010 programs, you can determine the availability of your colleagues, such as when co-authoring a document in Word or viewing your e-mails in Outlook. Initiate conversations directly from your application including instant messaging and even voice calls.

5. **Get the information you need when, where, and how you want:**
- MS-Office 2010 makes it easy for you to stay productive on the go by providing access to your Office documents and notes from anywhere through the Web browser, computer, or smartphone.
    - **(i)** **Office Web Apps** are online companions to your Microsoft Office 2010 applications. Post your files to a SharePoint site or your Windows Live SkyDrive folder, then access and edit them from virtually any computer with an Internet connection.
    - **(ii)** **Microsoft Office** Mobile brings powerful and familiar Microsoft Office tools you rely on to your Windows Phone 7 devices. Experience a rich interface specifically suited to your mobile device's screen and easily take action when you are on the go.
    - **(iii)** **SharePoint Workspace 2010**, formerly known as Microsoft Office Groove, expands the boundaries of your SharePoint 2010 content. Easily update on your documents and lists offline. When you are back online your revisions will synchronize to the server automatically.

8.2 MS-Word

- Microsoft Word is a word-processing program that is part of the ubiquitous Microsoft Office suite of productivity applications.
- Word is used to create, format, edit, save and print electronic documents.
- Microsoft Word is a word processor designed by Microsoft. It was first released in 1983 under the name Multi-Tool Word for Xenix systems.
- Microsoft Word, or Word as it is commonly known, is a software application that allows you (the user) to perform word processing.
- Microsoft Office Word is a non-free commercial word processor designed by Microsoft. It is part of the Microsoft Office Suite.
- Microsoft Word is currently the most common word processor ON the market. Because it is so common, the .doc/.docx format has become the de facto format for text documents.
- MS-Word is a popular word processing program used for creating documents such as letters, brochures, learning activities, tests, quizzes and students homework assignments.

Getting Started (Microsoft Word 2010):
- To start word application, follow the following steps:
    Step 1: Click Start button.
    Step 2: Click All Programs option from the menu.
    Step 3: Search for **Microsoft Office** from the sub menu and click it.
    Step 4: Search for Microsoft Word 2010 from the submenu and click it.

Explore Window (Microsoft Word 2010):
- Following is the basic window which we get when we start word application. Let us understand various important parts of this window.

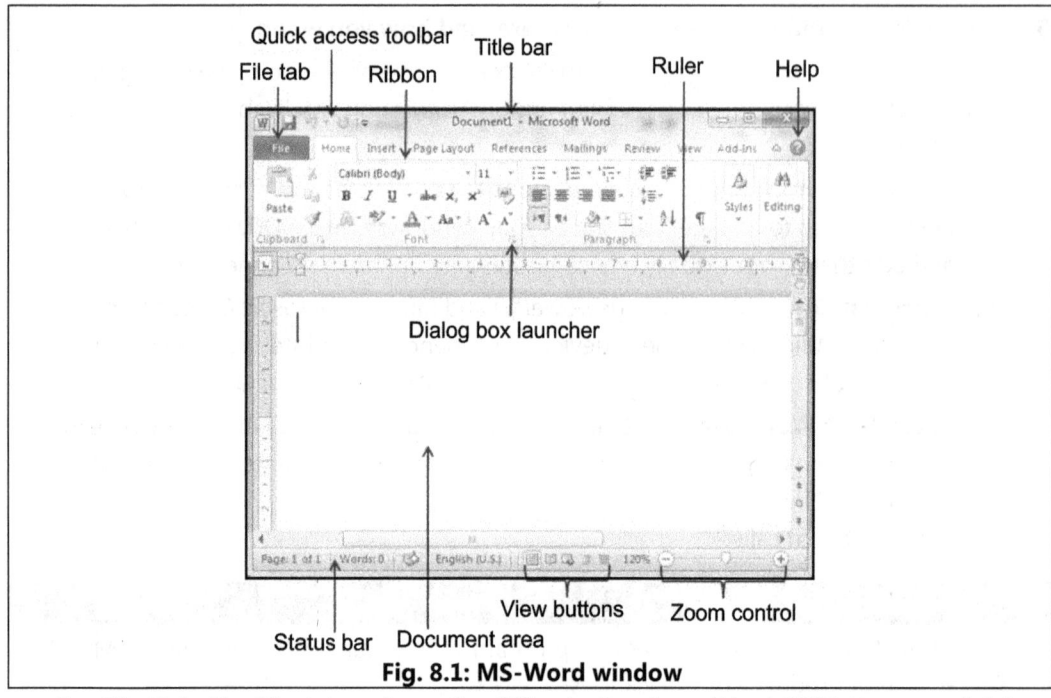

Fig. 8.1: MS-Word window

1. **File Tab:** The File tab replaces the Office button from Word 2007. You can click it to check Backstage view, which is the place to come when you need to open or save files, create new documents, print a document, and do other file-related operations.
2. **Quick Access Toolbar:** This you will find just above the File tab and its purpose is to provide a convenient resting place for the Word most frequently used commands. You can customize this toolbar based on your comfort.
3. **Ribbon:** Ribbon contains commands organized in three components:
    (i) **Tabs:** They appear across the top of the Ribbon and contain groups of related commands. Home, Insert, Page Layout are example of ribbon tabs.
    (ii) **Groups:** They organize related commands; each group name appears below the group on the Ribbon. For example group of commands related to fonts or or group of commands related to alignment etc.
    (iii) **Commands:** Commands appear within each group as mentioned above.

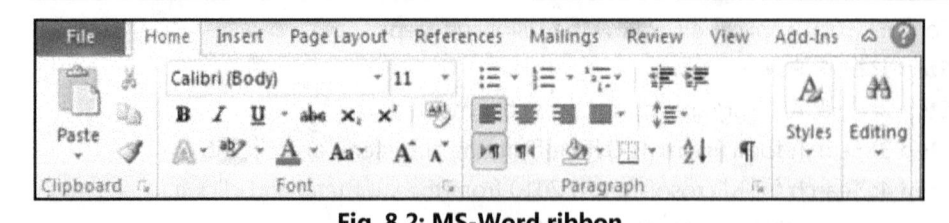

Fig. 8.2: MS-Word ribbon

4. **Title bar:** This lies in the middle and at the top or the window. Title bar shows the program and document titles.

5. **Rulers:** Word has two rulers - a horizontal ruler and a vertical ruler. The horizontal ruler appears just beneath the Ribbon and is used to set margins and tab stops. The vertical ruler appears on the left edge of the Word window and is used to gauge the vertical position of elements on the page.
6. **Help:** The Help Icon can be used to get word related help anytime you like. This provides nice tutorial on various subjects related to word.
7. **Zoom Control:** Zoom control lets you zoom in for a closer look at your text. The zoom control consists of a slider that you can slide left or right to zoom in or out, . and + buttons you can click to increase or decrease the zoom factor.
8. **View Buttons:** The group of five buttons located to the left of the Zoom control, near the bottom of the screen, lets you switch among Word's various document views.
   (i) **Print Layout view:** This displays pages exactly as they will appear when printed.
   (ii) **Full Screen Reading view:** This gives a full screen look of the document.
   (iii) **Web Layout view:** This shows how a document appears when viewed by a Web browser, such as Internet Explorer (IE).
   (iv) **Outline view:** This lets you work with outlines established using word's standard heading styles.
   (v) **Draft view:** This formats text as it appears on the printed page with a few exceptions. For example, headers and footers aren't shown. Most people prefer this mode.
9. **Document Area:** The area where you type. The flashing vertical bar is called the insertion point and it represents the location where text will appear when you type.
10. **Status Bar:** This displays document information as well as the insertion point location. From left to right, this bar contains the total number of pages and words in the document, language etc.

    You can configure the status bar by right-clicking anywhere on it and by selecting or deselecting options from the provided list.
11. **Dialog Box Launcher:** This appears as very small arrow in the lower-right corner of many groups on the Ribbon. Clicking this button opens a dialog box or task pane that provides more options about the group.

8.2.1 Creating a Letter

- Some of the content in this topic may not be applicable to some languages:
  1. On the File menu, click New.
  2. In the New Document task pane, under Templates, click On my computer.
  3. Click the Letters & Faxes tab.
  4. Double-click Letter Wizard.
  5. If you do not see this wizard in the Templates dialog box, you might need to install it.
  6. Follow the instructions in the Letter Wizard.

8.2.2 Tables

- Using tables in Word can provide you with additional elements to any document.
- Tables can be used to create lists or format text in an organized fashion.

1. Inserting a Table:

- Following the following steps for inserting a table in a document:
  (i) Click where to insert a table.
  (ii) On the Insert tab, in the Tables group, click Table.
  (iii) A drop down box will appear; click and hold your mouse then drag to select the number of rows and columns that you want inserted into your document. You will see your table appearing in your document as you drag on the grid.
  (iv) Once you have highlighted the rows and columns you would like let go of your mouse and the table will be in your document.

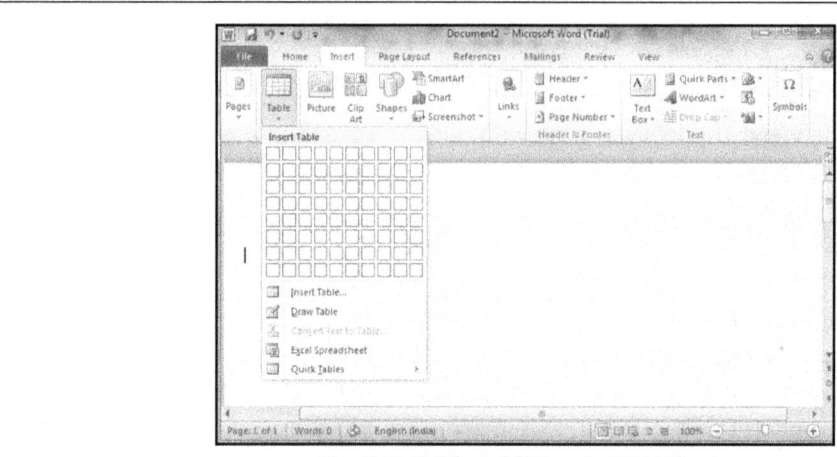

Fig. 8.3: Table addition in MS-Word

2. Add Row/Column to Table:

  (i) Click on the table.
  (ii) Under Table Tools, go to the Layout tab.
  (iii) Click on the Insert Above or Insert Below to add a row, Click on Insert Left or Insert Right to insert a column.
  (iv) Click on Delete to remove a column, row or cell.

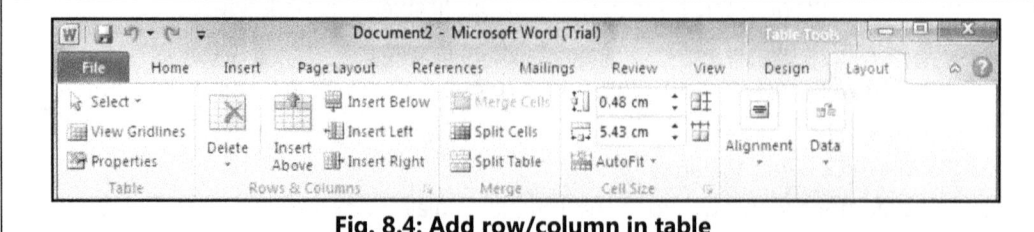

Fig. 8.4: Add row/column in table

3. **Delete a Table:**
   (i) Rest the pointer on the table until the table move ⊞ handle appears, and then click the table move handle.
   (ii) Press BACKSPACE on your keyboard.

8.2.3 Fonts
- Microsoft word allows you to use different fonts with different size.
- You can change your document's appearance by changing the fonts and their size.
- Usually you use different fonts for paragraphs and headings. So it is important to learn how to use different fonts. This chapter will teach you how to change a font and its size using simple steps.

1. **Change the Font Type and Size:**
- Let us give a brief idea about font buttons which we are going to use in this point. Here, is a screen capture to show few font related buttons.

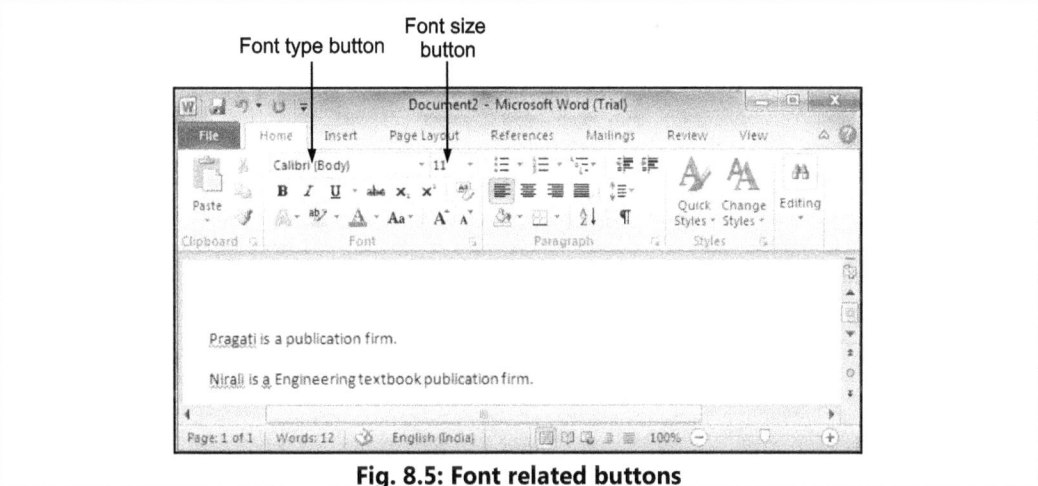

Fig. 8.5: Font related buttons

Step 1 : Select the text that is to be change to a different font and click Home tab. Now click Font Type button to list down all the fonts available as shown below.

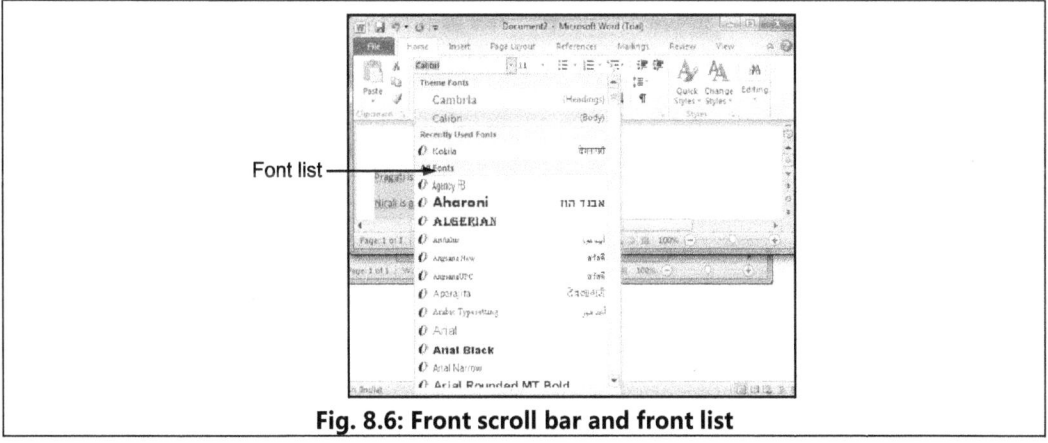

Fig. 8.6: Front scroll bar and front list

Step 2 : Try to move mouse pointer over different fonts listed. You will see that text font changes when you move mouse pointer over different fonts. You can use Font Scroll Bar to display more fonts available. Finally select a desired font by clicking over the font name in the list. Here we have selected Algerian for my sample text.

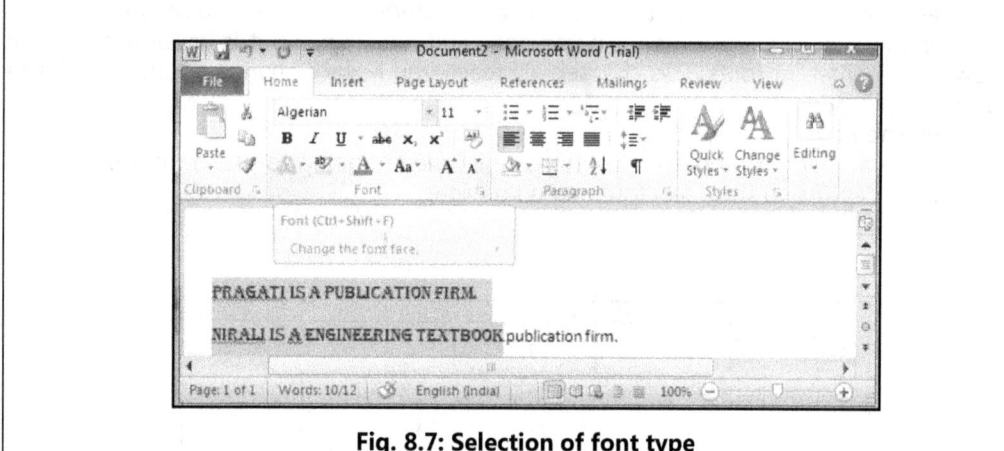

Fig. 8.7: Selection of font type

Step 3 : Similar way, to change the font size, click over the Font Size button which will display a font size list. You will use same procedure to select a desired font size what you have used while selecting a font type.

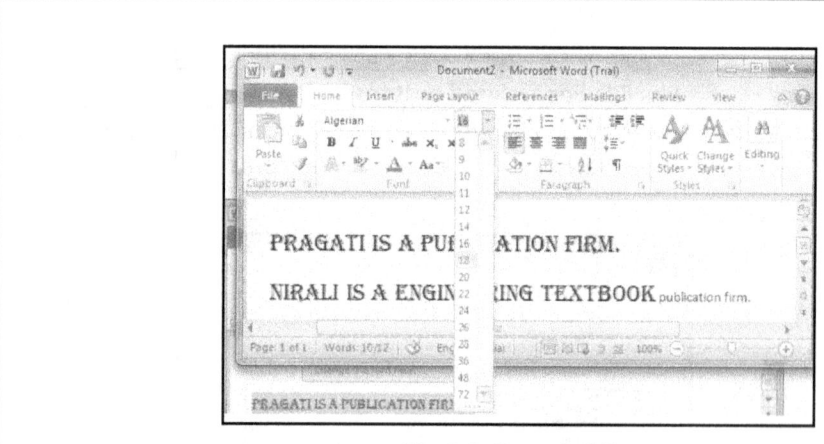

Fig. 8.8: Font size list

Use Shrink and Grow Buttons:

- You can use a quick way to reduce or enlarge the font size. As shown in first screen capture, Shrink Font button can be used to reduce the font size whereas Grow Font button can be used to enlarge font size.

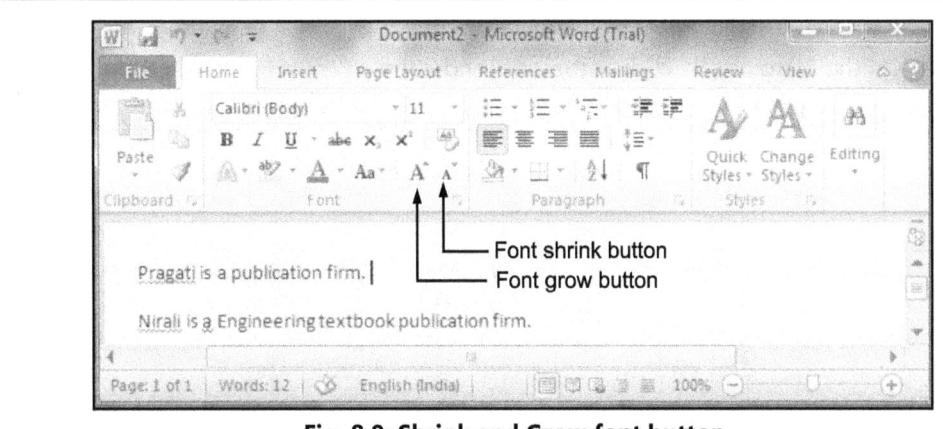

Fig. 8.9: Shrink and Grow font button

8.2.4 Page Layout

- This tab has commands to adjust page elements such as margins, orientation, inserting columns, page backgrounds.

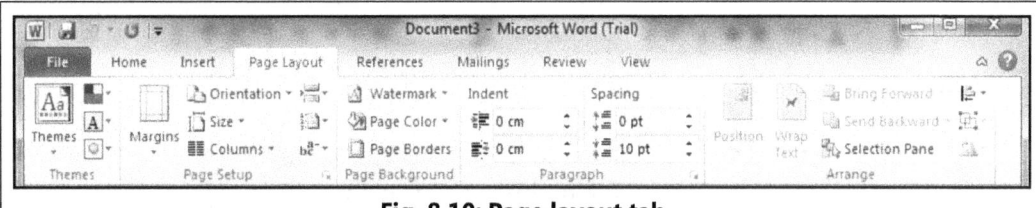

Fig. 8.10: Page layout tab

1. **Page Orientation:**
- You can choose either portrait (vertical) or landscape (horizontal) orientation for all or part of your document.
2. **Change Page Orientation:**
   (i) On the Page Layout tab, in the Page Setup group, click Orientation.
   (ii) Click Portrait or Landscape.

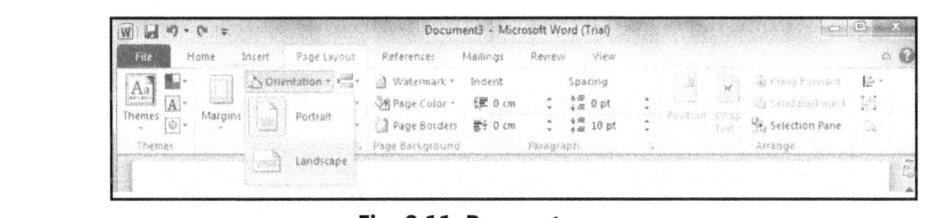

Fig. 8.11: Page setup group

3. **Different Page Orientations on same Document:**
   (a) Highlight the pages or paragraphs that you want to change to portrait or landscape orientation.
   (b) On the Page Layout tab, in the Page Setup group, click Margins.
       (i) Click Custom Margins at the bottom of the drop down menu.

(ii) A Page Setup dialog box will appear.

(iii) On the Margins tab, click Portrait or Landscape.

(iv) In the Apply to list, click Selected text or This point forward.

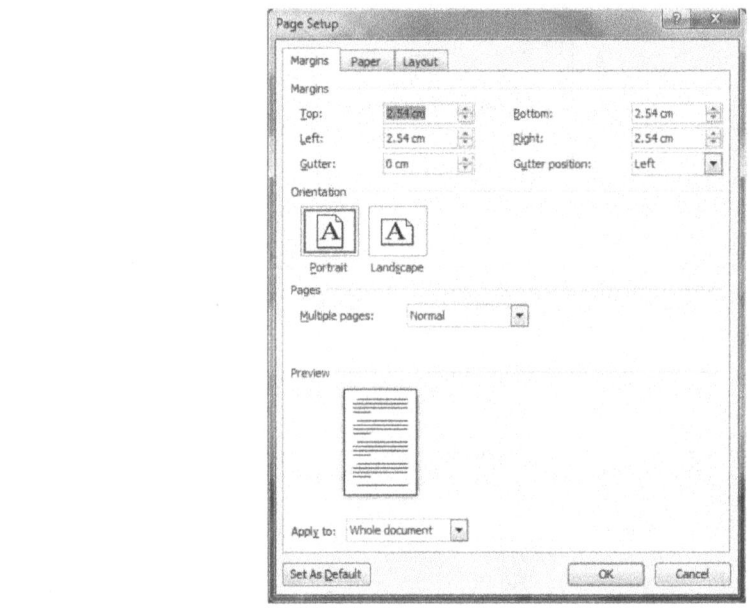

Fig. 8.12: Margins in page layout

4. Page Margins:

- Page margins are the blank space around the edges of the page. In general, you insert text and graphics in the printable area inside the margins.
- When you change a document's page margins, you change where text and graphics appear on each page.
- You can change the page margins either by choosing from one of Word's predefined settings in the Margins gallery or by creating custom margins.

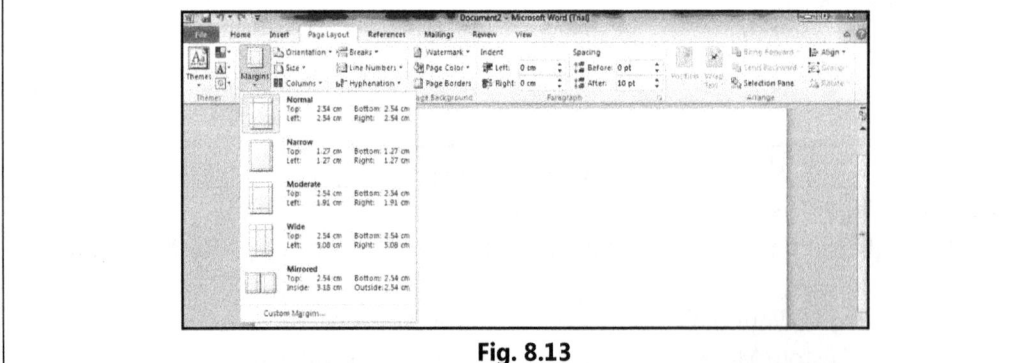

Fig. 8.13

(a) Setting Predefined Page Margins:
  (i) On the Page Layout tab, in the Page Setup group, click Margins. The Margins gallery drop down menu will appear.
  (ii) Click the margin type that is to be applied.

(b) Create Custom Margins:
  (i) On the Page Layout tab, in the Page Setup group, click Margins.
  (ii) At the bottom of the Margins gallery drop down menu, click Custom Margins.
  (iii) The Page Setup dialog box will appear.
  (iv) Enter new values for the margins in all or some of the Top, Bottom, Left or Right text boxes.
  (v) Click OK.

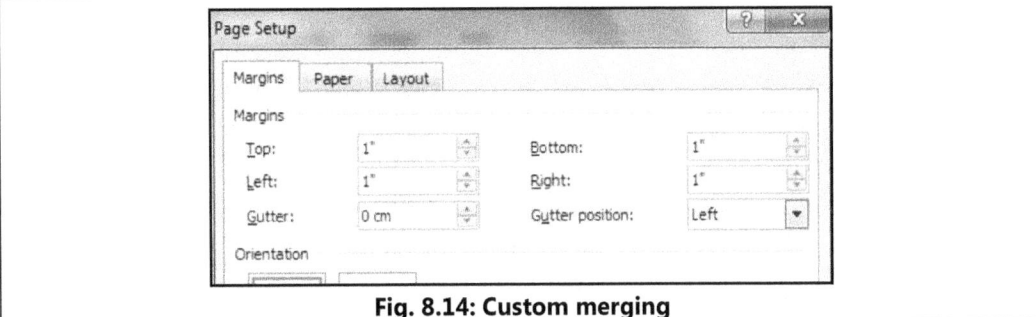

Fig. 8.14: Custom merging

8.2.5 Formatting Documents

1. Adjusting Line Spacing:
- The default spacing is 1.15 line spacing and 10 points after each paragraph. The default spacing in Office Word 2003 documents is 1.0 between lines and no blank line between paragraphs.

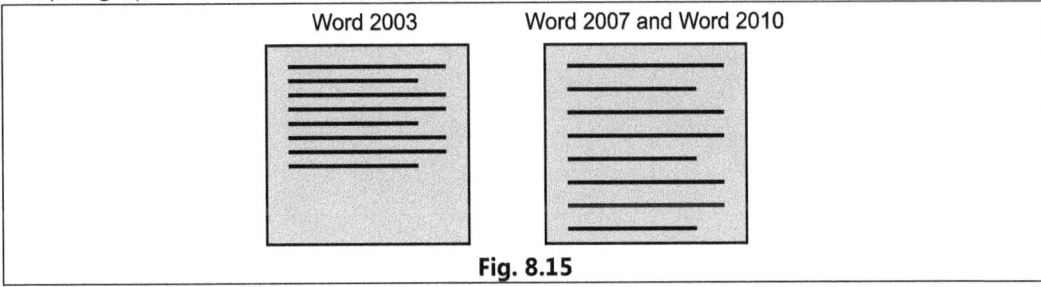

Fig. 8.15

- The easiest way to change the line spacing for an entire document is to highlight the paragraphs or entire document that you want to change the line spacing on.
  1. On the Home tab, in the Paragraph group, click Line Spacing.
  2. Do one of the following:
- Click the number of line spaces that you want.
- For example, click 1.0 to single-space with the spacing that is used in earlier versions of Word. Click 2.0 to double-space the selected paragraph. Click 1.15 to single-space with the spacing that is used in Word 2010.

- Click Remove Space Before Paragraph to remove any additional lines added after each paragraph as a default.

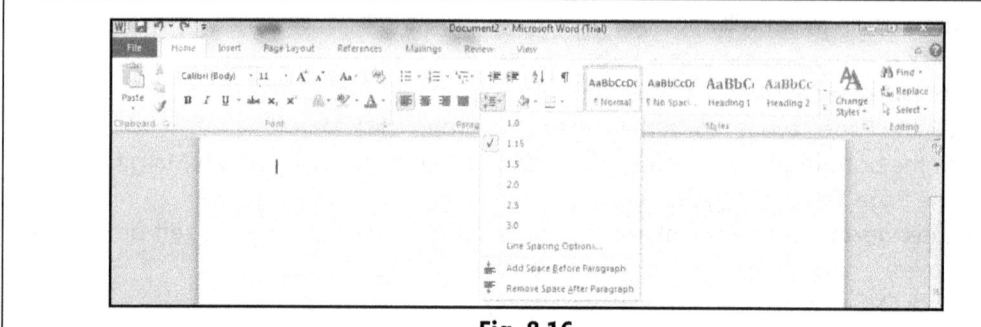

Fig. 8.16

2. Page Breaks:
- Word automatically inserts a page break when you reach the end of a page.
- If you want the page to break in a different place, you can insert a manual page break.

Inserting a Page Break:
1. Click where you want to start a new page.
2. On the Insert tab, in the Pages group, click Page Break.

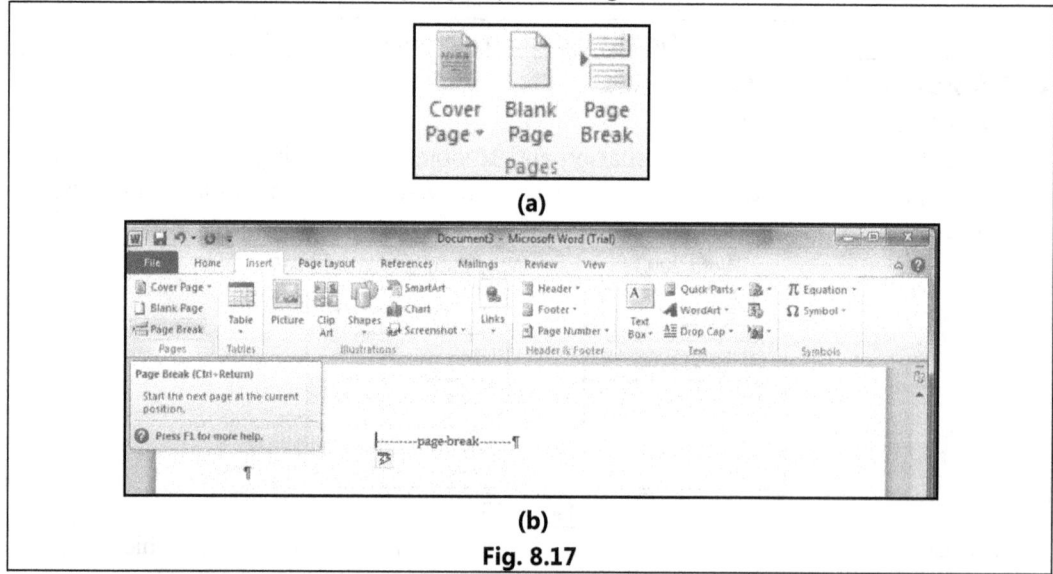

Fig. 8.17

3. Headers and Footers:
- You can add headers and footers numerous ways.
- The simplest way is to double click on the top or bottom of the page and the header and footer area will appear.
- Enter the text you wish to be displayed at the top or bottom of every page.

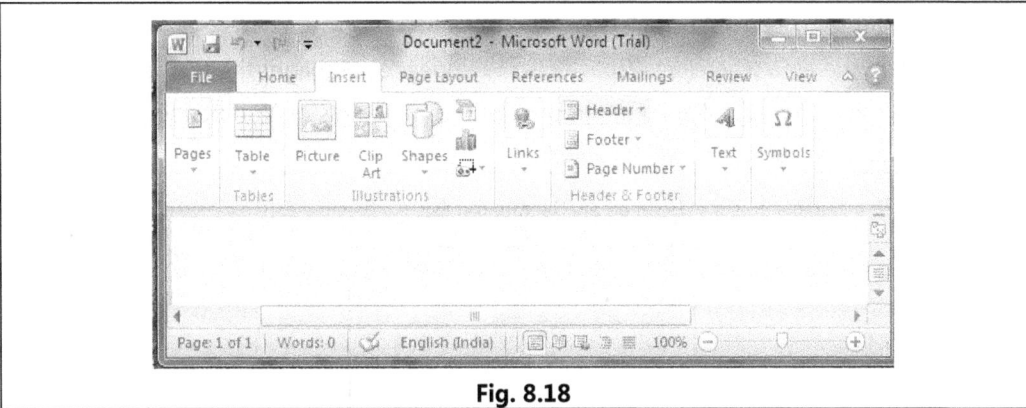

Fig. 8.18

Add Header or Footer:
1. On the Insert tab, in the Header & Footer group, click Header or Footer.
2. Click the header or footer that you want to add to your document and your header or footer area will open.
3. Type text in the header or footer area.
4. To return to the body of your document, click Close Header and Footer on the Design tab (under Header & Footer Tools).

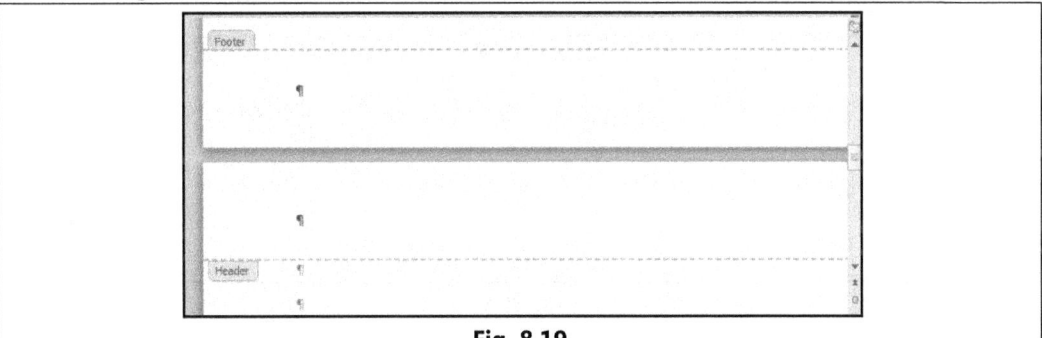

Fig. 8.19

4. Bulleted or Numbered List:
- You can quickly add bullets or numbers to existing lines of text, or Word can automatically create lists as you type.
- By default, if you start a paragraph with an asterisk or a number 1. Word recognizes that you are trying to start a bulleted or numbered list.

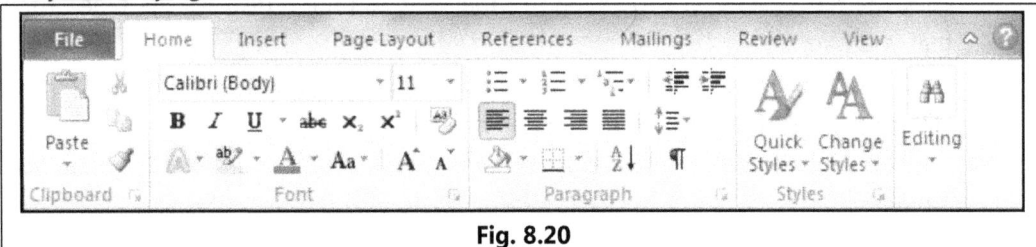

Fig. 8.20

(a) Insert Bulleted or Numbered List:
1. Click on the area where we want the list to appear or highlight the text to be in a list.
2. Go to the Home tab, in the Paragraph group, click Bullets or Numbering.
3. A bullet(s) or number(s) will be inserted.

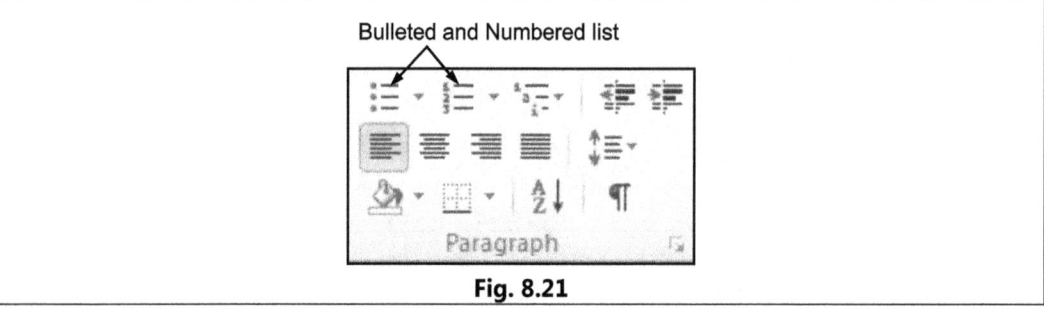

Fig. 8.21

(b) Select Bullets or Numbering Style:
1. Select the items that you want to add bullets or numbering to.
2. On the Home tab, in the Paragraph group, click the arrow next to the Bullets or Numbering command.
3. Select the bullet or number format you would like to be inserted.

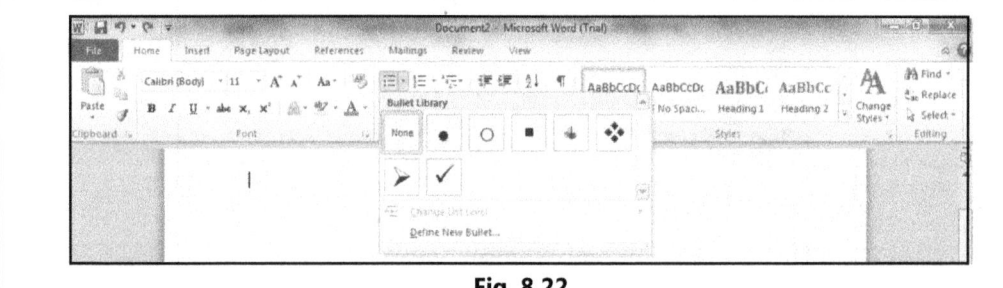

Fig. 8.22

5. Tab Stops:
- Creating tab stops can be helpful when creating a large number of documents such as flyers, table of contents or even when creating a resume. They help you to display and line up information correctly.

Setting Manual Tab Stops
1. Click the tab selector at the left end of the ruler 🔲 until it displays the type of tab that you want.
2. Then click in the ruler at the top of your page, where you want to set the tab stop.

- The different types of tab stops found on the ruler are:
    - 🔲 A Left Tab stop sets the start position of text that will then run to the right as you type.

- A Center Tab stop sets the position of the middle of the text. The text centers on this position as you type.
- A Right Tab stop sets the right end of the text. As you type, the text moves to the left.
- A Decimal Tab stop aligns numbers around a decimal point. Independent of the number of digits, the decimal point will be in the same position, you can align numbers around a decimal character only.
- A Bar Tab stop does not position text. It inserts a vertical bar at the tab position.

Setting Detailed Tab Stops:
- If you want you tab stops at precise positions that you cannot get by clicking the ruler, or if you want to insert a specific character (leader) before the tab, you can use the Tabs dialog box.
    1. Click the Home tab, click the Paragraph Dialog Box Launcher.
    2. A Paragraph box will appear, click on the Tabs button at the bottom left of the dialog box.
    3. A Tabs dialog box will appear.
    4. Under Tap stop position area, type the location where you want to set the top stop. Hit enter.
    5. Under Alignment, click the type of tab stop that you want.
    6. To add dots with your tab stop, or to add another type of leader, click the option that you want under Leader.
    7. Click Set.
    8. Repeat steps 4-5 to add another tab stop, or click OK.
    9. The Tabs dialog box will disappear and you should see you tabs set on the document ruler.

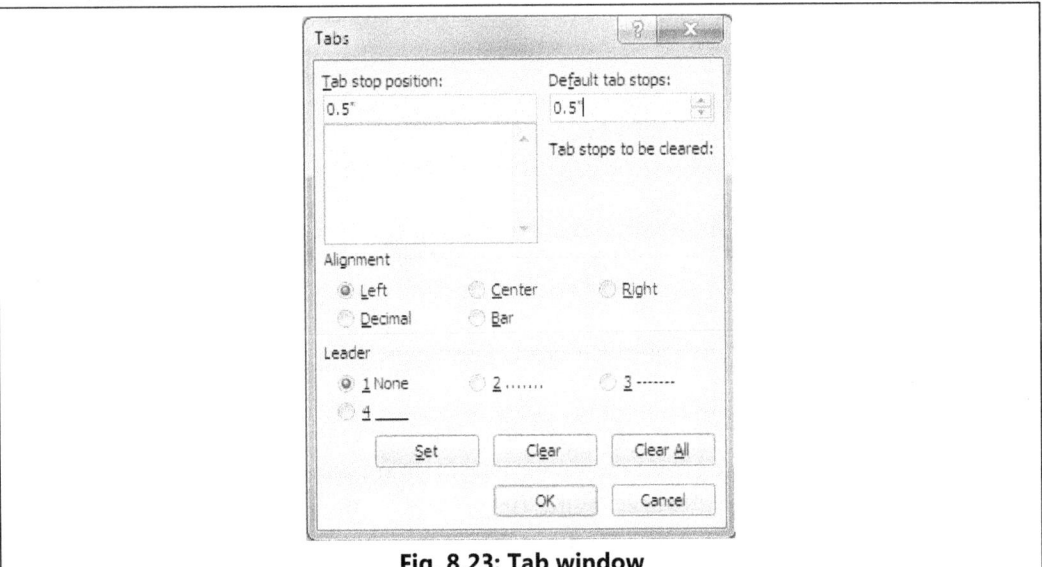

Fig. 8.23: Tab window

8.2.6 Spell Check

- As you type your document, red wavy lines will appear under any word that is spelled incorrectly. The fastest way to fix spelling errors is to:
  1. Put your cursor over the misspelled word and right click.
  2. A drop down box will appear with correct spellings of the word.
  3. Highlight and left click the word you want to replace the incorrect word with.

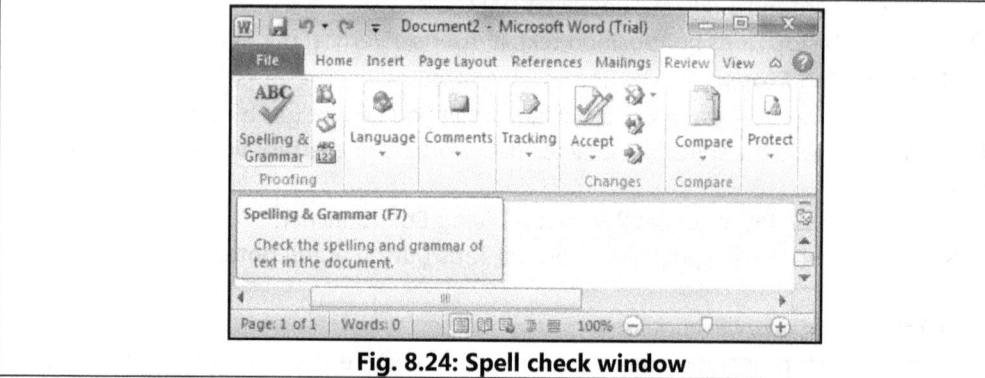

Fig. 8.24: Spell check window

- To complete a more comprehensive Spelling and Grammar check, you can use the Spelling and Grammar feature.
  1. Click on the Review tab
  2. Click on the Spelling & Grammar command (a blue check mark with ABC above it).
  3. A Spelling and Grammar box will appear.
  4. You can correct any Spelling or Grammar issue within the box.

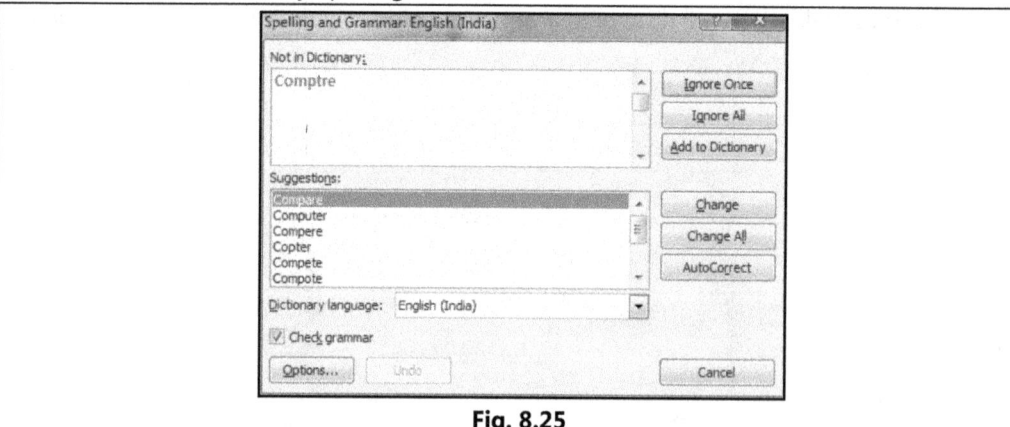

Fig. 8.25

8.2.7 Print Preview

- Print Preview automatically displays when you click on the Print tab. Whenever, you make a change to a print-related setting, the preview is automatically updated.
  1. Click the File tab, and then click Print. To go back to your document, click the File tab.
  2. A preview of your document automatically appears. To view each page, click the arrows below the preview.

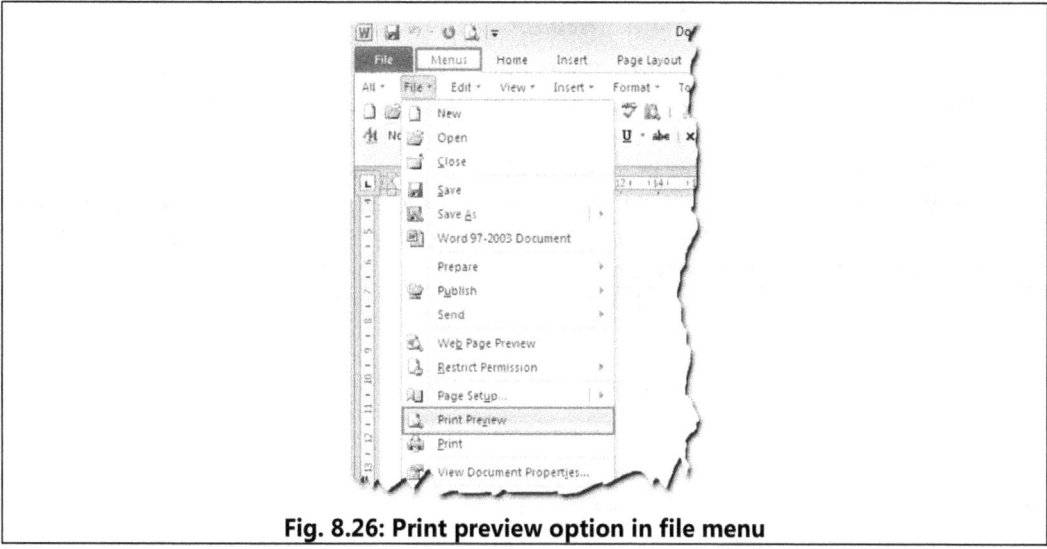

Fig. 8.26: Print preview option in file menu

- With Classic Menu for Word 2010 installed, you can click Menus tab to get back the classic style interface. It is so fast to get the Print Preview button in the toolbars. The following picture shows its position as clear as possible.

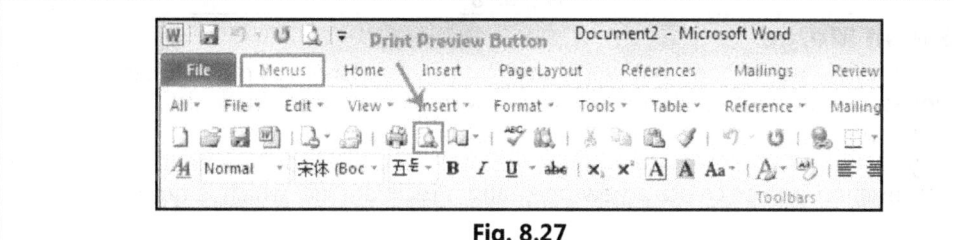

Fig. 8.27

8.2.8 Template

- Word 2010 allows you to apply built-in templates from a wide selection of popular Word templates, including resumes, agendas, business cards and faxes.
- To find and apply a template in Word, do the following:
  1. On the File tab, click New.
  2. Under Available Templates, do one of the following:
     o To use one of the built-in templates, click Sample Templates, click the template that you want and then click Create.
     o To reuse a template that you have recently used, click Recent Templates, click the template that you want and then click Create.
     o To find a template on Office.com, under Office.com Templates, click the template category that you want, click the template that you want and click Download to download the template from Office.com to you computer.
  3. Once, you have selected your template you can modify it in any way to create the document you want.

8.2.9 Colours
- When you will change the **Word page background color** through following process then it will only be affective for that specific Word document, it does not change the default Word background color which is normally set to white.

Change Page Background Color in Word 2010:
- Simply open Word document and navigate to "Page Layout" menu. Click "Page Color" button and rollover different colors available in list for preview and click on your desired one to **change background color**.

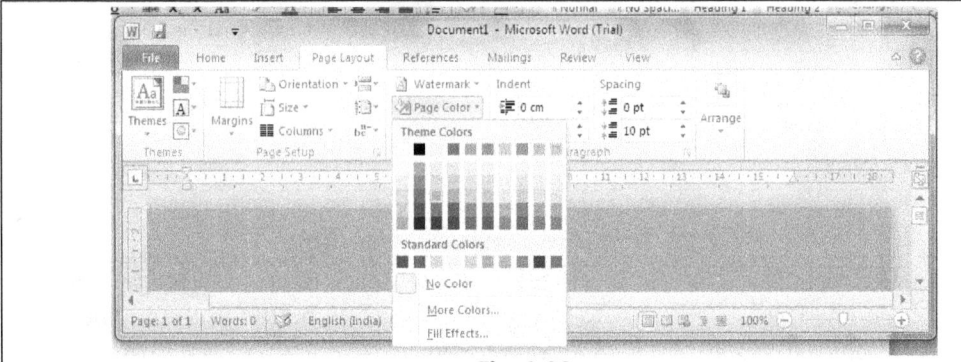

Fig. 8.28

8.2.10 Mail Merge
- Mail merge is a useful tool that will allow you to easily produce multiple letters, labels, envelopes, name tags and more using information stored in a list, database, or spreadsheet.
- When you are performing a Mail Merge, you will need a Word document (you can start with an existing one or create a new one), and a recipient list, which is typically an Excel workbook.
- Follow the following steps for mail merge;
    1. Open an existing Word document, or create a new one.
    2. Click the Mailings tab.
    3. Click the Start Mail Merge command.
    4. Select Step by Step Mail Merge Wizard.

Fig. 8.29: Selecting step by step mail merge wizard

- The Mail Merge task pane appears and will guide you through the six main steps to complete a mail merge.
- The following is an example of how to create a form letter and merge the letter with a recipient list.

  Step 1: Choose the type of document you wish to create. In this example, we select Letters.

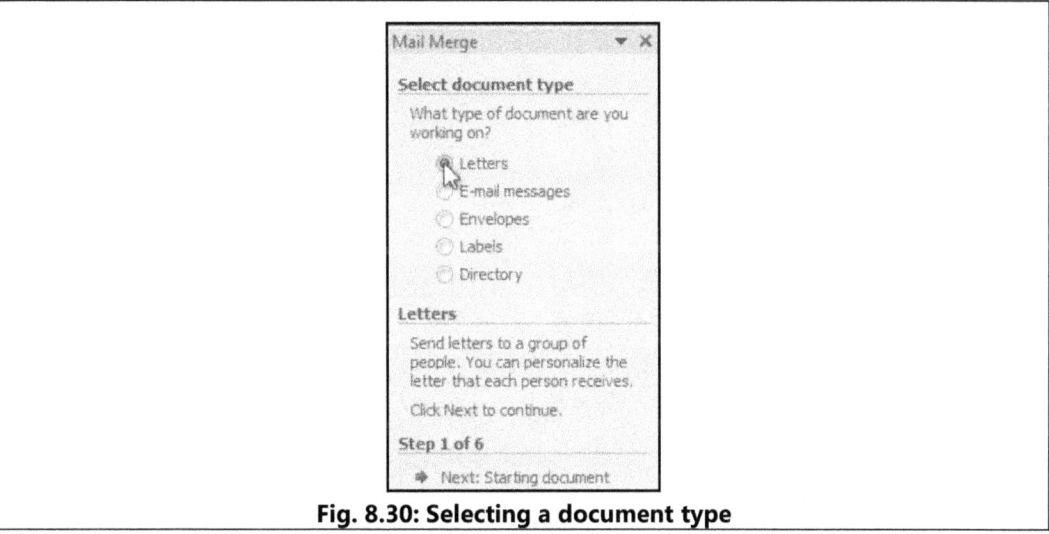

Fig. 8.30: Selecting a document type

Click Next: Starting document to move to Step 2.

Step 2: Select Use the current document.

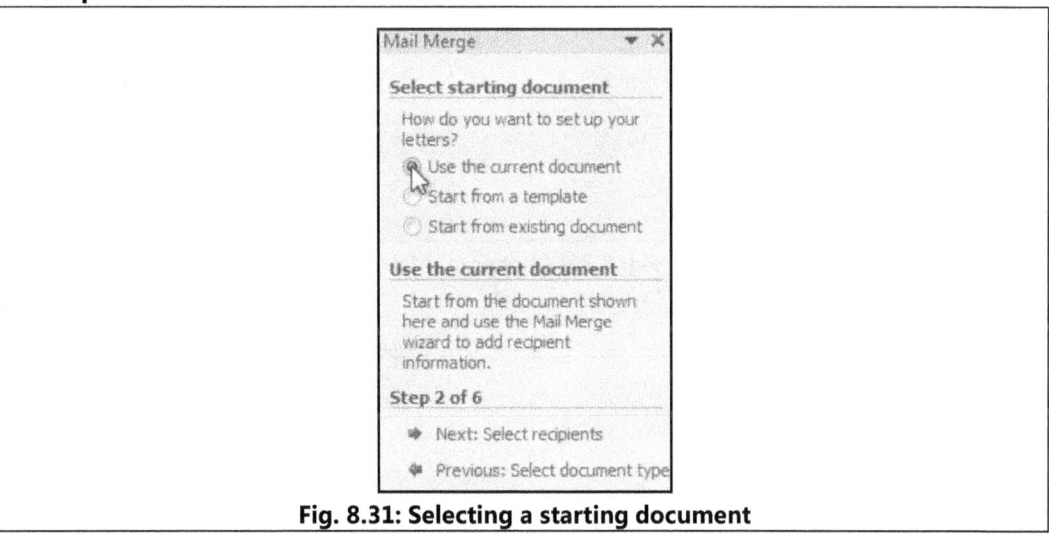

Fig. 8.31: Selecting a starting document

Click Next: Select recipients to move to Step 3.

Step 3: Now you will need an address list so that Word can automatically place each address into the document. The list can be in an existing file, such as an Excel workbook, or you can type a new address list from within the Mail Merge Wizard.

(i) From the Mail Merge task pane, select Use an existing list and then click Browse.

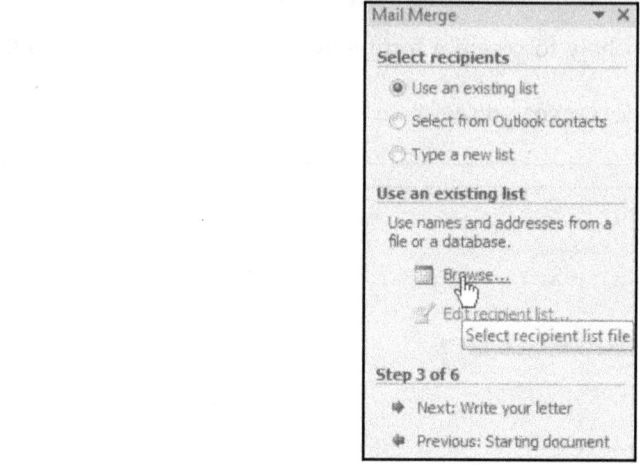

Fig. 8.32: Browsing for a data source

(ii) Locate your file in the dialog box (you may have to navigate to a different folder) and click Open.

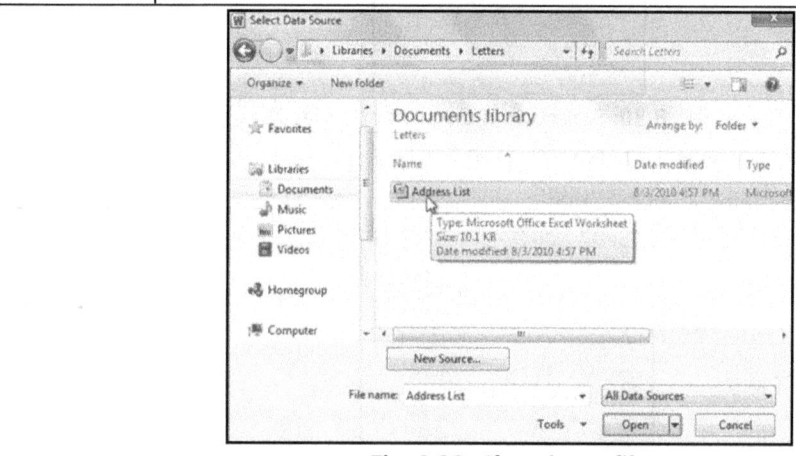

Fig. 8.33: Choosing a file

(iii) If the address list is in an Excel workbook, select the worksheet that contains the list and click OK.

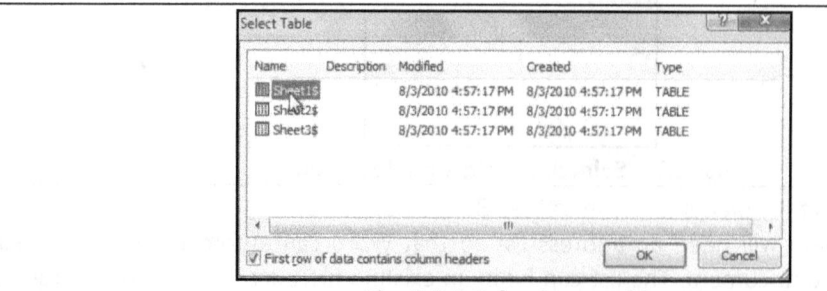

Fig. 8.34: Selecting a table

(iv) In the Mail Merge Recipients dialog box, you can check or uncheck each recipient to control which ones are used in the mail merge. When you are done, click OK to close the dialog box.

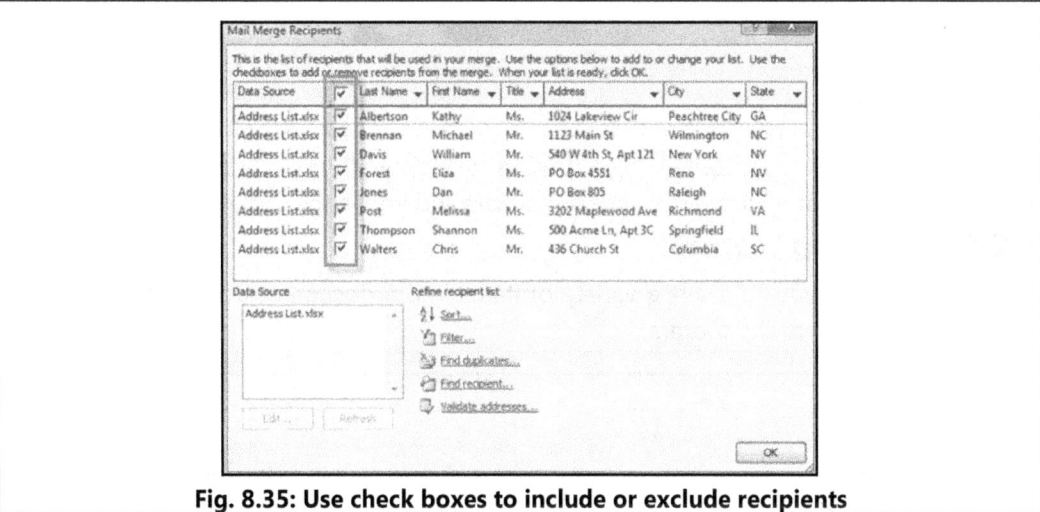

Fig. 8.35: Use check boxes to include or exclude recipients

(v) From the Mail Merge task pane, click Next: Write your letter to move to Step 4.

8.2.11 AutoText

- Classic Menu for Office brings back classic view into Ribbon of Office with familiar drop down menus and toolbar.
    1. Click the Menus tab;
    2. Click the Insert drop down menu;
    3. Click the Quick Parts item;
    4. Then you will view the AutoText sub-item.

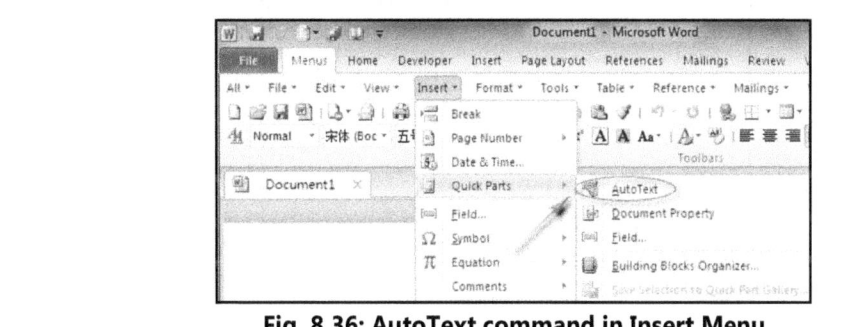

Fig. 8.36: AutoText command in Insert Menu

- Seek for AutoText on Ribbon (2010) if you do not have Classic Menu for Office as:
    1. Click the Insert tab;
    2. Go to Text group;
    3. Click the Quick Parts button;
    4. Then we will view the AutoText from Quick Parts button drop down list.

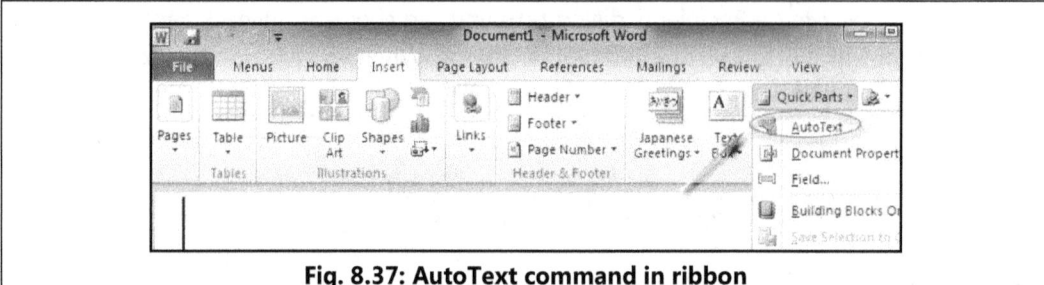

Fig. 8.37: AutoText command in ribbon

- The AutoText feature saves you time if you type and retype the same text.

8.2.12 Inserting Picture

- This tab allows you to insert a variety of items into a document from pictures, clip art, tables and headers and footers.

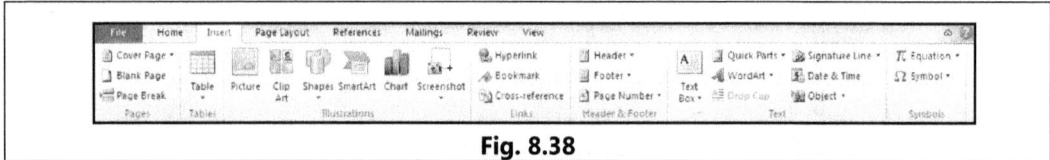

Fig. 8.38

Insert Picture/Clip Art:

- Pictures and clip art can be inserted or copied into a document from many different sources, including downloaded from a clip art Web site provider, copied from a Web page, or inserted from a folder where you save pictures.

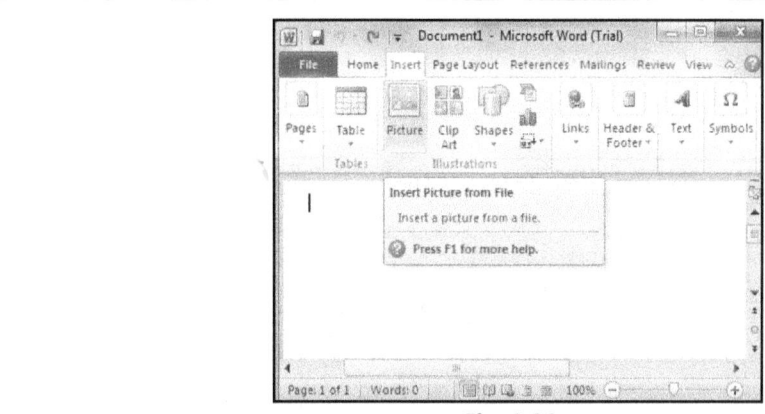

Fig. 3.39

1. **Insert Picture from Web:**
   (i) Open the document.
   (ii) From the Web page, drag the picture into the Word document.
2. **Insert Picture from File:**
- To insert a picture saved in your computer, insert it by following these steps:
   (i) Click where you want to insert the picture in your document.

(ii) On the insert tab, in the illustrations group, click Picture.

(iii) Locate the picture that you want to insert. For example, you might have a picture file located in My Documents.

(iv) Double-click the picture that you want to insert and it will appear in your document.

3. Insert Clip Art:
   (i) On the Insert tab, in the Illustrations group, click Clip Art.
   (ii) A Clip Art task pane will appear on the right of your screen, in the Search for box, type a word or phrase that describes the clip art that you want.
   (iii) Click Go.
   (iv) In the list of results, double click on the clip art to insert it into your document.

4. Inserting Shapes:
- You can add one shape to your file or combine multiple shapes to make a drawing or a more complex shape.
- Available shapes include lines, basic geometric shapes, arrows, equation shapes, flowchart shapes, stars, banners, and callouts.
- After you add one or more shapes, you can add text, bullets, numbering, and Quick Styles to them.
   1. On the Insert tab, in the Illustrations group, click Shapes.
   2. A drop down menu will appear, click the shape that you want.
   3. Click anywhere in the document, and then drag to place the shape.

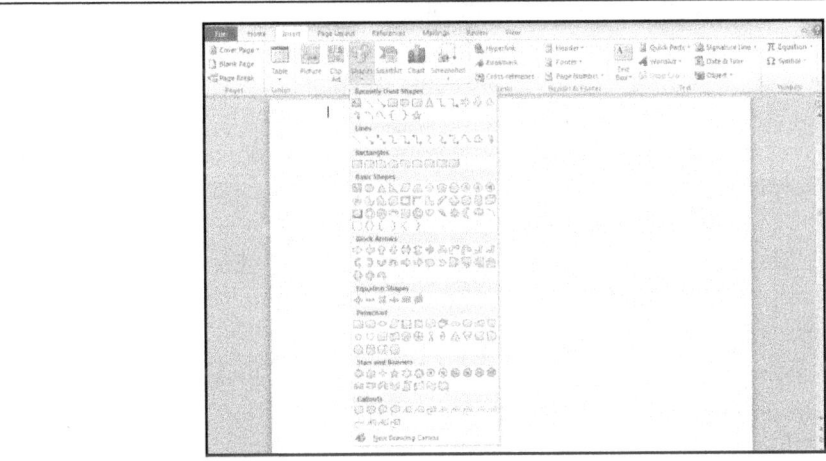

Fig. 8.40

5. Insert Text to Shapes:
- Once, you have added a shape, you may want to add text inside the shape. All you have to do is click on the inside of the shape and start typing.

8.2.13 WordArt
- WordArt can be used to add special text effects to your document. For example, you can stretch a title, skew text, make text fit a preset shape, or apply a gradient fill.

- This WordArt becomes an object that you can move or position in your document to add decoration or emphasis. You can modify or add to the text in an existing WordArt object whenever you want.
- To add WordArt to text in your document, complete the following steps:
  1. On the Insert tab, in the Text group, click WordArt.
  2. A Drop down menu will appear, click the WordArt style that you want.
  3. A Text Box will appear with the words" Enter your text here", Enter your text.

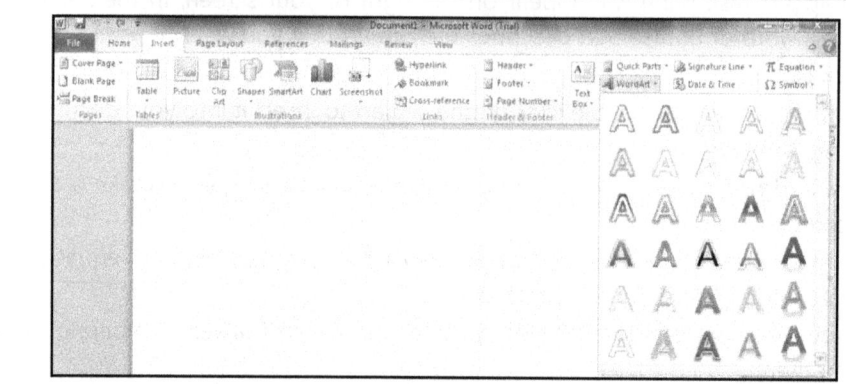

Fig. 8.41

8.3 MX-Excel

- Excel is a spreadsheet program in the Microsoft Office system.
- You can use Excel to create and format workbooks (a collection of spreadsheets) in order to analyze data and make more informed business decisions. Specifically, you can use Excel to track data, build models for analyzing data, write formulas to perform calculations on that data, pivot the data in numerous ways, and present data in a variety of professional looking charts.
- Common scenarios for using Excel include:
  1. **Accounting:** You can use the powerful calculation features of Excel in many financial accounting statements - for example, a cash flow statement, income statement, or profit and loss statement.
  2. **Budgeting:** Whether your needs are personal or business related, you can create any type of budget in Excel - for example, a marketing budget plan, an event budget, or a retirement budget.
  3. **Billing and sales:** Excel is also useful for managing billing and sales data, and you can easily create the forms that you need - for example, sales invoices, packing slips, or purchase orders.
  4. **Reporting:** You can create various types of reports in Excel that reflect your data analysis or summarize your data - for example, reports that measure project performance, show variance between projected and actual results, or reports that you can use to forecast data.

5. **Planning:** Excel is a great tool for creating professional plans or useful planners - for example, a weekly class plan, a marketing research plan, a year-end tax plan, or planners that help you organize weekly meals, parties, or vacations.
6. **Tracking:** You can use Excel to keep track of data in a time sheet or list - for example, a time sheet for tracking work, or an inventory list that keeps track of equipment.
7. **Using calendars:** Because of its grid-like workspace, Excel lends itself well to creating any type of calendar - for example, an academic calendar to keep track of activities during the school year, or a fiscal year calendar to track business events and milestones.

8.3.1 Introduction to Excel

- Microsoft Excel is one of the most popular spreadsheet applications that helps you manage data, create visually persuasive charts, and thought-provoking graphs.
- Excel is supported by both Mac and PC platforms.
- Microsoft Excel can also be used to balance a checkbook, create an expense report, build formulas, and edit them.
- Fig. 8.42 shows Excel 2010 Screen.

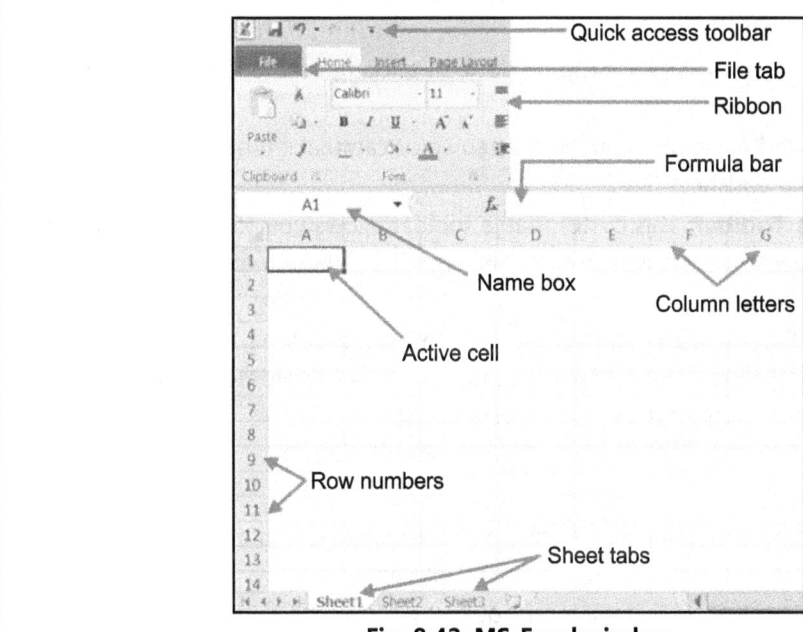

Fig. 8.42: MS-Excel window

- Various parts of Excel 2010 screen are given below:
    1. **Active Cell:** The active cell is recognized by its black outline. Data is always entered into the active cell. Different cells can be made active by clicking on them with the mouse or by using the arrow keys on the keyboard.
    2. **File Tab:** The File tab is new to Excel 2010 and it is a replacement for the Office Button in Excel 2007 which was a replacement for the file menu in earlier versions of Excel.

Like the old file menu, the File tab options are mostly related to file management such as opening new or existing worksheet files, saving, printing, and a new feature (saving and sending Excel files in PDF format).

3. **Formula Bar:** Located above the worksheet, this area displays the contents of the active cell. It can also be used for entering or editing data and formulas.

4. **Name Box:** Located next to the formula bar, the Name Box displays the cell reference or the name of the active cell.

5. **Column Letters:** Columns run vertically on a worksheet and each one is identified by a letter in the column header.

6. **Row Numbers:** Rows run horizontally in a worksheet and are identified by a number in the row header. Together a column letter and a row number create a cell reference. Each cell in the worksheet can be identified by this combination of letters and numbers such as A1, F456, or AA34.

7. **Sheet Tabs:** By default there are three worksheets in an Excel file.

   The tab at the bottom of a worksheet tells us the name of the worksheet - such as Sheet1, Sheet2, Sheet3 etc.

   Switching between worksheets can be done by clicking on the tab of the sheet to be accessed.

   Renaming a worksheet or changing the tab color can make it easier to keep track of data in large spreadsheet files.

8. **Quick Access Toolbar:** This customizable toolbar allows you to add frequently used commands. Click on the down arrow at the end of the toolbar to display the toolbar's options.

9. **Ribbon:** The Ribbon is the strip of buttons and icons located above the work area. The Ribbon is organized into a series of tabs - such as File, Home, and Formulas. Each tab contains a number of related features and options.

Types of Ribbon:

(i) Home Tab:

- This is one of the most common tabs (ribbon) used in Excel. You are able to format the text in your document, cut, copy, and paste information.
- Change the alignment of your data, insert, delete, and format cells. The Home Tab also allows you to change the number of your data (i.e. currency, time, date).

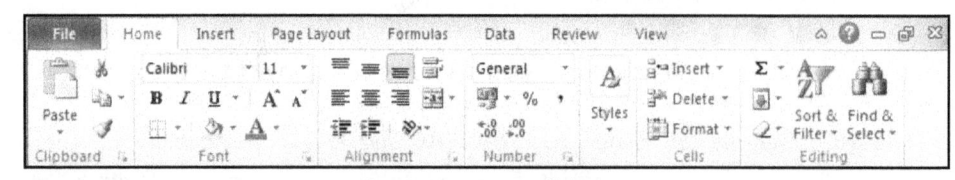

Fig. 8.43: Home ribbon

(ii) Insert Tab:

- This tab is mainly used for inserting visuals and graphics into your document. There are various different things that can be inserted from this tab such as pictures, clip art, charts, links, headers and footers, and word art.

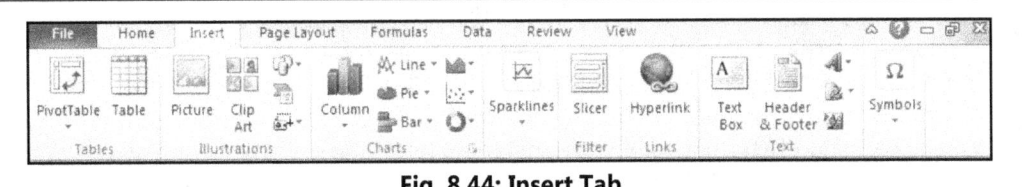

Fig. 8.44: Insert Tab

(iii) Page Layout Tab:

- Here, you are able to add margins, themes to your document, change the orientation, page breaks, and titles. The scale fit of your document is also included as a feature within this tab, if needed.

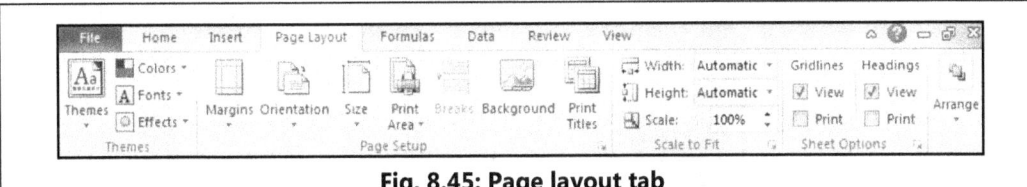

Fig. 8.45: Page layout tab

Formatting in Excel:

1. Working with cells:

- Cells are an important part of any project being used in Microsoft Excel.
- Cells hold all of the data that is being used to create the spreadsheet or workbook.
- To enter data into a cell you simply click once inside of the desired cell, a black border will appear around the cell (Fig. 8.45). This border indicates that it is a selected cell. You may then begin typing in the data for that cell.

Fig. 8.46: Entering data

2. Cut, Copy, and Paste:

- You can use the Cut, Copy and Paste features of Excel to change the data within your spreadsheet, to move data from other spreadsheets into new spreadsheets, and to save yourself the time of re-entering information in a spreadsheet.
- Cut will actually remove the selection from the original location and allow it to be placed somewhere else.
- Copy allows you to leave the original selection where it is and insert a copy elsewhere.
- Paste is used to insert data that has been cut or copied.

To Cut or Copy:
- Highlight the data or text by selecting the cells that they are held within.
- Go to the Home Tab → Copy (CTRL + C) or Home Tab → Cut (CTRL + X).
- Click the location where the information should be placed.
- Go to Home Tab → Paste (CTRL + V) to be able to paste your information.

3. Formatting Cells:
- There are various different options that can be changed to format the spreadsheets cells differently.
- When changing the format within cells you must select the cells that you wish to format.
- To get to the Format Cells dialog box select the cells you wish to change then go to Home Tab → Format → Format Cells. A box will appear on the screen with six different tab options (Fig. 3.47). Explanations of the basic options in the format dialog box are bulleted below.

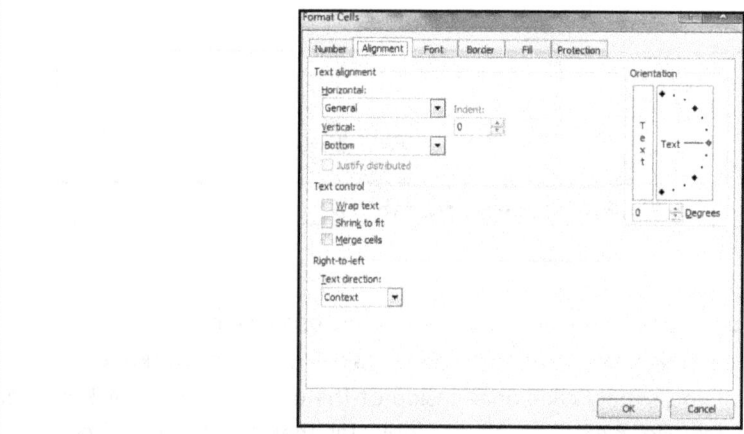

Fig. 8.47: Formatting Cells

(i) **Number:** Allows you to change the measurement in which your data is used.

(ii) **Alignment:** This allows you to change the horizontal and vertical alignment of your text within each cell. You can also change the orientation of the text within the cells and the control of the text within the cells as well.

(iii) **Font:** Gives the option to change the size, style, color, and effects.

(iv) **Border:** Gives the option to change the design of the border around or through the cells.

4. Formatting Rows and Columns:
- When formatting rows and columns you can change the height, choose for your information to autofit to the cells, hide information within a row or column, un-hide the information.
- To format a row or column go to Home Tab → Row Height (or Column Height), then choose which height you are going to use, (Fig. 3.48).
- The cell or cells that are going to be formatted need to be selected before doing this. When changing the row or column visibility (hidden, un-hidden) or autofit, you will go to the Home Tab and click Format. The drop down menu will show these options.

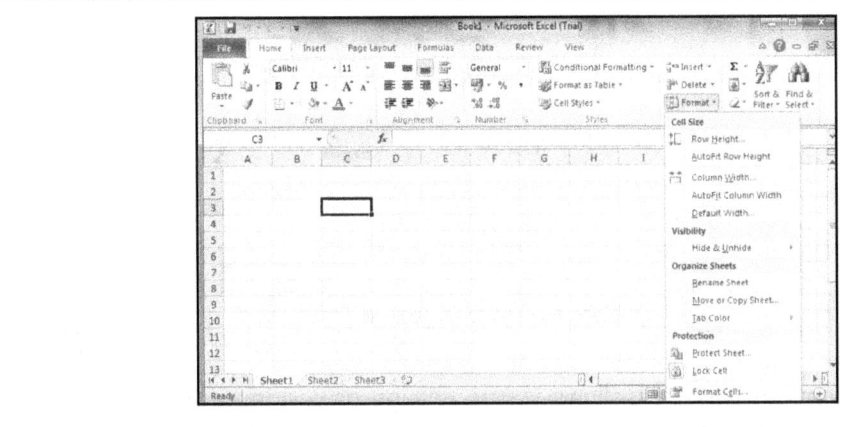

Fig. 8.48: Formatting rows and columns height

5. **Adding Rows and Columns:**
- When adding a row or column you are inserting a blank row or column next to your already entered data. Before you can add a Row you are going to have to select the row that you wish for your new row to be placed, (Rows are on the left hand side of the spreadsheet).
- Once, the row is selected it is going to highlight the entire row that you chose. To insert the row you have to go to Home Tab → Insert → Insert Sheet Rows, (Fig. 8.49).
- The row will automatically be placed on the spreadsheet and any data that was selected in the original row will be moved down below the new row.

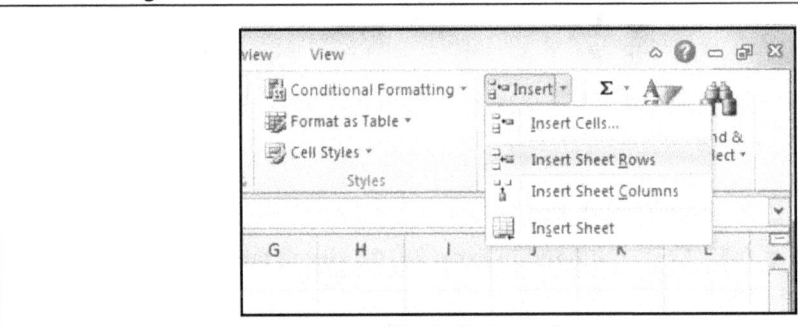

Fig. 8.49: Inserting rows

- Before you can add a Column you are going to have to select a column on the spreadsheet that is located in the area that you want to enter the new column. (Columns are on the top part of the spreadsheet.)
- Once, the column is selected it is going to highlight the entire row that you chose. To insert a column you have to go to Home Tab → Insert → Insert Sheet Column, (Fig. 8.50).
- The column will automatically be place on the spreadsheet and any data to the right of the new column will be moved more to the right.

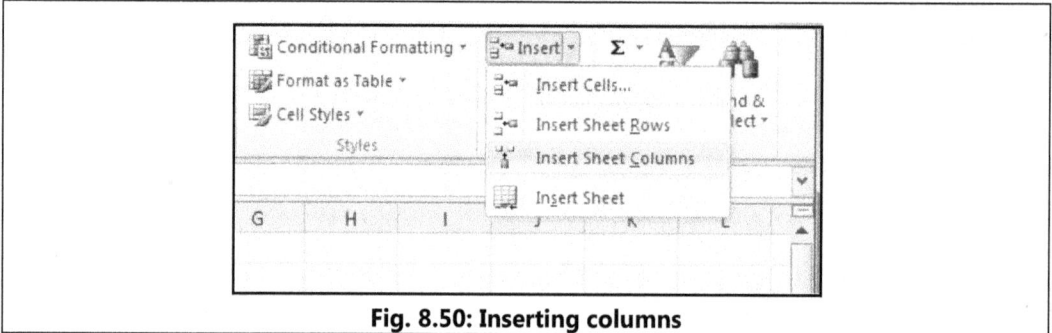

Fig. 8.50: Inserting columns

8.3.2 Sorting

- Sorting is a common task that allows you to change or customize the order of your spreadsheet data. For example, you could organize an office birthday list by employee, birthdate, or department, making it easier to find what you're looking for.
- Custom sorting takes it a step further, giving you the ability to sort multiple levels such as department first, then birthdate, to group birthdates by department, and more.

1. Sort button in Home tab:

- In the Editing group under Home tab, you will easily get the Sort & Filter button. Click the drop down button besides Sort & Filter button, and then you will get more sorting options: Sort A to Z, Sort Z to A, and Custom Sort.

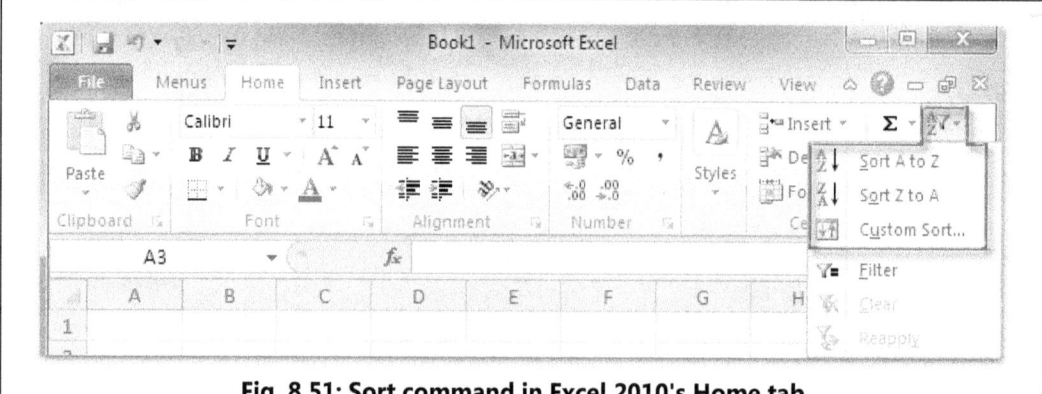

Fig. 8.51: Sort command in Excel 2010's Home tab

2. Sort button in Data tab:

- Go to the Sort & Filter group under Data tab, you will view three sorting button at ease: Sort A to Z button, Sort Z to A button, and Custom Sort button.

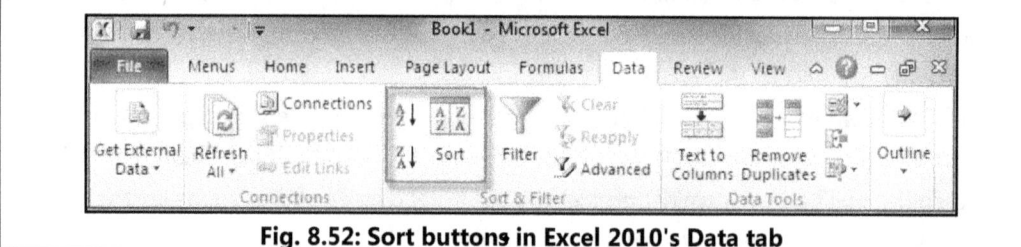

Fig. 8.52: Sort buttons in Excel 2010's Data tab

1. **To Sort in Alphabetical Order:**
   (i) Select a cell in the column to be sorted by. In this example, we will sort by Last Name.

	C	D	E
1	Last Name	Payment	T-Shirt Color
2	Olivera	1-Oct	White
3	Richards	4-Oct	Dark Red
4	Hanlon	5-Oct	Heather Grey
5	Means	5-Oct	Dark Red

   Fig. 8.53: Selecting a column to sort

   (ii) Select the Data tab, and locate the Sort and Filter group.
   (iii) Click the ascending command $\begin{smallmatrix}A\\Z\end{smallmatrix}\downarrow$ to Sort A to Z, or the descending command $\begin{smallmatrix}Z\\A\end{smallmatrix}\downarrow$ to Sort Z to A.
   (iv) The data in the spreadsheet will be organized alphabetically.

	C	D	E
1	Last Name	Payment	T-Shirt Color
2	Ackerman	1-Oct	Heather Grey
3	Albee	13-Oct	Heather Grey
4	Bell	11-Oct	Dark Red
5	Benson	11-Oct	White
6	Chen	5-Oct	Dark Red
7	Del Toro	13-Oct	White
8	Ellison	Pending	Dark Red
9	Flores	6-Oct	White
10	Hanlon	5-Oct	Heather Grey
11	Kelly	11-Oct	Dark Red
12	Kelly	11-Oct	Heather Grey
13	Lazar	14-Oct	White
14	MacDonald	Pending	Dark Red
15	Means	5-Oct	Dark Red
16	Naser	14-Oct	Dark Red
17	Nichols	6-Oct	Dark Red

   Fig. 8.54: Sorted by last name, from A to Z

   Sorting options can also be found on the Home tab, condensed into the **Sort & Filter** command.

2. To Sort in Numerical Order:

(i) Select a cell in the column you want to sort by.

	A	B	C
1	Homeroom #	First Name	Last Name
2	110	Kris	Ackerman
3	105	Nathan	Albee
4	220-B	Samantha	Bell
5	110	Matt	Benson

Fig. 8.55: Selecting a column to sort

(ii) From the Data tab, click the ascending command $^A_Z\downarrow$ to Sort Smallest to Largest, or the descending command $^Z_A\downarrow$ to Sort Largest to Smallest.

(iii) The data in the spreadsheet will be organized numerically.

	A	B	C
1	Homeroom #	First Name	Last Name
2	105	Nathan	Albee
3	105	Christiana	Chen
4	105	Sidney	Kelly
5	105	Derek	MacDonald
6	105	Melissa	White
7	105	Esther	Yaron
8	110	Kris	Ackerman
9	110	Matt	Benson
10	110	Gabriel	Del Toro
11	110	Regina	Olivera
12	135	Anisa	Naser
13	135	James	Panarello
14	135	Lia	Richards
15	135	Jordan	Weller
16	135	Chantal	Weller
17	135	Alex	Yuen

Fig. 8.56: Sorted by homeroom number, from smallest to largest

3. **To Sort by Date or Time:**
   (i) Select a cell in the column you want to sort by.

	D	E	F
1	Payment	T-Shirt Color	T-Shirt Size
2	13-Oct	Heather Grey	Medium
3	5-Oct	Dark Red	Medium
4	11-Oct	Dark Red	Medium
5	Pending	Dark Red	Large

Fig. 8.57: Selecting a column to sort

(ii) From the Data tab, click the ascending command $\overset{A}{\underset{Z}{\downarrow}}$ to Sort Oldest to Newest, or the descending command $\overset{Z}{\underset{A}{\downarrow}}$ to Sort Newest to Oldest.

(iii) The data in the spreadsheet will be organized by date or time.

	D	E	F
1	Payment	T-Shirt Color	T-Shirt Size
2	1-Oct	Heather Grey	Large
3	1-Oct	White	Large
4	4-Oct	Dark Red	X-Large
5	5-Oct	Dark Red	Medium
6	5-Oct	Heather Grey	Large
7	5-Oct	Dark Red	Medium
8	5-Oct	Heather Grey	X-Large
9	6-Oct	White	X-Large
10	6-Oct	Dark Red	X-Large
11	7-Oct	Heather Grey	Small
12	7-Oct	Dark Red	Small
13	7-Oct	Heather Grey	Small
14	7-Oct	Heather Grey	Small
15	11-Oct	Dark Red	Medium
16	11-Oct	White	Medium
17	11-Oct	Dark Red	Medium

Fig. 8.58: Sorted by payment date, from oldest to newest

8.3.3 Queries

- You know that the data is out there and you want to bring it into your homely Microsoft Excel. Here's how you do it.
    1. If you don't have a data source pointing to your database yet, create one.
    2. In Microsoft Excel choose Data, Import External Data and thenNew Database Query.

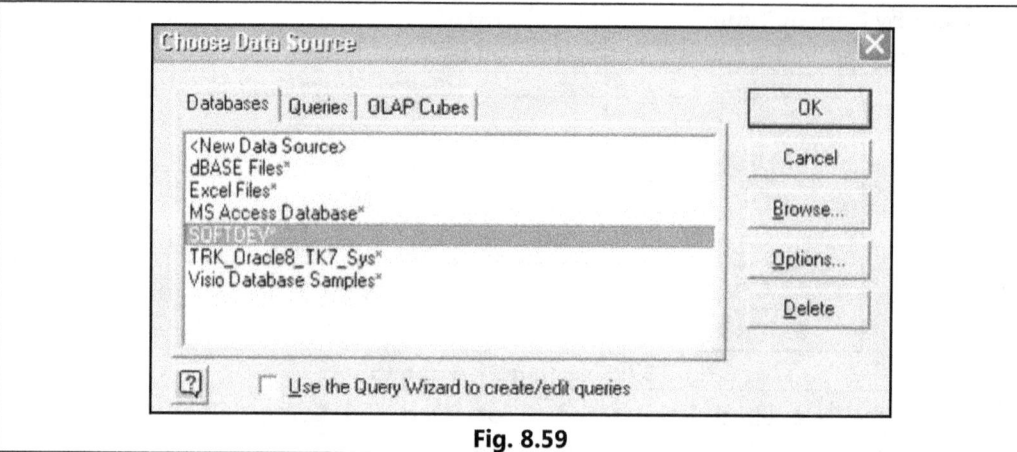

Fig. 8.59

1. Select your data source and click OK.
2. For interesting queries un-check Use the Query Wizard to create/edit queries.
3. Click OK and Microsoft Query appears.
4. Choose tables, fields, joins, filters, groups and sort orders as you like or write your SQL SELECT directly by clicking on SQL button (View, then SQL).
5. When you're done, click Return Data button on the toolbar (File, then Return Data to Microsoft Office Excel) and you're back in Excel with selected data.

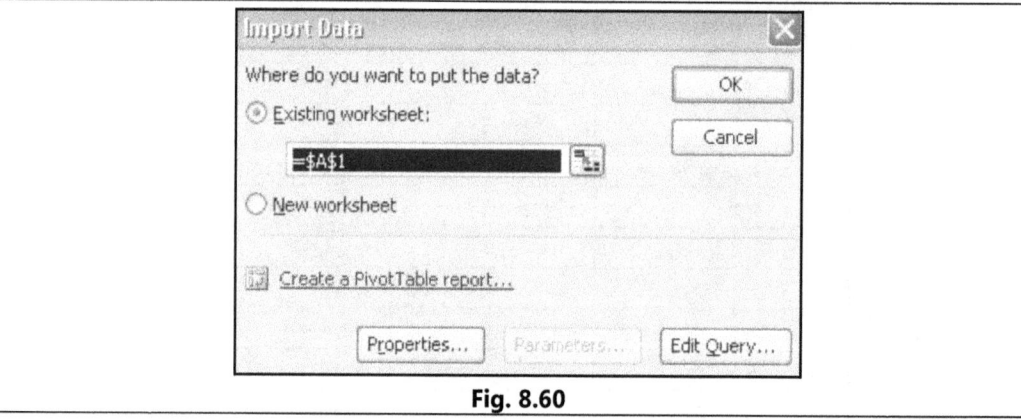

Fig. 8.60

- Just choose where exactly do you want that data. You can also choose Create a PivotTable report to have Microsoft Excel create a PivotTable report right away or click Properties, to tweak some settings on how this data is imported or Edit Query, to return to Microsoft Query.
- Now you can right click anywhere on the table and either Refresh the data, Edit Query or change the External Data Range Properties.

8.3.4 Graphs/Charts
- Charts are an important part to being able to create a visual for spreadsheet data.
- In order to create a chart within Excel the data that is going to be used for it needs to be entered already into the spreadsheet document.

- Once, the data is entered, the cells that are going to be used for the chart need to be highlighted so that the software knows what to include. Next, click on the Insert Tab that is located at the top of the screen, (Fig. 8.61).

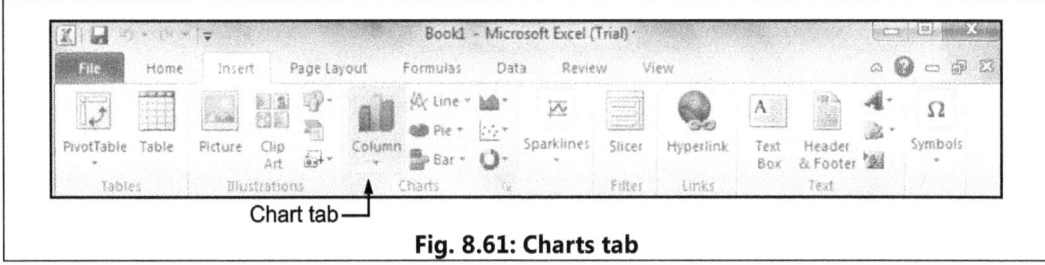

Fig. 8.61: Charts tab

- You may choose the chart that is desired by clicking the category of the chart you will use. Once, the category is chosen the charts will appear as small graphics within a drop down menu.
- To choose a particular chart just click on its icon and it will be placed within the spreadsheet you are working on. To move the chart to a page of its own, select the border of the chart and Right Click. This will bring up a drop down menu, navigate to the option that says Move Chart.
- This will bring up a dialog box that says Chart Location. From here you will need to select the circle next to As A New Sheet and name the sheet that will hold your chart. The chart will pop up larger in a separate sheet (Fig. 8.62), but in the same workbook as your entered data.

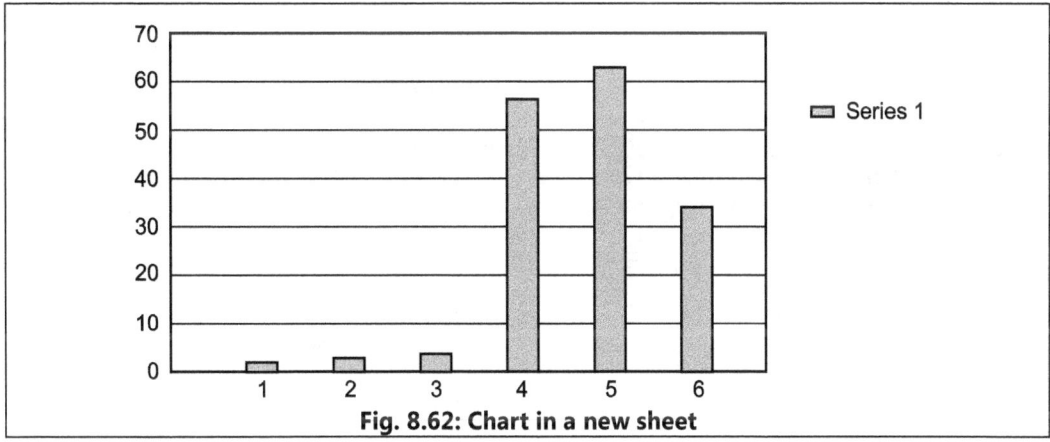

Fig. 8.62: Chart in a new sheet

Chart Design:
- There are various different features that you can change to make your chart more appealing. To be able to make these changes you will need to have the chart selected or be viewing the chart page that is within your workbook.
- Once you have done that the Design Tab will appear highlighted with various different options to format your graphic (Fig. 8.63).

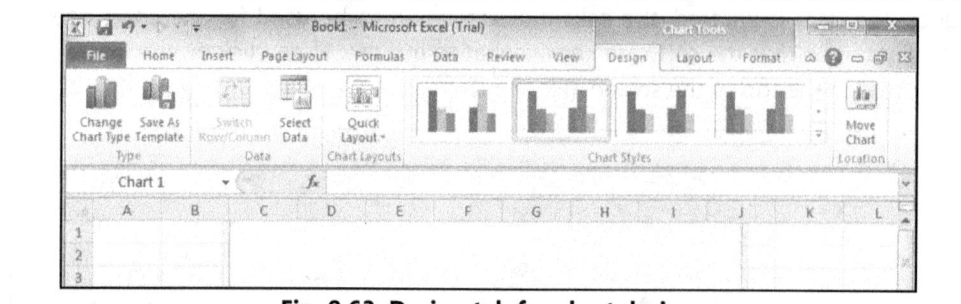

Fig. 8.63: Design tab for chart design

Pictures:
   (i) To insert Pictures: Go to the Insert Tab → Picture, a dialog box will appear and then you can select the desired picture from the location that is it stored (Fig. 8.64). The picture will be inserted directly onto your document, where you can change the size of it as desired.

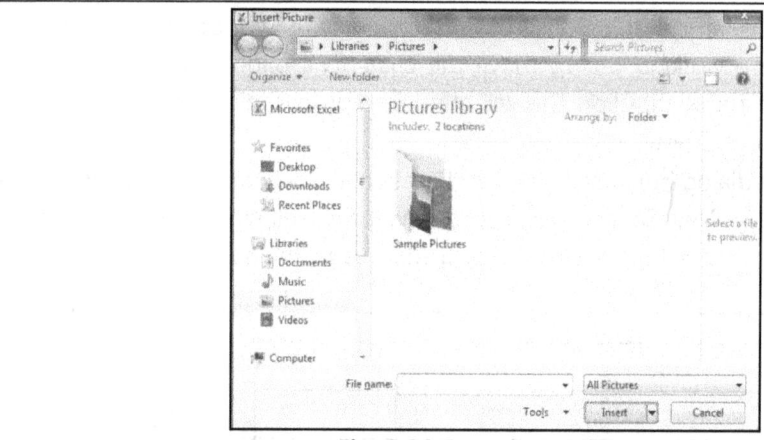

Fig. 8.64: Inserting a picture

   (ii) Inserting Clipart: To insert Clip Art you will need to go to the Insert Tab → Clip Art. A navigation pane will appear on the left hand side of the screen where you can search for words that pertain to the picture you are looking for.

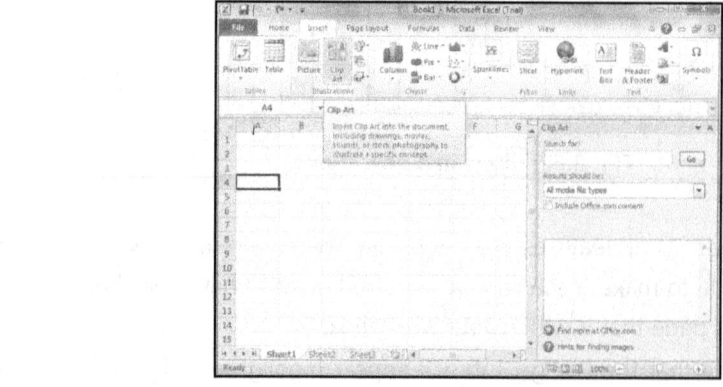

Fig. 8.65: Clip art

8.3.5 Formulas and Functions

- A formula is an expression which calculates the value of a cell. Functions are predefined formulas and are already available in Excel.
- You can specify mathematical relationship between the numbers using the formula. Formulas are used for simple addition, subtraction, multiplication and division as well as for complex calculations.
- Functions are built in formulas. The users have to provide cell references and addresses only. These are called arguments of the function and are given between the left and right parenthesis.
- A formula can have any or all of the following elements:
   - Must begin with the 'equal to' = sign.
   - Mathematical operators, such as + (for addition) and / (for division) and logical operators such as <, >.
   - References of cell (including named ranges and cells).
   - Text or Values.
   - Functions related to the worksheets, for example SUM or AVERAGE.

Inserting Formula:

- For example, cell A3 below contains a formula which adds the value of cell A2 to the value of cell A1.
- When you select a cell, Excel shows the value or formula of the cell in the formula bar.

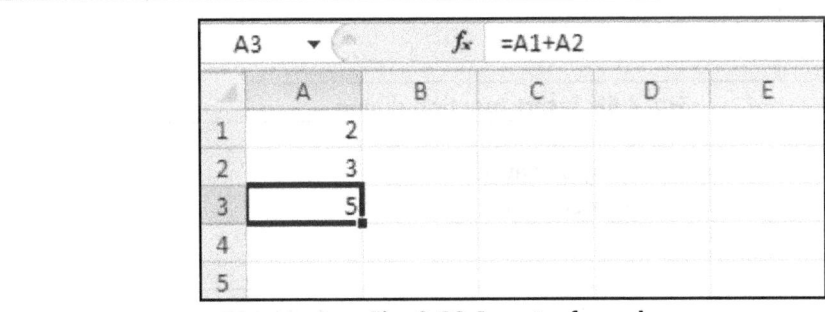

Fig. 8.66: Insert a formula

Inserting Function:

- Every function has the same structure. For example, SUM(A1:A4). The name of this function is SUM. The part between the brackets (arguments) means we give Excel the range A1:A4 as input. This function adds the values in cells A1, A2, A3 and A4. It's not easy to remember which function and which arguments to use for a specific task. Fortunately, the Insert Function feature in Excel helps you with this.
- To insert a function, execute the following steps.
    1. Select a cell.
    2. Click the Insert Function button.

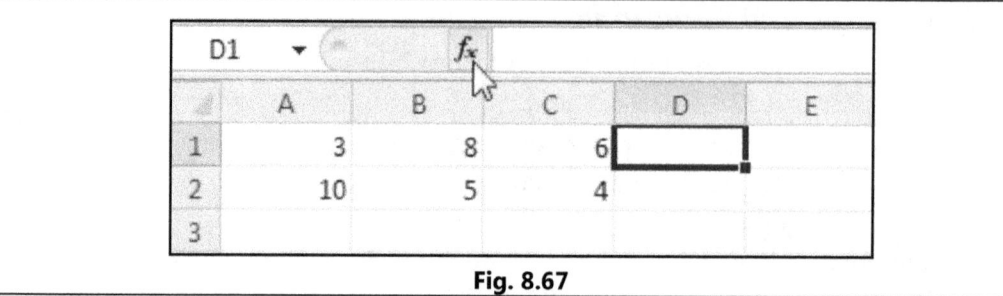

Fig. 8.67

The 'Insert Function' dialog box appears.

3. Search for a function or select a function from a category. For example, choose COUNTIF from the Statistical category.

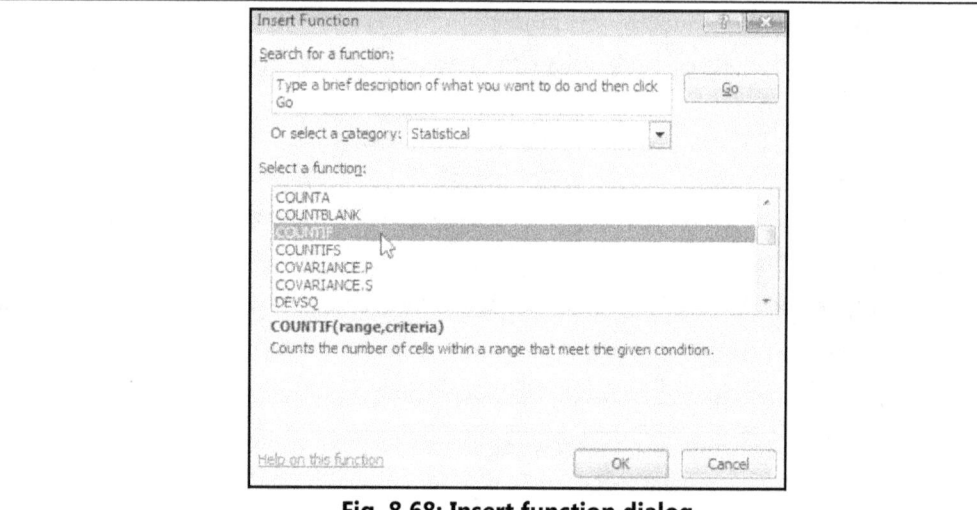

Fig. 8.68: Insert function dialog

4. Click OK.
   The 'Function Arguments' dialog box appears.
5. Click in the Range box and select the range A1:C2.
6. Click in the Criteria box and type >5.
7. Click OK.

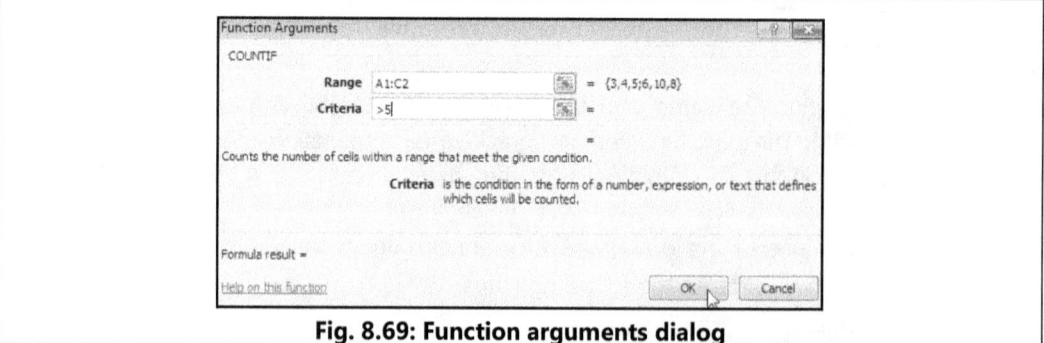

Fig. 8.69: Function arguments dialog

- **Output:** Excel counts the number of cells that are higher than 5.

Logical Functions

1. **If Function:** The IF function checks whether a condition is met, and returns one value if TRUE and another value if FALSE.

   Select cell C2 and enter the following function.

   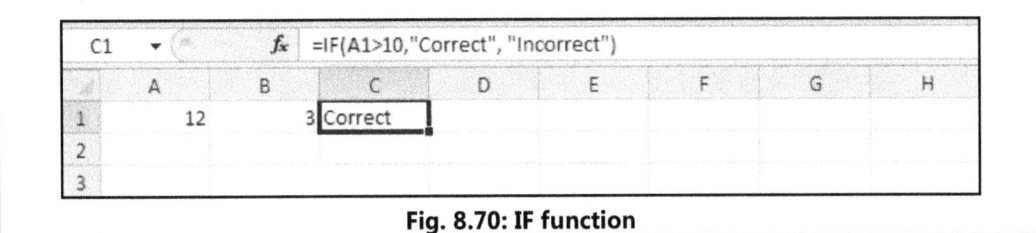

   Fig. 8.70: IF function

- The IF function returns Correct because the value in cell A1 is higher than 10.

2. **AND Function:** The AND function returns TRUE if all conditions are true and returns FALSE if any of the conditions are false.

   Select cell D2 and enter the following formula.

   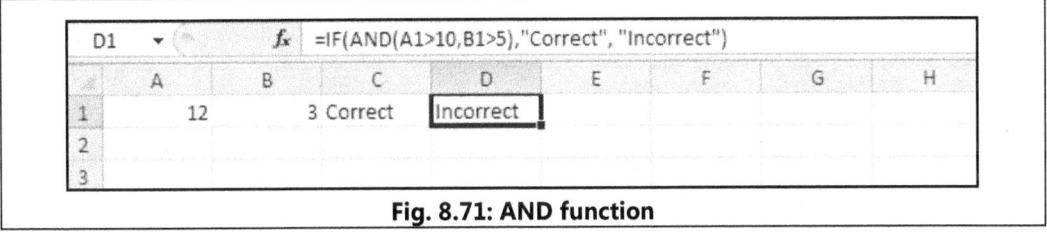

   Fig. 8.71: AND function

- The AND function returns FALSE because the value in cell B2 is not higher than 5. As a result the IF function returns Incorrect.

3. **OR Function:** The OR function returns TRUE if any of the conditions are TRUE and returns FALSE if all conditions are false.

   Select cell E2 and enter the following formula.

   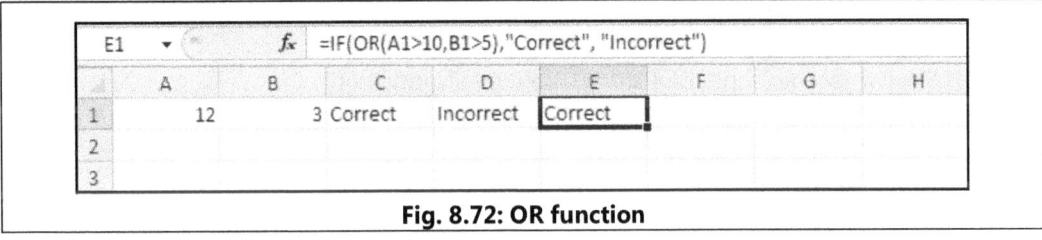

   Fig. 8.72: OR function

- The OR function returns TRUE because the value in cell A1 is higher than 10. As a result the IF function returns Correct.
- The AND and OR function can check up to 255 conditions.

Text Functions: Excel has many functions to offer when it comes to manipulating text strings.

1. **Join Strings:** We use the & operator to join strings.

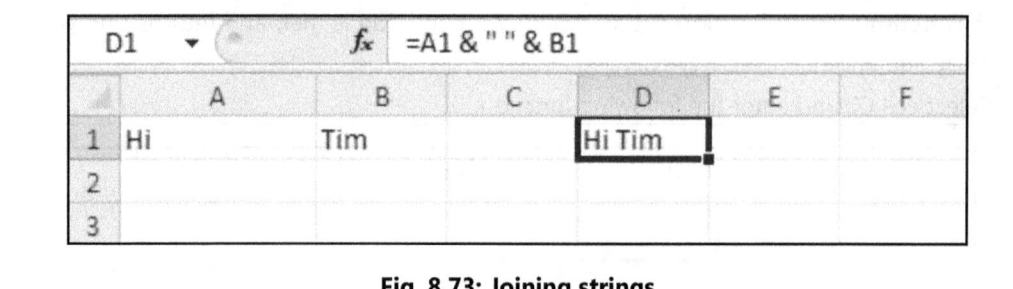

Fig. 8.73: Joining strings

2. **LEFT:** To extract the leftmost characters from a string, use the LEFT function.

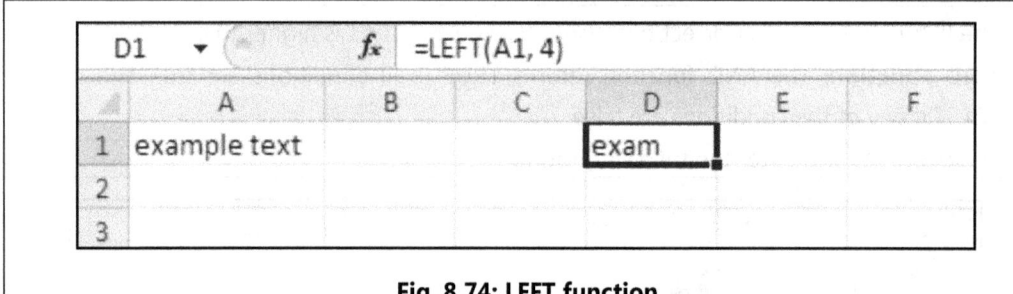

Fig. 8.74: LEFT function

3. **RIGHT:** To extract the rightmost characters from a string, use the RIGHT function.

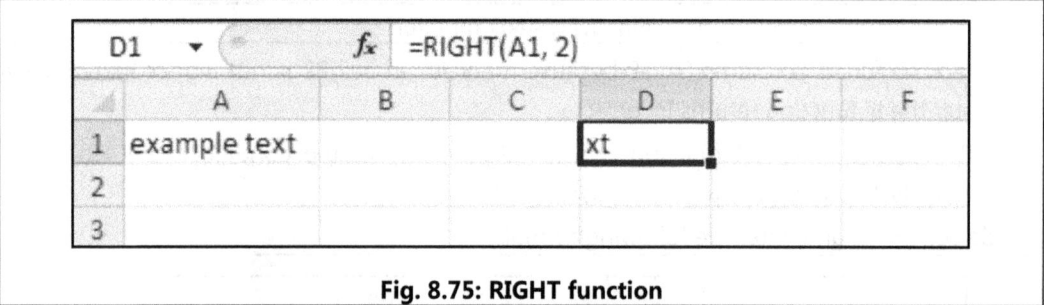

Fig. 8.75: RIGHT function

4. **LEN:** To get the length of a string, use the LEN function.

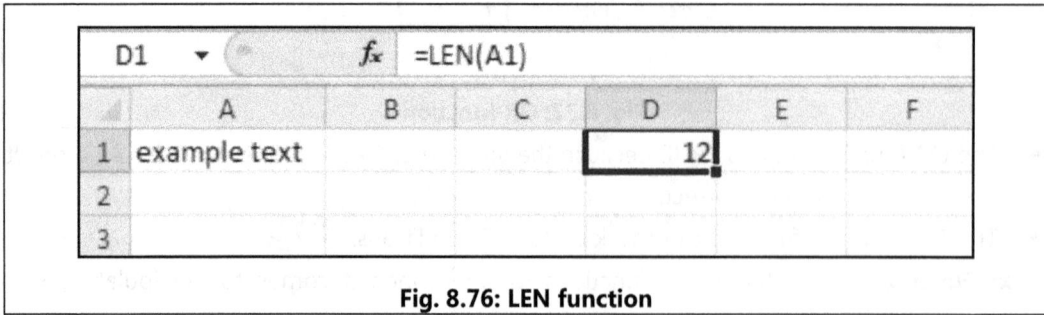

Fig. 8.76: LEN function

Note: space (position 8) included.

5. **FIND:** To find the position of a substring in a string, use the FIND function.

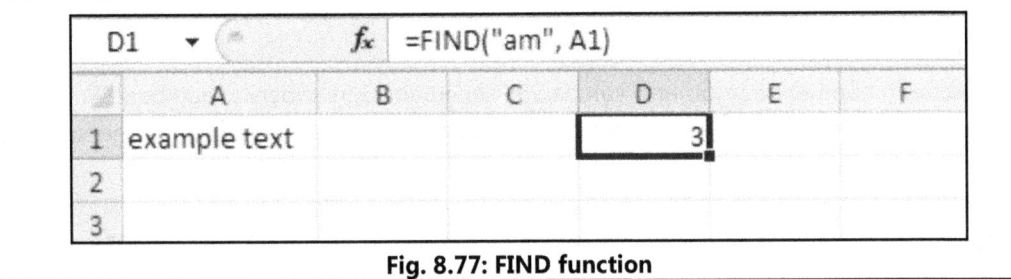

Fig. 8.77: FIND function

Note: string "am" found at position 3.

6. **MID:** To extract a substring, starting in the middle of a string, use the MID function.

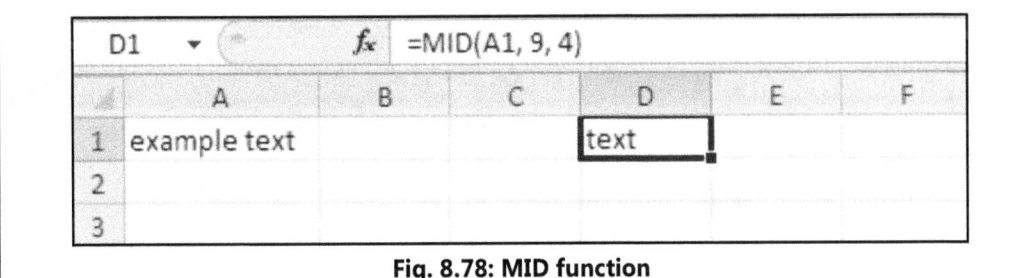

Fig. 8.78: MID function

Note: started at position 9 (t) with length 4.

7. **SUBSTITUTE:** To replace existing text with new text in a string, use the SUBSTITUTE function.

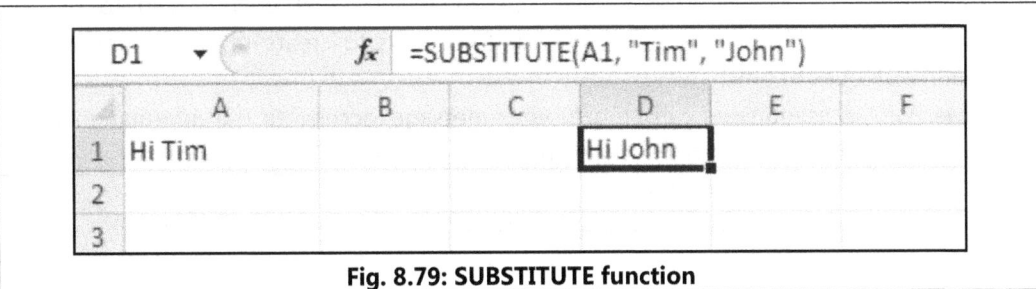

Fig. 8.79: SUBSTITUTE function

Other important functions in Excel:
1. **Sum:** This function adds all the numbers in a range of cells.
   Syntax: SUM(number1,number2, ...)
   Maximum number of arguments can be 255 i.e. number1, number2 ... number255. Sum function is having different forms. You can choose as per the requirement.
2. **SUMIF(range, criteria, sum_range):** This form of sum functions is used to add the cells with respective to a given criteria.
3. **Sum_range:** These are the actual cells to be added if their corresponding cells in range match criteria. In case the sum_range is avoided, then the cells in range are both evaluated by criteria and added if they match criteria.

4. **Average function:** It helps you to get the average of the numbers. It returns the average (arithmetic mean) of the arguments.
   Syntax: `AVERAGE(number, number2,...)`
   Maximum number of arguments can be 255 i.e. number1, number2 ... number255.
5. **Min function:** It helps you to get the minimum of the numbers. Returns the smallest number in a set of values.
   Syntax: `MIN(number1,number2,...)`
   Maximum number of arguments can be 255 i.e. number1, number2 ... number255.
6. **Max function:** It helps you to get the maximum of the numbers. Returns the largest number in a set of values.
   Syntax: `MAX(number1,number2,...)`
   Maximum number of arguments can be 255 i.e. number1, number2 ... number255.

8.4 MS-PowerPoint

- Microsoft PowerPoint is a software product used to perform computer based presentations.
- MS-PowerPoint is a presentation software.
- One way you can open Microsoft PowerPoint by: Clicking Start → (All) Programs → Microsoft Office → Microsoft Office PowerPoint 2010.
- Microsoft PowerPoint is the name of proprietary commercial presentation program.

8.4.1 Introduction to PowerPoint

- PowerPoint is a system in the Microsoft Office Suite that enables you to present information in office meetings, lectures and seminars to create maximum impact in a minimal amount of time.
- PowerPoint presentations can amplify your message, accelerate the information being absorbed and assist with comprehension enabling faster decision-making.

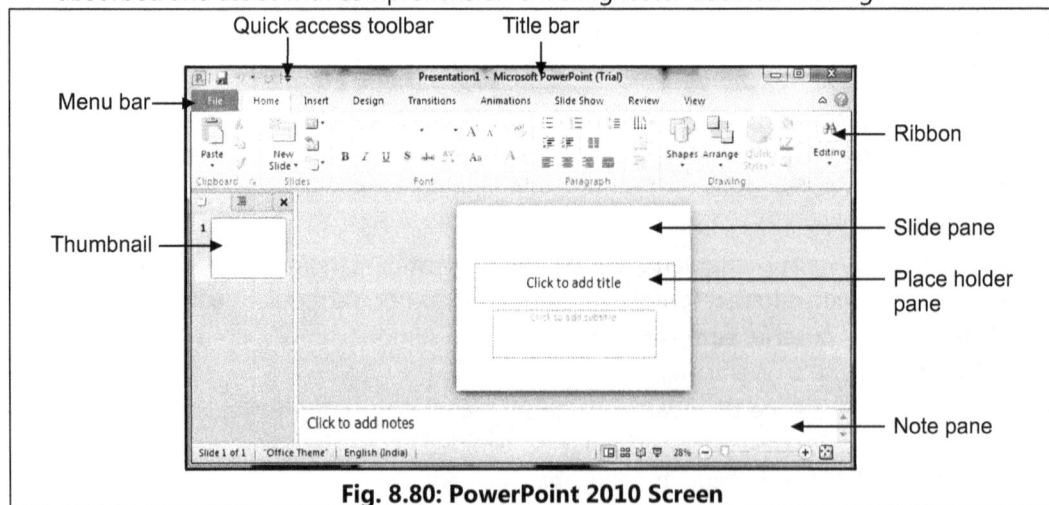

Fig. 8.80: PowerPoint 2010 Screen

Parts of the PowerPoint 2010 Screen:
- When you first open PowerPoint you will se what is called the Normal view.
- The slide pane is the big area in the middle. This is the area you will work into create your slides.
- On each slide, you will see various boxes with the dotted borders which are called placeholders. This is where you type your text. Placeholders can be customized to different sizes and can contain pictures, charts and other non-text items.
- On the left of the screen are thumbnail versions of the slides in your presentation; the slide you are working will be highlighted.
- The bottom area is the notes pane, this is where you type speaker notes that you can refer to when you present. You can also print speaker notes to use when presenting a slide show.
- For anyone new to PowerPoint, it is always a good practice to get accustomed to the parts of the screen.
    1. **File Tab:** The new File tab in the left corner of the ribbon, replaces the Office button. Many of the same features are present and some new features have been added.
    2. **Ribbon:** The ribbon replaces the toolbar in older versions of PowerPoint, prior to PowerPoint 2010.
    3. **Quick Access Toolbar:** This toolbar appears in the top left corner of the PowerPoint 2010 screen. This is a customizable toolbar, so that you may add icons for features that you use frequently.
    4. **Tabs on the Ribbon:** These tabs on the ribbon are headings for groups of tasks. These tabs look similar to the headings on the menus in older versions of PowerPoint.
    5. **Help Button:** This tiny question mark icon is how to access help for PowerPoint 2010.
    6. **Slides/Outline Pane:** The Slides/Outline pane is located on the left side of the window. The Slides pane shows thumbnail versions of each of the slides in the presentation. The Outline pane shows a text outline of all the information on the slides.
    7. **Notes:** The Notes section is a place for the speaker to jot down any hints or references for his presentation. Only the presenter will see these notes.
    8. **Status Bar:** The Status bar shows current aspects of the presentation, such as the current slide number and what design theme was used. A tiny Common tools toolbar gives quick access to features that the presenter would use often.

8.4.2 Creation of Slides
- When you open a new PowerPoint document you will only see one slide. In order to add more slides you need to create them, to do this you have a few options.
- Clicking on the top portion of the New Slide command, on the Home tab is the easiest method because a new slide will be added immediately. PowerPoint will automatically insert a Title and Content slide when using this method of adding slides.

- If you click the bottom part of the New Slide command, a box will appear and you will see a gallery of layouts for you to choose from which will be inserted after your previous slide once you click on your preferred slide option.

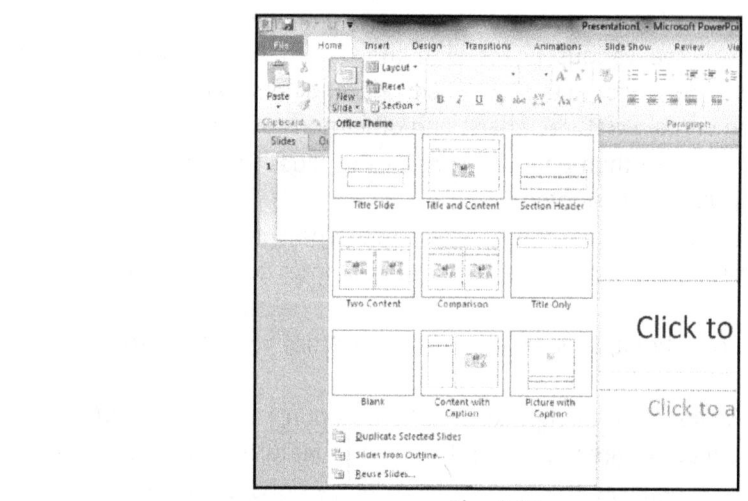

Fig. 8.81

1. Formatting Text:
- Many of your slides will require you to enter text in the placeholder boxes.
    (i) When typing text PowerPoint will automatically place the text into bulleted lists to make minor points under major points. PowerPoint will also automatically text fit the text reducing font size and line spacing to fit everything into the placeholder boxes.
    (ii) To change the text font, color and size use commands in the Font group.
    (iii) To change paragraph formatting such as bullet type, text indentation and line spacing use the commands in the Paragraph group.

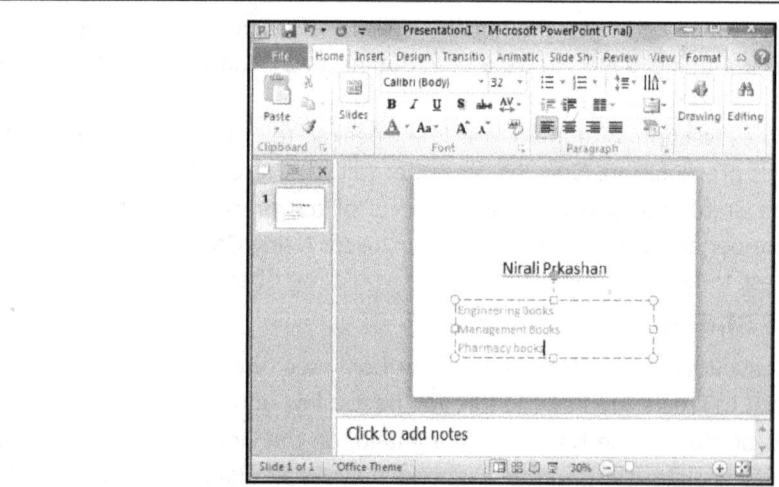

Fig. 8.82

2. Inserting Clip Art:

- If you would like to add an additional dimension to PowerPoint slide you can add Clip Art to your slides.
- Clip Art includes pictures, sounds and videos. There are two ways to initiate inserting Clip Art depending on where you would like the graphic to be located.
    - (i) The first method is to go to the Insert Ribbon and click on the Clip Art command. You can also click on the Audio and Video commands and opt to pick from the Clip Art gallery. The second method is to click on the Clip Art icon in a placeholder.
    - (ii) The Clip Art task pane will then open on the right. Type a keyword in the Search for box that suggests the type of clips you may want. Use the Results should be drop down to select the media type to search in then click Go.
    - (iii) Clips that fit the keyword will appear in the box below. Click on the clip that you would like on your slide and it will be automatically appear.

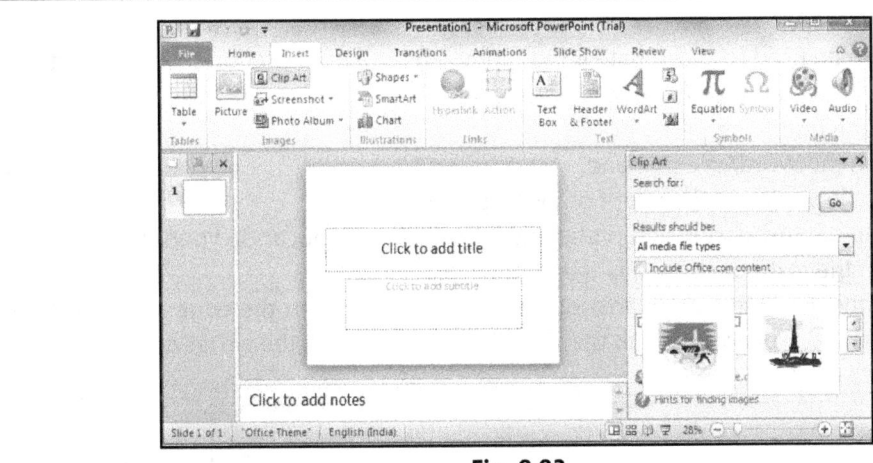

Fig. 8.83

3. Insert Shapes:

- Shapes can be used in PowerPoint as a graphic to enhance the presentation or to insert text into to add visual appeal to a slide.
- Follow the following steps for inserting shape to slide:
    - (i) Go to the Insert Tab.
    - (ii) Click on Shapes command.
    - (iii) A large selection of shapes will appear in a drop down menu.
    - (iv) Double click on the shape you want to insert then the shape will appear on the slide.
    - (iv) Move the shape to any area of the slide by clicking on the edge of the shape and dragging it. Expand or shrink the shape by clicking on the circles surrounding the shape and drag.

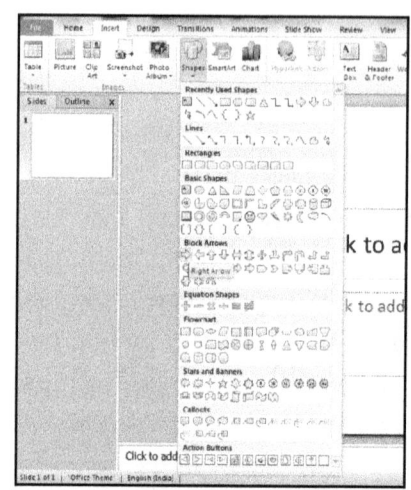

Fig. 8.84

4. Inserting WordArt:
- WordArt can be used to accentuate important words in a presentation such as the title.
- Follow the following steps for inserting WordArt:
    (i) Go to the Insert Tab.
    (ii) Click on the WordArt command.
    (ii) A drop down menu of text options will appear.
    (iv) Click on the text design you prefer and a text box will appear on your slide.
    (v) Click in the text box to modify the text.
    (vi) Move the WordArt to any area of the slide by clicking on the edge of the text and dragging it. Expand or shrink the WordArt by clicking on the circles surrounding the text and drag.

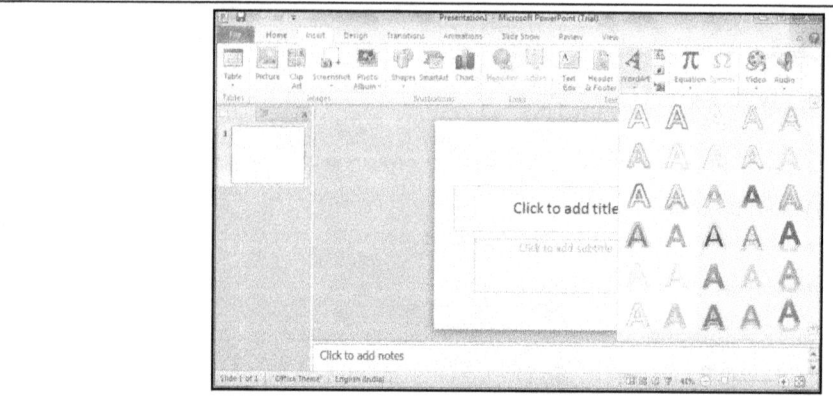

Fig. 8.85

5. Inserting Tables and Charts:
- Tables and Charts can be used to express data in a presentation. First, go to the Insert Tab.

- **To insert a chart:**
  (i) Click on the Chart command.
  (ii) An Insert Chart box will appear.
  (iii) Click on the chart you prefer.
  (iv) An Excel worksheet will open, enter the data in the Excel Document that you want displayed on the chart.

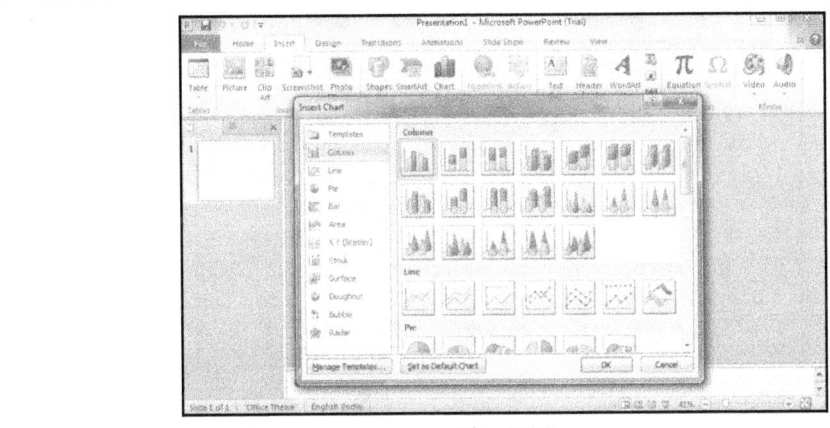

Fig. 8.86

- **To insert a Table:**
  (i) Click on the Table command.
  (ii) Highlight the number of cells you want in your table.
  (iii) Click for the table to appear on your slide.
  (iv) Click on each cell to enter the data you need displayed.

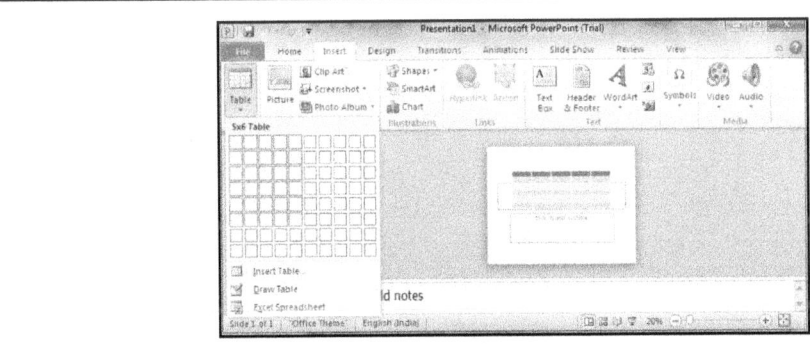

Fig. 8.87

8.4.3 Inserting Pictures

- Pictures are another way to include graphics into a PowerPoint presentation.
- Many people like using this feature to incorporate pictures from their personal collection to distinguish their presentation.

- Follow the following steps for inserting picture:
  1. Go to the Insert Tab.
  2. Click on the Picture command.
  3. A Insert Picture box will appear.
  4. Select the picture to insert using the folders on the left of the Insert Picture box.
  5. Click Open. The picture will appear on the slide.
  6. Move the picture to any area of the slide by clicking on the edge of the picture dragging it. Expand or shrink the picture by clicking on the circles surrounding the picture and drag.

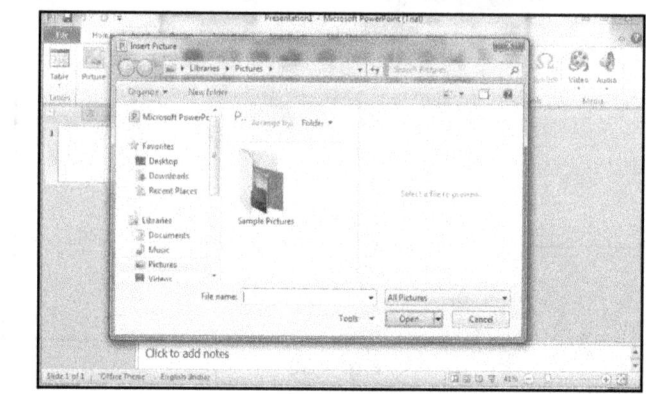

Fig. 8.88

Slide Transitions:
- Slide transitions provide an animated effect to each slide when moving from one slide to the next during a slide show.
- There are variety of transitions that can be applied to each or all slides including sounds.

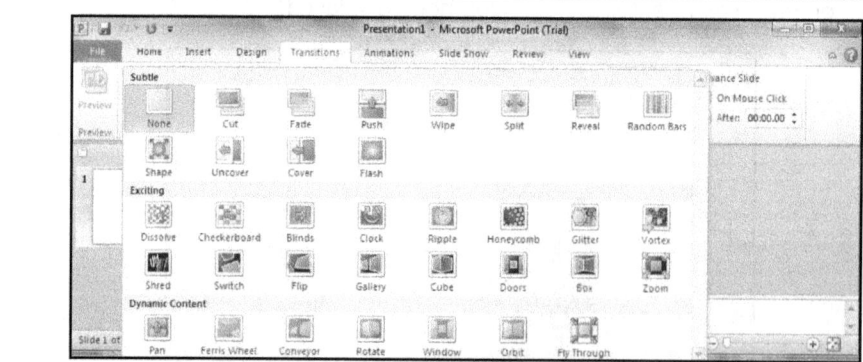

Fig. 8.89: Slide transition window

1. The transition to this Slide group provides thumbnails of various slide transition options. To see all of the transitions options click on the up and down arrows or the More arrow to the right of this group.
2. When you point and hover (mouse over) over any transition thumbnail, a preview of the theme will play. To apply the transition to your slide, click on the thumbnail you like.

3. To apply the same transition to all of your slides click on the Apply To All command after selecting the transition of you choice. To apply a Sound, click on the sound drop down arrow. Then Click on the sound you would like to chime during the slide transition. Click to Apply To All command to have the chime occur during each transition.
4. The Advance Slide group, allows you to decide if a transition should appear when the mouse is clicked or after a specified time. Click the On Mouse Click box for transitions to occur only when forced. Click on the After box for the slide to transition at the time specified such as 5 seconds or 1 minute. Finally, when all transitions are applied you can preview the current slide by clicking on the Preview command.

8.4.4 Preparing Slide Show with Animation

1. **Slide Animations:**
- Slide animations create animated effects to text and graphics during a slide show.
- There are a variety of animations that can be applied to text or graphics in multiple ways from a single word to all of the text on a slide.

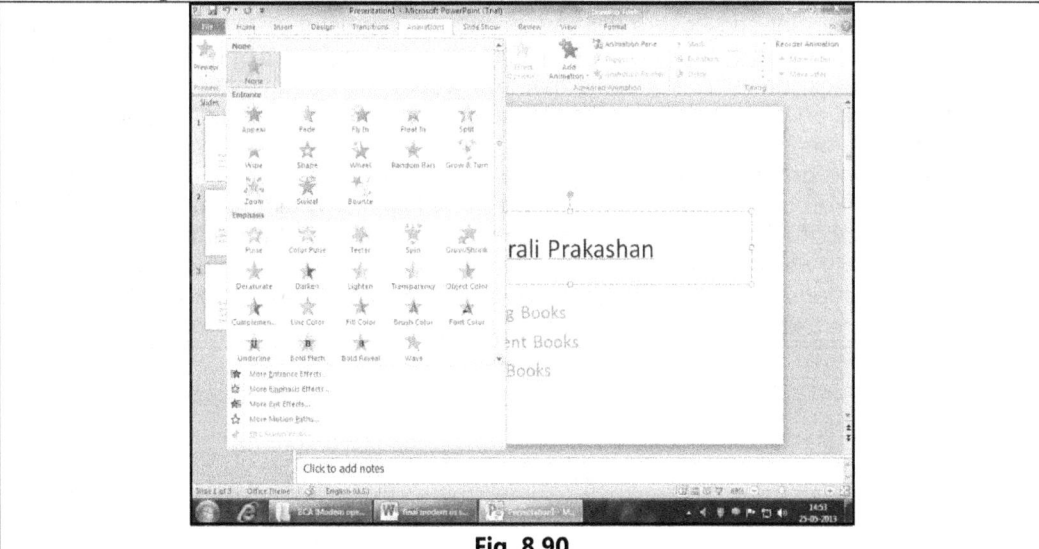

Fig. 8.90

1. The Animation group provides a variety of option to apply animations to text and graphics within each slide.
   (i) To see all of the animation options click on the Up Row, Down Row and More arrows to the right of the Animation group.
   (ii) The Effect Options command provides additional animation options for each animation command in the Animation group.
   (iii) The Add Animation command provides a visual of all of the animation options to animate text and graphics upon Entrance, Exit and as an Emphasis. These commands are the same as the commands in the Animation group.

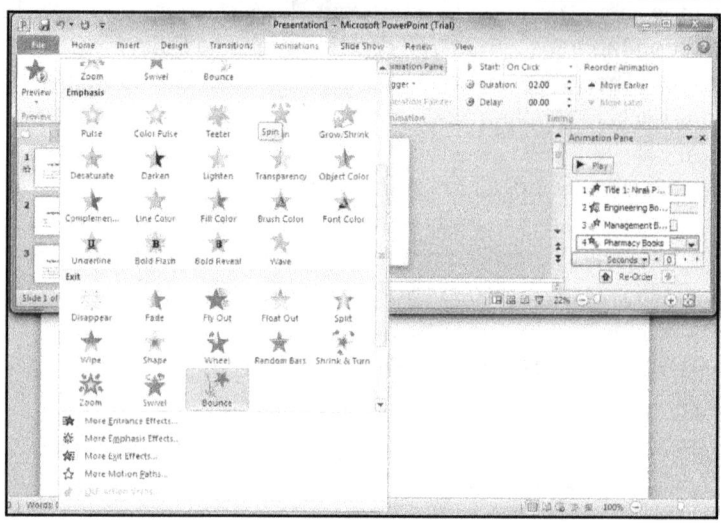

Fig. 8.91

2. When you point and hover over any animation command, it will be highlighted in a golden color and a preview of the animation will appear. To apply an animation, highlight text or select a graphic that you would like the animation to be used on, then click on the command, the selected command will remain highlighted in a golden color.

3. The Timing group allows you to modify the sequence and timing of the animations selected. You can decide if an animation should appear when the mouse is clicked or after a specified time. You can also decide if text should be animated together or separate as well as reordering the animations. Use the Start drop down arrow to opt for animations to occur only when clicked or with other text. Click on the Duration box for the text or graphic to animate at a specified time.

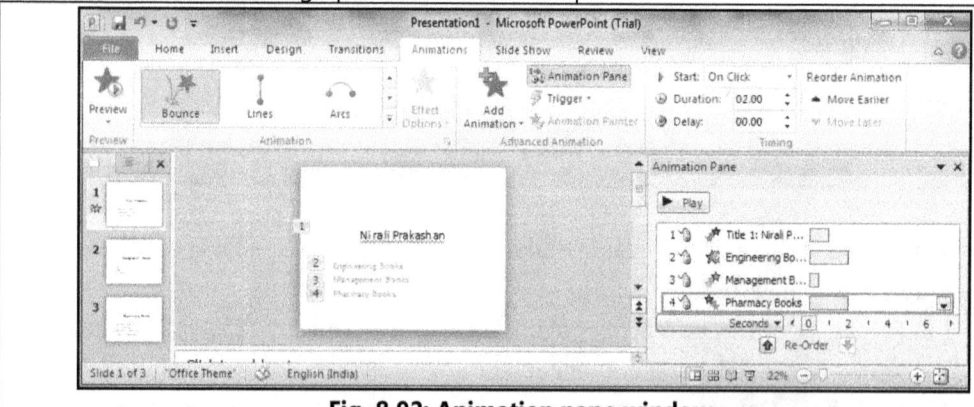

Fig. 8.92: Animation pane window

4. The Animation Pane displays all of the animations you have applied to each slide. It also enables you to modify each animation similar to the Timing group and play the animations applied to the slide.

5. Finally, when all animations are applied you can preview the current slide by clicking on the Preview command.

2. Starting a Slide Show:

- The best way to view you slides as a show, whether you are previewing your documents or presenting to an audience, go to the Slide Show tab on the Ribbon.

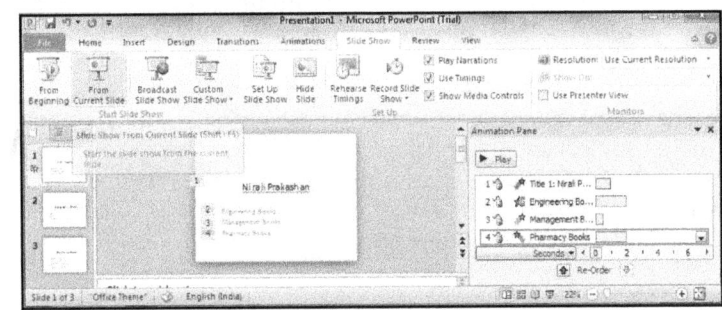

Fig. 8.93

(i) To view your slide show go to the Start Slide Show group. To start on the first slide click the From Beginning command. To start on the current slide click the Form Current Slide command.
(i) You computer screen will disappear and a slide show will fill you computer screen.
(iii) To move from slide to slide can use the Slide Show toolbar at the bottom left of the screen.
(iv) Navigational arrows will appear when you position your cursor in that area. You can also move from slide to slide by clicking the mouse button or using the right and left arrows on the keyboard.
(v) To end you slide show press the ESC button on your keyboard. This return you to your screen as you left.

Fig. 8.94: Slide after running animation effect

8.5 MS Access (Creation and Manipulation of Files)

- Microsoft Access is a computer application used to create and manage computer-based databases on desktop computers and/or on connected computers (a network).
- Microsoft Access can be used for Personal Information Management (PIM), in a small business to organize and manage data, or in an enterprise to communicate with servers.
- Microsoft Access is an application used to create computer databases.
- Database is a collection of data. DBMS (Database Management System) is a software which relies upon to organize the storage of data.

How to Start Microsoft Access 2010?

- An important part of Access 2010 comes from how easy it can be to open up the program. A user can easily use a desktop icon to open Access 2010 in the event that an icon has been created. Otherwise, a person can use this process on the Start menu to get to Access 2010:

    Start → All Programs → Microsoft Office → Microsoft Access 2010

- Microsoft Access 2010 introduces numerous features those are not supported in Office Access 2007. The Office 2010 release of Access offers some improvements that make the application more usable, including reliability enhancements.
- To get started, launch Microsoft Access, on File menu click New, you can either choose Blank database from Available templates or any other form of database from Office.com Templates. Give it an appropriate name and hit Create.

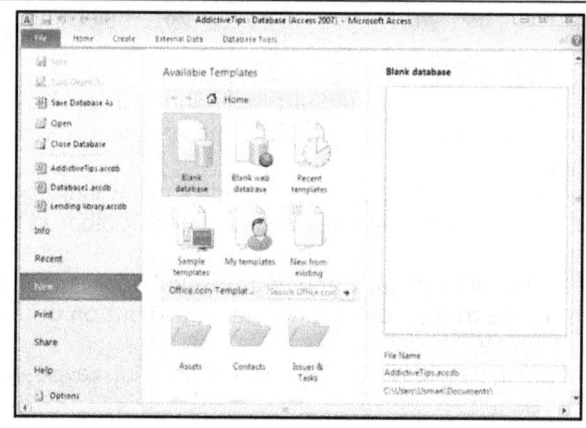

Fig. 8.95: MS-Access window

- Navigate to Create tab, click Table to add another Table. From the left pane right-click Table1 and hit Design View, or you can also click a small button on the bottom-right corner of the window.

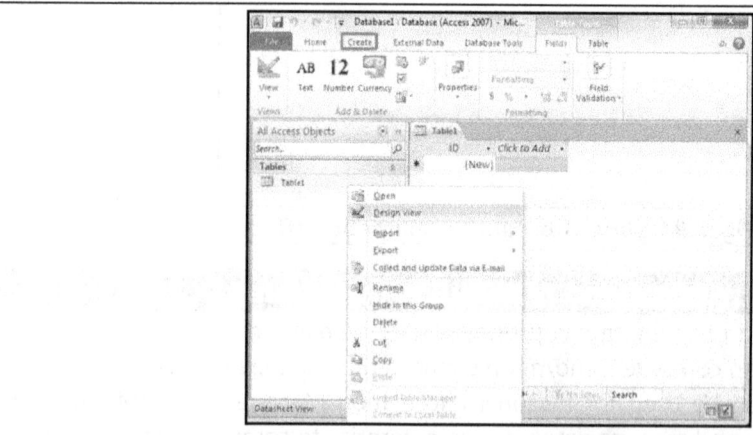

Fig. 8.96: Creating tables

- Give this table an appropriate name and hit OK. In Design view you can name table columns and apply desired constraints over them from Field Properties. Choose Primary key to uniquely identify each record in the table.

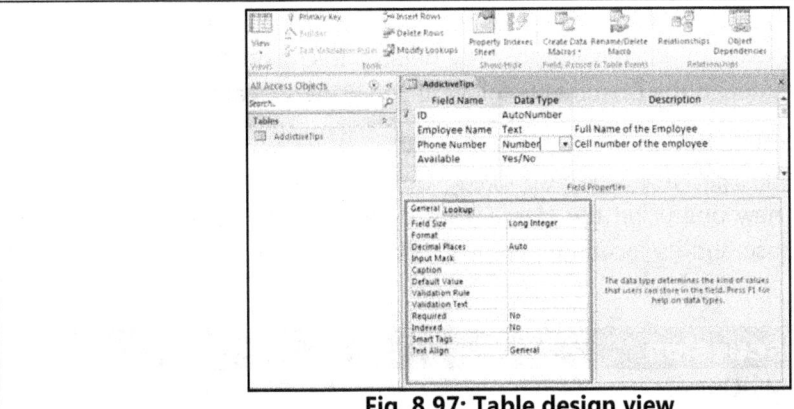
Fig. 8.97: Table design view

- To start filling tables, switch to table view by clicking the small button on the bottom-right of the window. You will see the columns created in design view and constraints applied.

1. **Designing of Database:**
- Before creating a database, you should plan and design it. For example, you should define the type of database you want to create. You should create, in writing, a list of the objects it will contain: employees, customers, products, transactions, etc.
- For each object, you should create a list of the pieces of information the object will need for its functionality: name(s), contact information, profession, etc. You should also justify why the object needs that piece of information.
- You should also define how the value of that piece of information will be given to the object.

2. **Creating of Database:**
- Follow the following steps for creating a new database in MS-Access.
    (i) To create a blank database, in the middle section, under Available Templates, click Blank Database
    (ii) To create a database using one of the samples, under Available Templates, click a category from one of the buttons, such as Sample Templates. Then click the desired buttons:

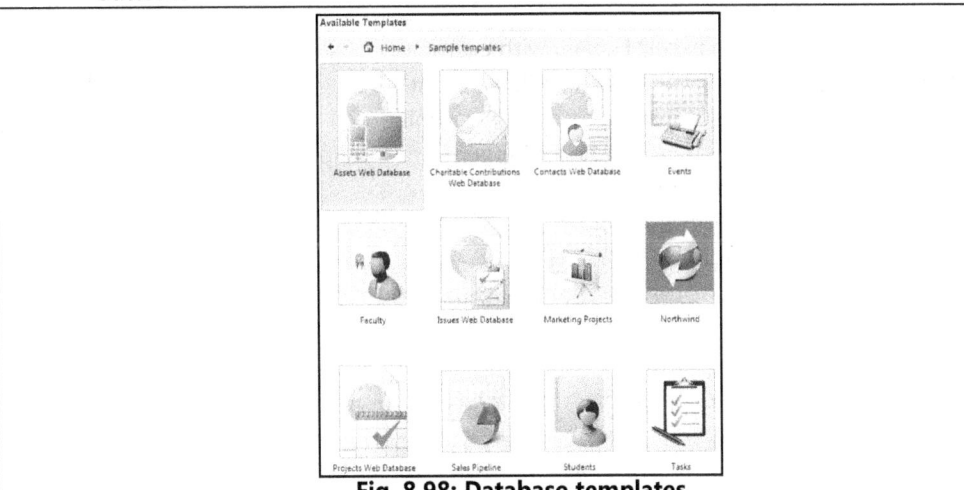
Fig. 8.98: Database templates

- Microsoft Access always suggests a name for the database. You can accept or change it. Use the File Name text box for this purpose. By default, Microsoft Access suggests that the database be created in the Documents folder. If you want it located in another folder, you can click the Browse button .
- This would open the File New Database dialog box where you can select an existing folder or create a new one using the New Folder button. Once you have specified the name of the database and its location, you can click Create. After specifying the name, click Create.

Questions for Discussion

1. What is meant by MS-Office?
2. What are the components of MS-Office?
3. What is MS-Word? Explain its uses.
4. What are the different features of Excel that provide the ease of work?
5. What is the significance of formulas in Excel?
6. Explain the formulas of MS-Excel.
7. What are functions? Explain logic and text function in Excel.
8. How to create database in Access?
9. What is the purpose of queries? Explain with example.
10. Describe MS-Word in detail.
11. How to prepared tables in word. Explain briefly.
12. Explain the term Mail-merge.
13. Describe formatting and editing in MS-Word.
14. Explain MS-Excel. Enlist various characteristics of MS-Excel.
15. Describe the term editing and formatting in MS-Excel.
16. Write short notes on:
    (i) Function in Excel, and
    (ii) Formulae in Excel.
17. How to prepare charts in Excel? Explain with example.
18. With the neat diagram explain screen of PowerPoint.
19. Describe how to prepare a presentation in PowerPoint.
20. What is slide? How to create slide show? Explain with example.
21. Write short note on: Spell check.
22. How to insert picture in Word?
23. How to insert pictures in PowerPoint?
24. What is the meaning of WordArt? What are its uses?
25. Describe slide animation in detail.
26. Write short note on: Templates.
27. How to create graphs in Excel? Explain with example.
28. Explain page layout concept of word in detail.

■■■

Annexure A

Contents ...

1.1 Introduction
1.2 Algorithm
    1.1.1 Uses of Algorithm
1.3 Flowchart
    1.3.1 Symbols
    1.3.2 Principles of Flowchart
1.4 Converting Algorithm to Flowchart
    1.4.1 Read a Number to the Computer and Display on the Screen
    1.4.2 Addition of Integers
    1.4.3 Subtraction of Integers
    1.4.4 Multiplication of Integers
    1.4.5 Determining if a Number is +ve/−ve
    1.4.6 Determining if a Number is Even/Odd
    1.4.7 Maximum of 2 Numbers
    1.4.8 Maximum of 3 Numbers
    1.4.9 Algorithm and Flowchart for Sum of Digits
    1.4.10 Sine Value of Angle
    1.4.11 Cosine Value of Angle
    1.4.12 Algorithm and Flowchart for Table Generation of n Numbers
    1.4.13 Algorithm and Flowchart for Finding a Prime Number
    1.4.14 Algorithm and Flowchart to Find Factors of a Number
    1.4.15 Algorithm and Flowchart for Pascal Triangle
    1.4.16 Algorithm and Flowchart of Factorial of a Number (N)
    1.4.17 Algorithm to Exchange the Values of 2 Variables A and B without using Third Temporary Variable
    1.4.18 Algorithm to display first n Fibonacci number
- Questions

1.1 Introduction

To write effective computer program, one must plan the logic of the program. This logic is written into steps. It is necessary that every instruction is written in the proper sequence. The programmer has to write each and every step for solving a given problem. This process is algorithm writing. Algorithm represents a logic of the program and also specify how to solve a given problem. There are different ways in which an algorithm can be expressed. It can be written in pseudo code or it can be expressed in a programming language. If it expressed in programming language, it becomes a program. Algorithms can also be expressed in the form of flowcharts.

Flowchart is a pictorial representation of an algorithm. It has special boxes of different shapes for specific purpose i.e. to denote different types of instructions.

This chapter deals with writing algorithms and drawing flowcharts for some arithmetic problems.

1.2 Algorithm

An algorithm is a set of instructions for accomplishing a task. An algorithm is independent of the language. An algorithm is a sequence of instructions such that :

- The sequence is finite.
- Each instruction is executed only a finite number of times.
- Each instruction is unambiguous.

For practical application algorithm must have following properties :

- An algorithm is a computable set of steps to achieve a desired result.
- They should be efficiently making the best use of **space** and **time**.

1.1.1 Uses of Algorithms

- It gives a language independent layout of the program.
- Using the basic layout, we can develop the program in any desired language.
- Algorithms are easy to understand.
- Facilitates easy coding.

1. **Algorithm to swap two numbers**

   Step 1 : Read a and b.

   Step 2 : Let temp = a

   Step 3 : a = b

   Step 4 : b = temp

   Step 5 : Stop.

1. **Algorithm to find maximum of 3 numbers**

   Step 1 : Read the values of 3 numbers x, y and z.

   Step 2 : If x > y and x > z then print value of a, goto step 5

   Step 3 : If y > x and y > z then print y, goto step 5.

   Step 4 : If z > x and z > y then print value of z.

   Step 5 : Stop.

1.3 Flowchart

Flowchart is an important tool which is used by programmers and analysts for tracing the information flow and the logical sequence for data processing. It helps us in understanding of logical structure of the problem. Every problem can be represented symbolically with the help of flowchart. Flowchart is a pictorial representation of an algorithm that uses boxes of different shapes to denote different types of instructions. These boxes are connected by solid lines having arrows marks to indicate the flow of operation and the exact sequence in which the instructions are to be executed. Flowchart shows the flow of the whole process, which includes the data inputs, operations or computations performed, decision taken and output generated.

1.3.1 Symbols Used in Flowcharts

Flowcharting Symbols :

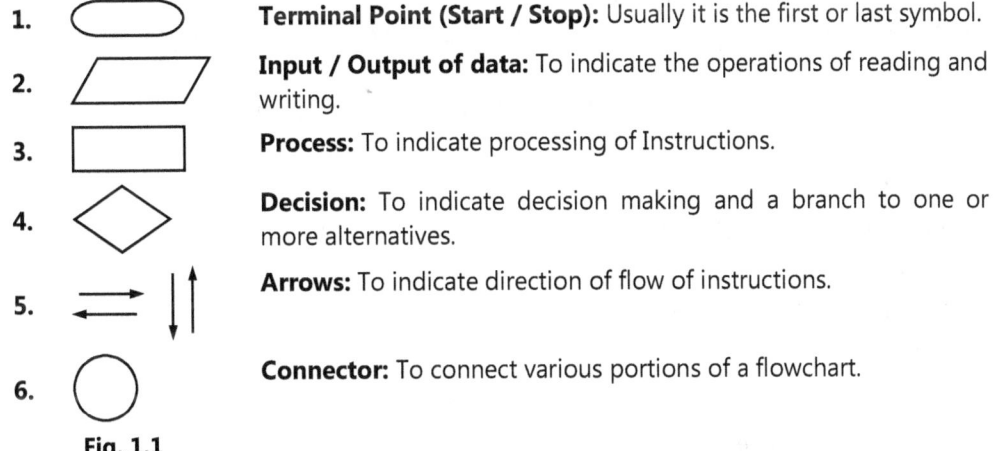

1. **Terminal Point (Start / Stop):** Usually it is the first or last symbol.
2. **Input / Output of data:** To indicate the operations of reading and writing.
3. **Process:** To indicate processing of Instructions.
4. **Decision:** To indicate decision making and a branch to one or more alternatives.
5. **Arrows:** To indicate direction of flow of instructions.
6. **Connector:** To connect various portions of a flowchart.

Fig. 1.1

1.3.2 Principles of Flowcharting

1. Pictorial representation makes it a convenient method of communication.
1. It promotes logical accuracy and is a key to correct programming.
3. Takes care that no path is left incomplete without any action being taken.
4. Helps to develop program logic and serves as documentation.
5. It is an important tool for planning and designing a new system.

1.4 Converting Algorithms to Flowcharts

1.4.1 Read a number to the computer and display on the screen

Algorithm :

Step 1 : Start
Step 2 : Read number X
Step 3 : Display number X
Step 4 : Stop

Flowchart :

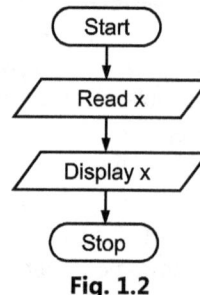

Fig. 1.2

Description:

The algorithm and flowchart above, illustrate the steps for solving the problem of program for read number to the computer and display on screen.

Both the algorithm and flowchart should always have a start step at the beginning of the algorithm.

In this example computer read the number from user and display on screen.

e.g. Step 1 : Start

Step 2 : Read X = 12

Step 3 : Display the value of X = 12

Step 4 : Stop

1.4.2 Addition of Integers

Algorithm:

Step 1 : Start

Step 2 : Read numbers x and y

Step 3 : z = x + y.

Step 4 : Display z

Step 5 : Stop

Flowchart:

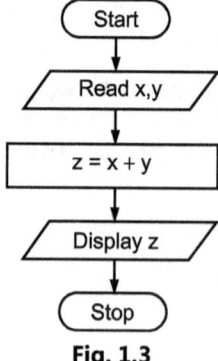

Fig. 1.3

Description:

The algorithm and flowchart above illustrate the steps for solving the problem of program for addition of two integers.

Both the algorithm and flowchart should always have a start step at the beginning.

In step 2 computer read number x and y.

In step 3 calculate the value of z.

$$z = x + y$$

In Step 4 it display the value of z.

e.g. Step 1 : Start
Step 2 : x = 16, y = 12
Step 3 : z = x + y
= 16 + 12
= 28
Step 4 : Display the value of Z is **28**.
Step 5 : Stop.

1.4.3 Subtraction of Integers

Algorithm:
Step 1 : Start
Step 2 : Read numbers x and y
Step 3 : z = x – y.
Step 4 : Display z
Step 5 : Stop

Flowchart:

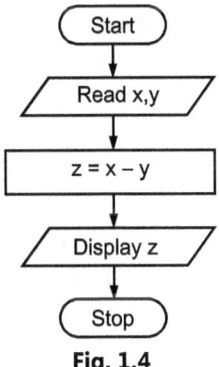

Fig. 1.4

Description:

The algorithm and flowchart illustrate the steps for solving the problem of program for subtraction of two integers.

Both the algorithm and flowchart should always have a start step at the beginning.

In Step 2 computer read number x and y.
In Step 3 computer calculate the value of z.
In Step 4 it displays value of z.

e.g.
  Step 1 : Start
  Step 2 : x = 42, y = 26
  Step 3 : z = x – y
           = 42 – 26
           = **16**
  Step 4 : Display the value of z = **16**
  Step 5 : Stop

1.4.4 Multiplication of Integers

Algorithm:
  Step 1 : Start
  Step 2 : Read numbers x and y
  Step 3 : z = x * y.
  Step 4 : Display z
  Step 5 : Stop

Flowchart:

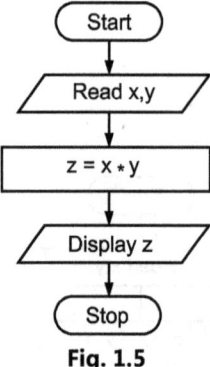

Fig. 1.5

Description:

The algorithm and flowchart illustrate the steps for solving the problem of program for multiplication of two numbers.

Both the algorithm and flowchart should always have a start step at the beginning.

In Step 2 : Computer read number x and y.

In Step 3 : Computer calculate the value of 1.

In Step 4 : It display the value of z.

e.g. Step 1 : Start
Step 2 : x = 80, y = 2
Step 3 : z * y
   = 80 * 2
   = **160**
Step 4 : Display the value of z = **160**.

1.4.5 Determining if a number is +ve/−ve

Step 1 : Start
Step 2 : Read number as X
Step 3 : If X > 0 then display number is positive
Step 4 : Stop 4.
Flowchart :

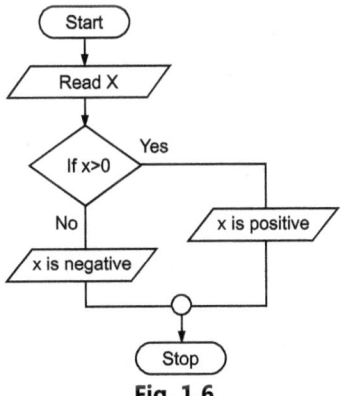

Fig. 1.6

Description:
The algorithm and flowchart illustrate the steps for solving the problem of program for determining its number is +ve or −ve.

Both the algorithm and flowchart should always have a start step at the beginning.
In Step 2 :   Computer read number x.
In Step 3 :   The number is greater than 0. It displays number is positive.
In Step 4 :   The number is less than 0. It displays number is negative.
e.g. Step 1 :
   Step 2 : X = 12
   Step 3 : X > 0. It display number is positive

1.4.6 Determining if a number is even/odd
Algorithm :
Step 1 : Read n
Step 2 : If (n mod 2) = 0, then
         Display "n is even"
         Otherwise display "n is odd".
Step 3 : Stop

Flowchart :

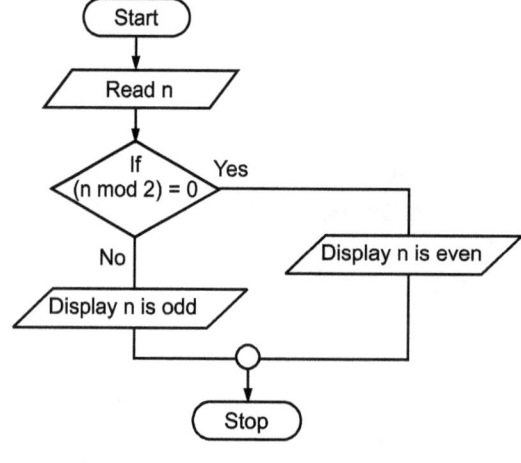

Fig. 1.7

Description :

The algorithm and flowchart illustrate the steps for solving the problem of program for determining if a number is even or odd.

Both the algorithm and flowchart should always have a start step at the beginning.

In Step 1 :   Read number n

In Step 3 :   Calculate

n mod 2 = (n%2) = 0, then display n is even.

Otherwise display n is odd.

e.g. Step 2 : n = 12

Step 3 : (n%2) = 0

Display n is even

1.4.7 Maximum of 2 numbers

Algorithm:

Step 1 : Start

Step 2 : Read number a and b

Step 3 : If a > b then display "a is greater"

Otherwise display "b is greater".

Step 4 : Stop

Flowchart:

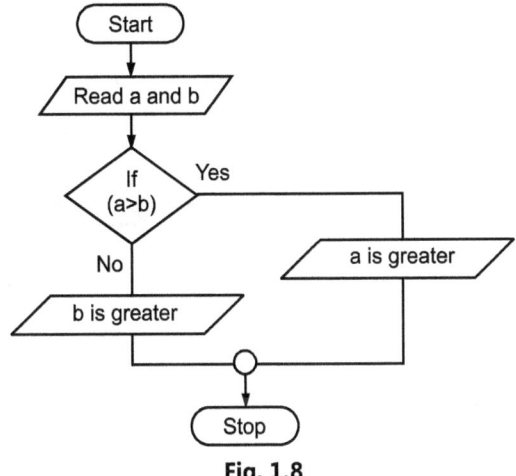

Fig. 1.8

Description:

The algorithm and flowchart illustrate the steps for solving the problem of maximum of 2 numbers. Both the algorithm and flowchart should always have a start step at the beginning.

Step 2 : Read the number 'a' and 'b' in

Step 3 : It display 'a' is greater otherwise "b" is greater.

Step 4 : Stop.

e.g. Step 2 : a = 20, b = 10

Step 3 : (20 > 10)

These pore prints a is greater.

Step 4 : Stop.

1.4.8 Maximum of 3 numbers

Algorithm :

Step 1 : Start

Step 2 : Read A, B, C

Step 3 : Assign max = A

Step 4 : If A > B and A > C then max = A

Step 5 : If B > A and B > C then max = B

Step 6 : If C > A and C > B then max = C

Step 7 : Stop

Flowchart :

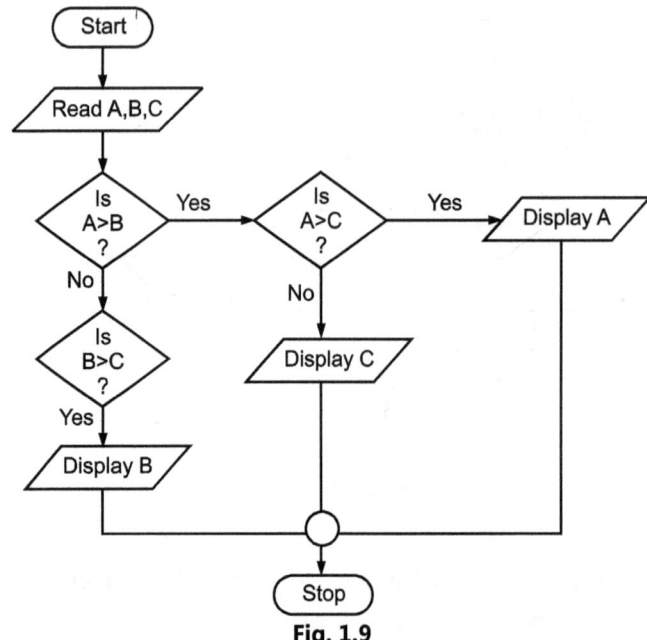

Fig. 1.9

Description:

The algorithm and flowchart illustrate the steps for solving the problem of program for determining maximum number in 3 number's.

Both algorithm and flowchart should always have start step at the beginning.

In Step 2 : Computer read A, B and C As A = 25, B = 30, C = 35
In Step 3 : Assign max = A
In Step 4 : If 'A' is greater than 'B' and 'A' is greater than 'C' then display B is greater. A ≯ B, and A ≯ C.
In Step 5 : If 'B' is greater than A and B is greater than 'C' then display B is greater. B > A but B ≯ C.
In Step 6 : If 'C' is greater than A and C is greater than B then display 'C' is greater. C > A and C > A. It displays 'C' is greater.

1.4.9 Algorithm and Flowchart for sum of digits

Algorithm:
    Step 1 : Start
    Step 2 : Read number as n
    Step 3 : Let sum = 0
    Step 4 : Calculate sum = sum + (N mod 10)
    Step 5 : N = N DIV 10
    Step 6 : If N > 0 then go to step 4
    Step 7 : Display sum and digits
    Step 8 : Stop

Flowchart:

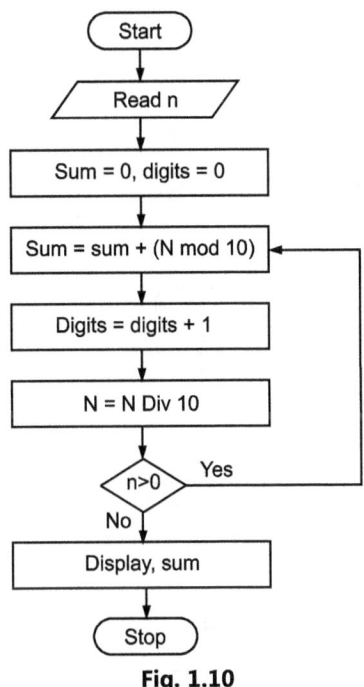

Fig. 1.10

Description:

The algorithm and flowchart illustrate the steps for solving the problem of program for sum of first 'n' numbers.

Both the algorithm and flowchart should always have a start step at the beginning.

Step 2 : Read number as N = 325

Step 3 : Sum = 0

Step 4 : Calculate the sum Iteration 1 : sum = 5
        sum = sum + (N Mod 10)

Step 5 : Calculate N
        N = N Div 10

Iteration 2 : sum = 7 (5 + 2)

Iteration 3 : sum = 10 (5 + 2 + 3)

Step 6 : If N > 0 then go to Step 4

Step 7 : It display the values of sum and digits

1.4.10 Sine Value of Angle

Algorithm:

Step 1 : Start

Step 2 : Read x and n

Step 3 : Convert x values into radian using formula
        X → x * 3.1412/180

Step 4 : t ← x
Step 5 : Sum ← X
Step 6 : Step for loop from i ← 1 until
(i < n + 1) increment 1
Step 7 : t ← (t * (pow((double(2 * I – 1)) * X * X)/(2 * i * (2 * i + 1)
Step 8 : sum ← sum + t
Step 9 : print sum
Step 10 : Stop

Flowchart:

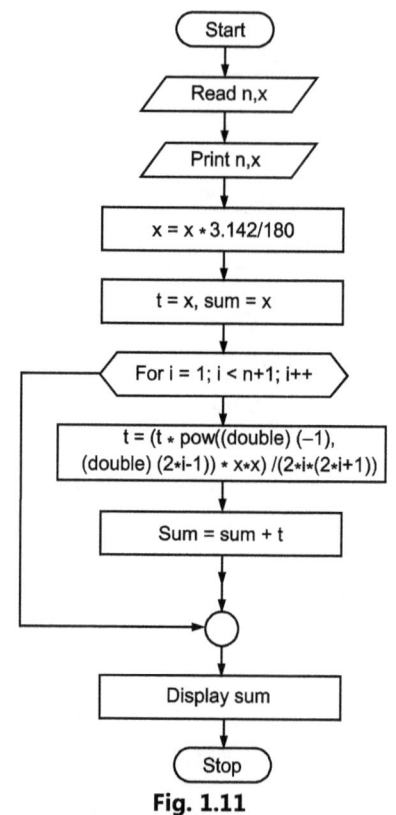

Fig. 1.11

Description:
Algorithm and flowchart illustrate step for finding sine value of angle (x).
Both algorithm and flowchart should have start and stop steps.
Step 2 : Read n, x as x = 45, n = 10
Step 3 : Print x and n, x = 45, n = 10
Step 4 : x = x * 3.142/180, x = 0.7855
Step 5 : t = x, sum = x
Step 7 : Calculating by formula provided in Step 7, for 10 time we get, sum = 0.71
Step 8 : Display sum = 0.71.
Thus, we get value of sin(x) = sum, sin(45) = 0.71.

1.4.11 Cosine Value of Angle

Algorithm:

Step 1 : Start
Step 2 : Initialise n ← 20;
Step 3 : Read X
Step 4 : Convert X values into radian using formula
  X ← X * 3.142/180
Step 5 : t ← 1, sum ← 1
Step 6 : Set up loop from i ← 1 until (i<n+1) increment
Step 7 : t ← (t*(pow(double) (−1), (double) (2 * i − 1)) X * X/(2 * i * (2 *i − 1))
Step 8 : sun ← sum + t
Step 9 : Display sum
Step 10 : Stop

Flowchart:

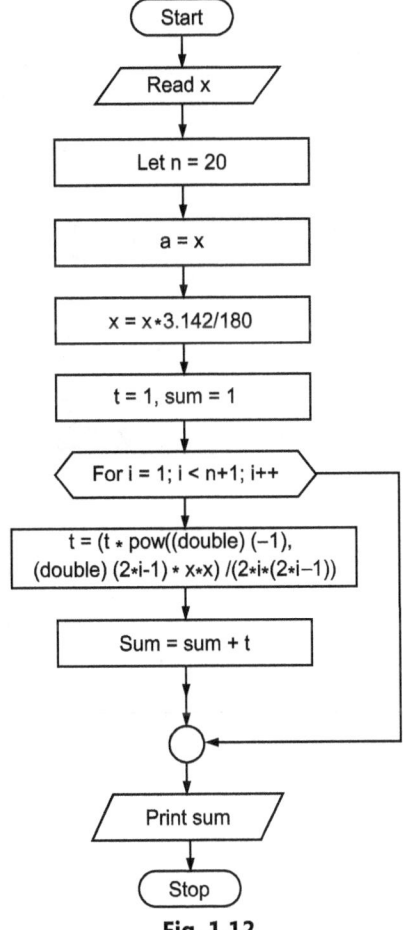

Fig. 1.12

Description:
The above algorithm and flowchart illustrate steps for finding cosine value of angle (x). Both algorithm and flowchart should have start and stop steps.
Step 2 : Read x. x as 60.
Step 5 : x = x * 3.142/180. x = 1.0473333
Step 8 : Calculating by formula provided in Step 8 for 20 times we get, sum = 0.500113
Step 9 : Display sum = 0.500113
Thus, we get cosine of 60 = 0.500113.

1.4.12 Algorithm and flowchart for table generation of n numbers

Algorithm:

Step 1 : Start

Step 2 : Read n

Step 3 : Let i = 2

Step 4 : Set up loop from i =2 until i <= n increment by 1

Step 5 : Set up loop from j = 1 until j <= 10 increment by 1

Step 6 : Print i * j = i * j, print new line character

Step 7 : Stop.

Flowchart:

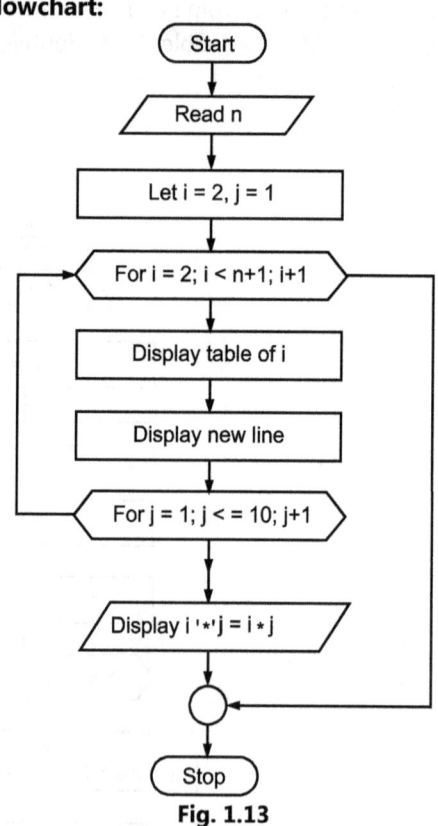

Fig. 1.13

Description:
Algorithm and flowchart illustrate steps for printing tables of n numbers.
Both algorithms and flowchart should have start and stop steps.
Step 2 : Read n. n = 5
Step 4 : Loop will start from i = 2 to i = 5
Step 6 : Loop will start from j = 1 to j = 10
Step 8 : The table of 2 will be displayed step by step as
   2 * 1 = 2
   2 * 2 = 4
The steps 4 to 8 will be repeated until table of 5 is displayed.

1.4.13 Algorithm and flowchart for finding a prime number

Step 1 : Start
Step 2 : Read n number
Step 3 : X = 2; flag = true
Step 4 : If nMODx=0
then flag=false, Goto Step 8.
Step 5 : X = X + 1
Step 6 : If x < n Goto Step 4
Step 7 : If flag = true then
Print "Number is prime"
Otherwise Goto Step 9
Step 8 : If flag=false, then
print "Number is not prime"
Step 9 : Stop.

Flowchart:

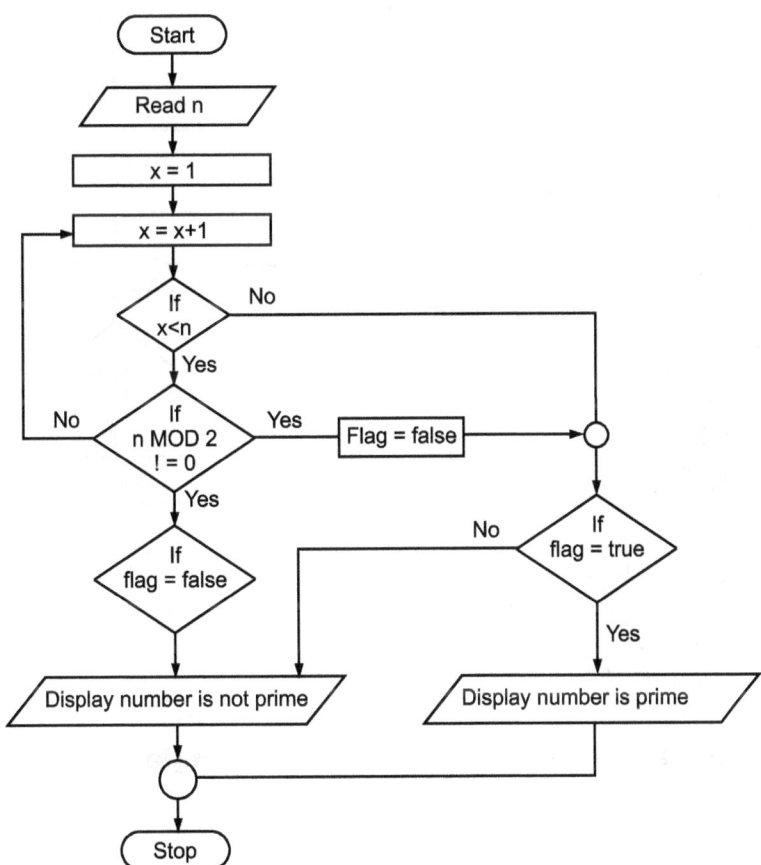

Fig. 1.14

Description:

The algorithm and flowchart illustrate the steps for finding whether given number is prime or not.

Both algorithm and flowchart should have start and stop steps.

Step 2 : Read n, n = 5
Step 4 : x = x + 1, x = 2
Step 5 : x < n, ∴ 2 < 5
Step 6 : 5 MOD 2 ! = 0
    ∴ x = x + 1,
    ∴ x = 3

Now, steps 4, 5 and 6 are repeated till x = 5.
Step 7 : flag = true as 5 is not divisible by 2, 3, 4.
Step 8 : Display number if prime.

1.4.14 Algorithm and flowchart to find factors of a number

Algorithm:

Step 1 : Start
Step 2 : Read n
Step 3 : i = 2
Step 4 : Set up loop from i = 2 until i < n increment by 1
Step 5 : if n MOD i = 0 then print i
Step 6 : Stop.

Flowchart:

Description:

The algorithm and flowchart illustrate the steps for finding factor of a number.

Both algorithm and flowchart should have start and stop steps.

Step 2 : Read n. n = 6.
Step 4 : A loop is started from i = 2 till i < 6
Step 5 : 6 % 2 = 0 – true
Step 6 : 2 is printed

Now, steps 4, 5, 6 will be iterated and 3 will be printed for i = 4 and i = 5, only steps 4 and 5 will be repeated as 6 is not divisible by 4 and 5, those values won't be printed.

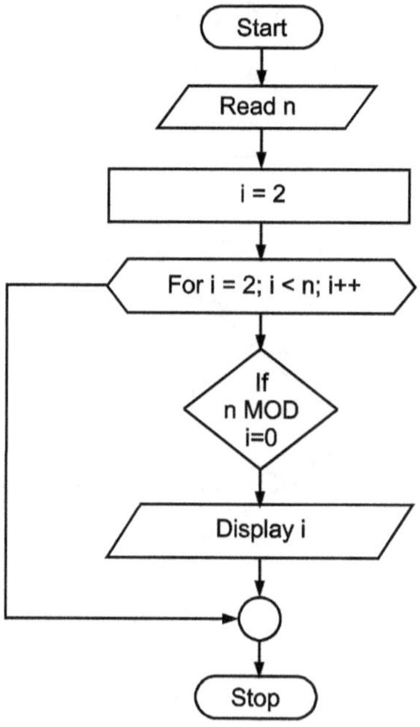

Fig. 1.15

1.4.15 Algorithm and Flowchart for Pascal Triangle

Algorithm:

Step 1 : Start
Step 2 : Read p
Step 3 : q = 0, binom = 1, x = 0
Step 4 : Set up loop from q = 0 until q < p, increment by 1

Step 5 : Set up loop from r = 40 – 3 * q until r > 0, decrement by 1
Step 6 : Print blank space
Step 7 : Setup loop from x = 0 until x <= q increment by 1
Step 8 : if x = 0 or q = 0 then binom = (binom * (q – x + 1))/x;
Step 9 : print binom (%6d)
Step 10: print new line character
Step 11 : Stop.

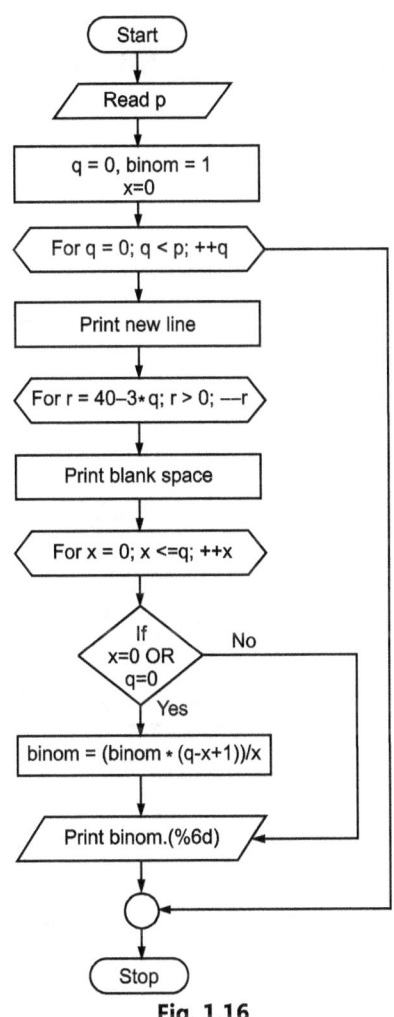

Fig. 1.16

Description:

The algorithm flowchart illustrate the steps for printing pascal triangle.
Both algorithm and flowchart should have start and stop steps.
Step 2 : Read p, p = 3.
Step 4 : Loop will be established from q = 0 to q < p
Step 6 : Loop will be established from r = 40 – 3 * q to r > 0
Step 7 : Loop will be established from x = 0 to x <= q

Step 8 : If x = 0 or q = 0 for first time true. Thus, binom = (binom * (q – x + 1))/x will be executed
Step 9 : Binom is printed
Step numbers 4, 6, 7, 8, 9 will be continued till q = p i.e. q becomes 3.
Thus, we get pascal triangle printed as

```
    1
   1 2 1
  1 3 3 1
```

1.4.16 Algorithm and flowchart of factorial of a number (N)

Algorithm:
Step 1 : Start
Step 2 : Input N
Step 3 : Factor = 1
Step 4 : Counter = 1
Step 5 : While (counter ≤ N)
Step 6 : Factor = factor * counter
Step 7 : Counter = Counter + 1
Step 8 : print(N, factor)
Step 9 : End

Flowchart:

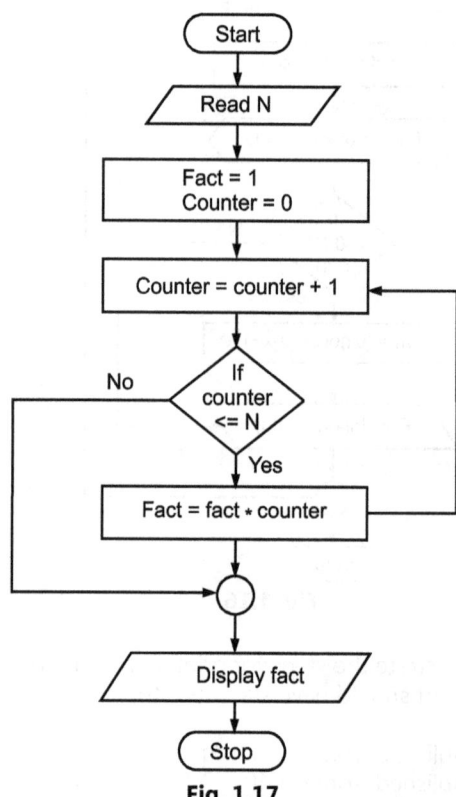

Fig. 1.17

Description:

Algorithm and flowchart illustrate steps to calculate factorial of a number.

Both algorithm and flowchart should have start and stop steps.

Step 2 : Read N. N = 3

Step 4 : counter +.

∴ Counter = 1

Step 5 : Counter <= N – true (1 < 3)

Step 6 : fact = fact * counter.

∴ Fact = 1

Step 4 – 6 will be repeated till counter = 4

∴ Value of factorial will be 1 × 2 × 3 = 6.

1.4.17 Algorithm to exchange the values of 2 variables A and B without using third temporary variable.

Algorithm :

    Step 1 : Start

    Step 2 : Read A and B

    Step 3 : A = A + B

    Step 4 : B = A – B

    Step 5 : A = A – B

    Step 6 : Display A, B

    Step 7 : Stop

Flowchart :

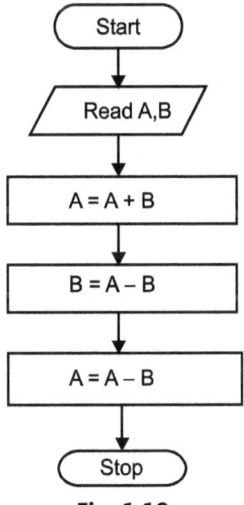

Fig. 1.18

Description:

The algorithm and flowchart illustrates the steps for solving a problem of program for exchange the values of 2 variables A and B without using third temporary variable.

Both the algorithm and flowchart should always have a start at the beginning.

Step 2 : Read A and B as
   A = 15, B = 30
Step 3 : Calculate A = A + B,
   A = 45
Step 4 : Calculate B = A − B,
   B = 15 (45 − 30)
Step 5 : Calculate A = A − B,
   A = 30 (45 − 15)
Step 6 : Display A and B,
   A = 30, B = 15

1.4.18 Algorithm to display first n Fibonacci number

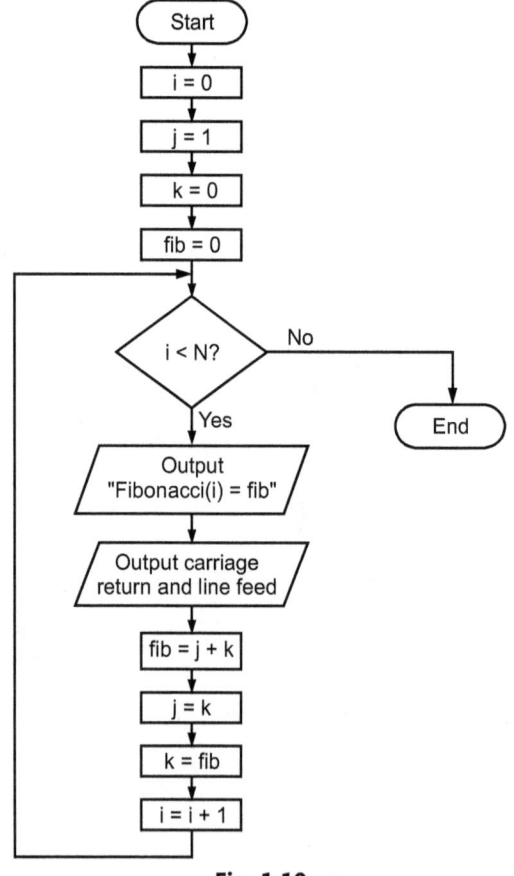

Fig. 1.19

Algorithm :

Step 1 : Start

Step 2 : Initialize the i, k, fib to 0 and j to 1.

Step 3 : Check condition i < N then condition is false then go to step 8

Step 4 : Fib = j + k

Step 5 : j = k

Step 6 : k = fib

Step 7 : i = i + 1 go to step 3

Step 8 : Stop

Description :

The algorithm and flow chart illustrate the steps for solving a problem of program for display first n Fibonacci numbers.

Step 2 : Initialize i = k = fib = 0 and j = 1

Step 3 : Check i < N

       go to step 8

Step 4 : fib = j + k

Step 5 : j = k

Step 6 : k = fib

Step 7 : i = i + 1

       go to step 3

Practice Questions

1. What is an algorithm? What are the advantages of writing an algorithm?
2. What is a flowchart? What are the principles of flowcharting?
3. Explain the flowcharting symbols with examples.
4. Draw a flowchart to calculate the sum and average of N numbers.
5. Draw a flowchart to check whether a given number is prime or not.
6. Draw a flowchart to generate N terms of Fibonacci series.
7. Draw a flowchart to calculate xn where x is real and n is an integer.
8. Draw a flowchart to find all divisors of an integer number N.

9. Accept the day of the week and display whether the day is a 'Working Day' or 'Week End'. Display proper 'Error Message' for all incorrect inputs.
10. Write an algorithm and draw a flowchart to check whether the given string is palindrome or not.
11. Define flowchart. Explain various symbols used for drawing flowchart with their usage.

■■■

University Question Papers

Time: 3 Hours **October 2013** Max. Marks: 80

Instructions:
1. All questions are compulsory
2. Figures to the right indicate full marks
3. Draw neat diagram wherever necessary.

1. Answer the following (any eight): [16]
(a) What is analog computer?
Ans. Refer Section 1.5.1.
(b) What is purpose of Address bus?
Ans. Refer Section 2.3.1.
(c) Which are different types of keyboard?
Ans. Refer Section 3.2.1.
(d) Write the following conversions.
  (i) 1 KB = (?) bytes, (ii) 1 MB = (?) KB
Ans. The basic unit used in computer data storage is called a bit. 8 Bits is equal to 1 Byte.
Bit : A Bit is a value of either a 0 or 1.
Byte : 1 Byte = 8 Bits
Kilobyte (KB) : 1 KB = 8,192 Bits
    1 kB = 1,024 Bytes
Megabyte (MB) 1MB = 1024 KB
Gigabyte (GB) 1GB = 1024 MB
Terabyte (TB) 1TB = 1024 GB
Petabyte (PB) 1PB = 1024 TB
Exabyte (EB) 1EB = 1024 PB
Zettabyte (ZB) 1ZB = 1024 EB
(e) What is function of Assembler?
Ans. Refer Section 5.5.
(f) What is operating system?
Ans. Refer Section 6.1.
(g) What is bus topology? Draw diagram.
Ans. Refer Section 7.9.1.
(h) Write any two statistical functions in MS-Excel.
Ans. Refer Section 8.3.
(i) Write any two features of MS-Word.
Ans. Refer Section 8.2.
(j) What is LAN?
Ans. Refer Section 7.5.

2. Answer the following (any four): [16]
(a) Explain different characteristics of computer.
Ans. Refer Section 1.2.
(b) Explain in detail static RAM.
Ans. Refer Section 4.5.1.
(c) Explain features of Linux operating system.
Ans. Refer Section 6.6.1.
(d) Draw a flowchart to find the even numbers from 1 to 100.
Ans. Refer Section 5.3.

3. Answer the following (any four): [16]
(a) Explain in detail components of MS-Office.
Ans. Refer Section 8.1.1.
(b) Write a note on MS-Access.
Ans. Refer Section 8.5.
(c) Explain primary memory.
Ans. Refer Section 4.2.
(d) What are the limitations of computer application?
Ans. Refer Section 1.7.
(e) Write a note on MICR.
Ans. Refer Section 3.2.4.

4. Answer the following (any four): [16]
(a) Explain in detail Magnetic Disc.
Ans. Refer Section 4.6.2.
(b) What is algorithm? Explain characteristics of algorithm.
Ans. Refer Sections 5.2.1 and 5.2.2.
(c) What is internet? Explain advantages of internet.
Ans. Refer Section 7.8.
(d) Which are different characteristics of good language?
Ans. Refer Section 5.4.
(e) How graphs are created in MS-excel?
Ans. Refer Section 8.3.4.

5. Answer the following (any four): [16]
(a) Write a note on Windows 2000.
Ans. Refer Section 6.5.
(b) Write a note on power point.
Ans. Refer Section 8.4.
(c) Explain concept of networking briefly.
Ans. Refer Section 7.2.
(d) Write a note on impact printer.
Ans. Refer Section 3.3.2.
(e) Write a note on application software.
Ans. Refer Section 5.9.2.

■■■

Modern Operating Environment & MS Office (BCA-I)   P.3   University Question Papers

Time: 3 Hours | **April 2014** | Max. Marks: 80

Instructions:
1. *All questions are compulsory*
2. *Figures to the right indicate full marks*
3. *Neat diagrams must be drawn wherever necessary.*

1. Answer the following (any eight): [16]
(a) Define Hardware.
Ans. Refer Section 1.3.1.
(b) What are different types of printers?
Ans. Refer Section 3.3.2.
(c) Define non-volatile memory.
Ans. Refer Section 4.2.
(d) What is function of compiler?
Ans. Refer Section 5.6.
(e) What is batch operating system.
Ans. Refer Section 6.4, Point (1).
(f) Define topology.
Ans. Refer Section 7.9.
(g) Write any two features of MS-PowerPoint.
Ans. Refer Section 8.4.
(h) Write full form of:
  (i) EPROM
  (ii) ROM
Ans. (i) EPROM: Refer Section 4.5.2.3.
  (ii) ROM: Refer Section 4.5.2.
(i) Write any two graph types in MS-Excel.
Ans. Refer Section 8.3.4.

2. Answer the following (any four): [16]
(a) Explain in detail limitations of computer in various fields.
Ans. Refer Section 1.7.
(b) Draw a block diagram of computer and explain.
Ans. Refer Section 2.2.
(c) Write a note on Scanner.
Ans. Refer Section 3.2.3.
(d) Compare between primary and secondary storage.
Ans. Refer Section 4.2.
(e) Draw a flowchart to find the greatest among three numbers a, b, c.
Ans. Refer Section 1.4.8, From Annexure.

3. Answer the following (any four): [16]
  (a) Explain in detail Real Time Operating System.
Ans. Refer Section 6.4, Point (7).
  (b) Draw a figure of Co-axial cable and explain.
Ans. Refer Section 7.4, Point (1).
  (c) Explain different types of functions in MS-Excel.
Ans. Refer Section 8.3.5.
  (d) Write a note on MS-Word.
Ans. Refer Section 8.2.
  (e) Explain tree topology.
Ans. Refer Section 7.9.5.

4. Answer the following (any four): [16]
  (a) Write an algorithm to display first n Fibonacci numbers.
Ans. Refer Sections 1.4.18 from Annexure A.
  (b) Compare between hard disk and floppy disk.
Ans. Refer Section 4.6.2.2.
  (c) Write a short note on Compact Disk.
Ans. Refer Section 4.6.3.1.
  (d) Which are different disadvantages of Internet?
Ans. Refer Section 7.8.

5. Answer the following (any four): [16]
  (a) Write a note on MS-Access.
Ans. Refer Section 8.5.
  (b) Compare between LAN and WAN.
Ans. Refer Section 7.7.
  (c) Explain the history of Windows Operating System.
Ans. Refer Section 6.5.
  (d) Explain the characteristics of Good Language.
Ans. Refer Section 5.4.
  (e) Explain analog and digital computer.
Ans. Refer Section 1.5.1 and 1.5.2.

■■■

University Question Papers
April 2015

Time: 3 Hours   Max. Marks: 80

Instructions:
1. All questions are compulsory.
2. Figures to the right indicate full marks.
3. Draw neat diagrams wherever necessary.

Q.1 Answer the following (any eight): [16]
(a) What is special purpose computer?
(b) What is purpose of control bus?
(c) Write any two examples of non-impact printers.
(d) Write the following:
  (i) 1 Byte = (?) bits.
  (ii) 1 KB = (?) bytes.
(e) Define Algorithm.
(f) What is interpreter?
(g) What is star topology? Draw diagram of star topology.
(h) Write any two statistical function in MS-Excel.
(i) Write full form of: (1) EPROM, (2) DRAM.
(j) What is LAN?

Q.2 Attempt any four of the following: [16]
(a) Explain applications of computer in various fields.
(b) Explain bus structure of digital computer.
(c) Explain difference between RAM and ROM.
(d) Write a note on MS-Access.
(e) Draw a flowchart to calculate sum of first N numbers.

Q.3 Attempt any four of the following: [16]
(a) Explain in detail Retail time operating system.
(b) Write a note on MS-Word.
(c) Which are different network components? Explain.
(d) Write a note on OMR.
(e) Draw Neat diagram of bus topology and explain.

Modern Operating Environment & MS Office (BCA-I)   P.2   **April 2015**

Q.4 Attempt any four of the following: [16]
(a) Draw neat diagram of magnetic disk and explain.
(b) Explain characteristics of algorithm.
(c) Compare between Floppy disk and CD-ROM.
(d) Explain the different types of charts used in excel.
(e) Explain advantages of LAN.

Q.5 Attempt any four of the following: [4 × 4 = 16]
(a) Write a note on MS-Power Point.
(b) Write a note on Laser Printer.
(c) Compare between Window and Linux Operating System.
(d) Compare between Impact and Non-Impact printer.
(e) Write a note on mail-merge.

www.ingramcontent.com/pod-product-compliance
Lightning Source LLC
Chambersburg PA
CBHW062133160426
43191CB00013B/2293